DISCARD

The Samurai Films of Akira Kurosawa

Studies in Cinema, No. 23

Diane M. Kirkpatrick, Series Editor

Associate Professor, History of Art
The University of Michigan

Other Titles in This Series

No. 13 *Bertolt Brecht,* Cahiers du Cinéma, *and Contemporary Film Theory*	George Lellis
No. 14 Casablanca *and Other Major Films of Michael Curtiz*	Sidney Rosenzweig
No. 15 *Old Hollywood/New Hollywood: Ritual, Art, and Industry*	Thomas Schatz
No. 16 *Donald Duck Joins Up: The Walt Disney Studio During World War II*	Richard Shale
No. 18 *The Spanish Civil War in American and European Films*	Marjorie A. Valleau
No. 20 *Cinema Strikes Back: Radical Filmmaking in the United States, 1930-1942*	Russell Campbell
No. 21 *Third Cinema in the Third World: The Aesthetics of Liberation*	Teshome H. Gabriel
No. 22 *Women's Reflections: The Feminist Film Movement*	Jan Rosenberg
No. 24 *Visions, Images, and Dreams: Yiddish Films Past and Present*	Eric A. Goldman

The Samurai Films of Akira Kurosawa

by
David Desser

UMI RESEARCH PRESS
Ann Arbor, Michigan

Photos appear courtesy of the following: From *Kagemusha*, provided by Eddie Brandt's Saturday Matinee; reprinted courtesy of Twentieth-Century Fox. © 1980 by Toho Company Ltd. From *Shogun Assassin*, provided by and reprinted courtesy of Roger Corman. From *Rashomon*, provided by the Museum of Modern Art, New York City; reprinted courtesy of Janus Films. From *Throne of Blood, Seven Samurai, Sanjuro, High and Low*, provided by the Museum of Modern Art, New York City; reprinted courtesy of Toho Company Ltd.

Copyright © 1981, 1983
David Michael Desser
All rights reserved

Produced and distributed by
UMI Research Press
an imprint of
University Microfilms International
Ann Arbor, Michigan 48106

Library of Congress Cataloging in Publication Data

Desser, David.
The samurai films of Akira Kurosawa.

(Studies in cinema ; no. 23)
Revision of thesis (Ph. D.)–University of Southern California, 1981.
Bibliography: p.
Includes index.
1. Samurai films–History and criticism. 2. Kurosawa, Akira, 1910-   . I. Title. II. Series.

PN1995.9.S24D47   1983   791.43'0233'0924   83-15563
ISBN 0-8357-1495-0

Contents

Acknowledgments   vii

1 Introduction   *1*
   Japanese Films and the West
   Kurosawa's Use of Genre
   Kurosawa and American Film Motifs

2 The Samurai Film   *13*
   The Mythicization of History
   The Field of View
   The Historical Background
   Sign Systems
   Genre Types
      The Nostalgic Samurai Drama
      The Anti-Feudal Samurai Drama
      Zen Fighters
      The Sword Film
   The Mythicization of History and the Samurai Film

3 The Samurai Films of Akira Kurosawa   *57*
   Kurosawa and the West
   The Period Films of Akira Kurosawa
   The Samurai Films
      Seven Samurai
      The Hidden Fortress
      Yojimbo
      Sanjuro
      Kagemusha
   Conclusion

4 Implications for Further Study   *133*

Notes   *147*

Bibliography   *155*

Index   *159*

Film Index   *163*

Acknowledgments

If I were to begin writing this book today it would turn out rather different than the volume you are holding. But that is because this volume was the necessary prelude to the study I would write. This is to say that much yet remains in the study of Kurosawa's cinema and that this book is offered in the spirit of inspiration, as a place to begin as it was, and is, for me.

I would like to acknowledge several individuals who assisted me during the preparation of this study: Allan Casebier and Edward Kaufman of the Division of Cinema/Television, and Noboru Inamoto of the Dept. of East Asian Languages and Literatures, at the University of Southern California. I would also like to thank other members of the Critical Studies section of USC Cinema for their help, especially Richard B. Jewell, Marsha Kinder, Joseph Andrew Casper, Arthur Knight, and Robert Knutson of the Special Collections library. I would also like to thank Prof. Chieko Mulhern of the Asian Studies Department at the University of Illinois at Urbana-Champaign for taking a keen interest in my work with help and encouragement. Most of all, I'd like to thank my parents and my wife Cathleen, the only true samurai in the family.

Akira Kurosawa stands with American admirers Francis Ford Coppola (left) and George Lucas on the location of *Kagemusha* (The Shadow Warrior).

1

Introduction

Japanese Films and the West

If Kipling's observation that "East is East and West is West and never the twain shall meet" is true, it would be impossible for us in America to discuss the Japanese cinema intelligently. And yet we can, to greater and lesser degrees, make sense out of the celluloid images that come to us from the Land of the Rising Sun. But it is those "greater and lesser degrees" that are most intriguing, for we quickly realize that there are some Japanese films to which Westerners respond with facility and pleasure and others that leave people wondering if indeed Kipling was on to something. There are certain Japanese films that seem to speak clearly to a Western audience, films to which they respond "naturally." There are others that indicate somehow that the Japanese cinema is an acquired taste.

Admiral Perry and his Black Ships steamed into Tokyo Bay in 1853 and forced the opening of Japan to the West; Akira Kurosawa's *Rashomon* came steaming into the Venice Film Festival in 1950 and opened up the West to Japanese films. "*Rashomon* opened the eyes of the international public to the existence of a major film industry in Japan...."[1] It is here we may begin to compare those films with a Western following and those which have proved to be more esoteric. Although many historians attribute *Rashomon*'s appeal to its "exoticism" and "stylization,"[2] its enduring popularity indicates that there was more to its popularity than that. Whatever the case, *Rashomon* gave rise to a veritable cottage industry of films produced specifically for export to the West. Few of these films attained the popularity of *Rashomon*, although they did prove to be prize winners, as well. Seen today, a film like *Gate of Hell* appears of mere historical interest (erroneously called the "first" color film produced in Japan,[3] although its use of color is exemplary), while Inagaki's excellent color film version of *Rickshaw Man*, as wonderful as it is, is little seen and therefore little studied. Other films produced in Japan during this early onslaught of exports to the West were deemed entirely "too Japanese" by the Japanese themselves. Films like *Late Autumn* (Ozu), *The Life of Oharu* (Mizoguchi), and *Floating Clouds* (Naruse) awaited the day when Western critics, particularly European ones, could lure them onto Western screens.

A pattern soon emerged with regard to Japanese films here in America. Some proved to be audience favorites among the arthouse circuit, while others remained too specialized even for this particular group. Works like *Seven Samurai, Yojimbo,* and *Sanjuro* found Americans firmly on their side. These films made Kurosawa unarguably Japan's best known director in the West. And it is still quite true that "if any living director can rightfully claim to represent the cinema of Japan throughout the world, that director can only be Akira Kurosawa."[4] His popular acceptance may be quickly demonstrated by the fact that *Dersu Uzala* received the Academy Award for Best Foreign Language Film, while both *Dodeskaden* and *Kagemusha* received Oscar nominations. No other Japanese director has been so well received. Kurosawa's influence in the West ranges from the well-known adaptations of his films like *The Magnificent Seven* and *A Fistful of Dollars* to more generalized influences on the film styles of many contemporary directors, especially Sam Peckinpah and Walter Hill, to name but two.

Naturally, it cannot be coincidental that one man who signs his name to a body of work should have achieved a fame and reputation that exceeds his fellow countrymen, especially when at least two of them (Ozu and Mizoguchi) must be considered his cinematic equals with regard to talent and ability. In seeking to account for this popularity here in the West, perhaps we must begin to understand something about the nature of intercultural communication; of Japan's culture and of America's perception of it, and how these are expressed and understood through cinematic modes. If Kurosawa is truly "Japan's most Western director," then we are implicitly stating the existence of a set of codes and structures that signify "Western" which Kurosawa utilizes in constructing his films. Implied in this is the further existence of a Japanese way of cinema, culture, and film culture that, for instance Ozu ("Japan's most Japanese director") embodies and that Kurosawa does not; or that Kurosawa embodies to a lesser degree. It remains to be demonstrated, however, just what Western and Japanese filmic modes are. If all agree that Kurosawa is Japan's most accessible director to Western sensibilities, it remains as yet unspecified just why this should be so.

There is a corollary when discussing Kurosawa, one that generally goes unexplored to a large degree. And that is, to what extent does Kurosawa speak to the Japanese? Given the unfortunate Japanese penchant for cultural chauvinism (which is combined with a feeling of cultural inferiority) that still largely exists, does not the mandating of Kurosawa to the West imply, at least on a comparative level, his lack of value to the Japanese themselves?

To deal with the above issues we must first understand that Japan built a culture by borrowing and adjusting what was of interest from other cultures. The native Japanese culture that arose in the first few centuries A.D. has continually been the foundation for a series of wholesale adaptations of foreign ideas. Things foreign seem always to have exerted a fascination for the

Japanese. Although never conquered or occupied until 1945, the Japanese have adapted the ideologies and technologies of a number of nations throughout their long and complex history. In particular, what seems to have fascinated the Japanese was the technology associated with ideology. For instance, the mirror and the sword that became the symbols of the Emperor in the Kofun period (fourth century A.D.) are the technological expressions of a superior metal-working culture. These implements, however, were perceived not as machines or as weapons of war, but rather as religious icons which assumed cosmological importance to the emerging rice-growing culture. This pattern of adapting technology (in a broad sense) along with ideology is again apparent in the Nara period with the adaptation of Buddhism from China. The architecture and sculpture that were borrowed outright from the "middle kingdom" marked an implicitly different world view from the native Japanese culture. It is a tribute to this native culture that it formed an important part of the dialectic of cultural formation that marks the Nara and Heian periods.

Even the vaunted Tokugawa era (1615–1868) and the so-called closing of Japan does not put an end to the growth of Japanese culture through the adaptation and transformation of alien ways. The introduction of the musket and the cannon changed not only the nature of Japanese warfare by turning even a common peasant into a deadly killer (an important idea in *Kagemusha*), but also the nature of castle building and territorial fortifications. In the late sixteenth century, technology made the Samurai warrior obsolete at the very moment he reached his true glory. By the time Perry forcefully requested the Japanese to begin trade relations with the West, the Japanese themselves were ripe for the idea. Their economy was in a state of stagnation and by 1863 there was open warfare between pro- and anti-Shogunate forces, a warfare which led to the Meiji Restoration of 1868.

From this date on, Japan enters the modern, or Western world, achieving a surprising "equality" with the West as demonstrated by their victory in the Russo-Japanese War. Along with this modernization campaign to achieve parity with the highly technologized nations of the West comes the introduction of the motion picture. It was only natural for the Japanese to take to the movies with a passion. As a way of discovering and learning about life in the West, movies were unequaled. And, although many Japanese were equally fascinated by the projector itself as by the subject,[5] to most Japanese the West finally came alive and the craze for things Western was solidified.

As the Japanese soon discovered, again as it were, technology implies ideology. With the new form of film, a whole new way of perceiving the world, of reconstructing it along social, cultural, and political lines, came into their country and forced them into dynamic confrontation with the West.

Early Japanese films show the same hesitant explorations with regard to the proper use of the motion picture medium that we see in the West. Some interesting experiments were undertaken, such as photographing a Kabuki troupe in an outdoor setting and incorporating the footage into the evening's performance.[6] However, the Japanese industry quickly became a static and derivative one. There was no one working in Japan in the teens and early twenties to compare with D.W. Griffith, F.W. Murnau, or Sergei Eisenstein. However, the Japanese did manage to see the films of these and other important cinema pioneering geniuses, and so eventually their filmic techniques became more sophisticated along with their audiences.[7] By this time, the Japanese film industry had already established its pattern of genre, or formula pictures, becoming even more rigidified in this area than America ever would (outside of television, of course). The industry in Japan established a rigid system of advancement for directors,[8] much like the medieval mode of forming schools and training craftsmen in the ways of the particular family head. It was not a situation likely to encourage great originality, but, not unlike the American cinema of the thirties and forties, we do find a number of creators (or *auteurs*) emerging nonetheless. The rise of Japanese militarism in the middle and late thirties soon put a stop to what little genuine creativity had asserted itself so that directors like Ozu, Mizoguchi, and Kinugasa had to reduce their output or make films acceptable to the authorities.

The war years are not proud ones for Japan or her cinema. The few genuine masterworks, by Mizoguchi and Ozu for the most part, are overshadowed by militaristic, feudalistic paeans to the war effort. The same cannot be said of the years under the American occupation forces. America, through its occupation army, virtually forced Japan to adopt Western ideals. It was no longer a case of gradual adaptation. There was no choice. Through a complex series of edicts, some basically misguided and others fair attempts to install a true democracy in Japan (or as true as America's at any rate), Japanese society was changed forever. Subtler but just as crucial changes were wrought simply by the presence of great numbers of American servicemen and bureaucrats. As Americans tend to bring America with them wherever they go, Japan, particularly Tokyo, was changed into a little U.S.A..

Filmmakers were as much a part of the occupation army's attentions as any other segment of society. America had discovered the power of film for propaganda during the war and was determined to utilize the medium to bring democratic ideas to Japan after the war. As in Russia of the twenties, there was a revolutionary fervor surrounding film production, an explicit recognition of the importance of the new mass medium. Yet the two cultures were not without their differences.

Perhaps no film director embodies the tension between Japanese culture and the new American ways of the occupation better than Kurosawa. Part of the reason can perhaps be found in the fact that Kurosawa came to directorial maturity during the late forties. He came up through the ranks much as many Japanese directors had in the thirties, being exposed to the world of the genre film of this period. Kurosawa's first solo directorial effort came in 1943 with the semi-period piece *Sanshiro Sugata,* a film about a Judo master. This was followed by a modern story in 1944, *The Most Beautiful,* and then by two films in 1945, *Sanshiro Sugata Part II* and *They Who Tread on the Tiger's Tail.* Although it is generally regarded that the latter one is the best of this period,[9] *Sanshiro Sugata* actually seems the most mature and satisfying work. No doubt the losing war effort and the collapse of the film industry contributed to the disjointed feel of these films.

During the post-war Occupation, all film scripts had to be submitted to the American censor for approval.[10] While directors like Ozu and Mizoguchi had created fully mature masterpieces in the thirties and remained blissfully outside of America's influence, at least overtly, Kurosawa was still young and inexperienced enough to be swayed by the edicts and desires of the American censors. While Ozu, for instance, could go about blithely refining his already rarefied style, Kurosawa was in the midst of discovering his, all the while watched over by foreign eyes overseeing his every move. Kurosawa was in fact faced with the task of making films whose themes and subjects could be seen to be appropriate propaganda for the United States' desire to demilitarize and defeudalize Japanese attitudes. His solution to this may be seen in *No Regrets for Our Youth* (1946) and in *One Wonderful Sunday* (1947). The former film centers around a woman, in keeping with America's desire to change the status of women in Japan; the latter tries to defray tensions brought about by the post-war economic depression. To Kurosawa's credit, his films are both meaningful to his fellow Japanese on the thematic level and are interesting artistic experiments.

The same pressures were of course exerted upon other young Japanese filmmakers, such as Kon Ichikawa and Keisuke Kinoshita. But it was to be Kurosawa's peculiar genius that he could seemingly speak to the Western world with such great facility so early in his career. What Kurosawa did then was to adapt Western modes in a deliberate manner so as to explore the nature of Western ideals as they impact upon Japan.

One way to explore Western modes of thought and technique was through the adaptation of Western literature and formulas. We see Kurosawa drawn toward this idea rather early in his career. He has called *Drunken Angel* (1948) "a film in the Dostoevsky manner,"[11] as he tells a tale about a doctor's involvement with a gangster. *Rashomon* (1950), although adapted from a Japanese source, clearly owes much to Western existentialist philosophy. When the success of *Rashomon* enabled him to choose his own film projects, Kurosawa began in earnest to demonstrate his strong attraction for Western works. *The Idiot* (1951), *Throne of Blood* (1957), and *The Lower Depths* (1957), show his attraction to Western literary classics while *Stray Dog* (1949), *Yojimbo* (1961), and *High and Low* (1963) reveal his all-important fondness for pulp or formulaic works.

Kurosawa's attraction toward Western literature, and Western motifs, and his love of generic works, does not negate his interest in, and contributions to, works more traditionally Japanese. If he led the way in synthesizing Japanese and American tensions in his films, he also led the way in transforming pre-war forms into vital post-war structures. We should realize that *Seven Samurai* (1954) virtually created the serious contemporary Samurai film, paving the way for Masaki Kobayashi and Hideo Gosha to create their own brilliant and serious efforts.[12] I might also point out that it was *Yojimbo* that inspired the visual delights and violent excesses of the popular "Zato Ichi" series and the emerging *yakuza* form in the early sixties.

What we are faced with in Akira Kurosawa, then, is a filmmaker influential in his own country and highly respected, and influential, abroad. We are confronted with a filmmaker drawn to high art and literature as well as to popular art; a filmmaker deliberately operating dialectically to create works of narrative brilliance which reveal their own tensions; a filmmaker, moreover, who has mastered the craft of filmmaking yet who seems willing to violate some of its basic rules. In short, we have a puzzling genius, one who has been seriously neglected by film scholars.

Kurosawa's Use of Genre

If Kurosawa utilizes Western motifs and makes them his own, we are still left with the question of the specificity of such motifs. In other words, what is the nature of the themes, techniques, the codes in fact, that Kurosawa adapts and transforms? This question has remained previously unresolved for three reasons. One, because the question has never been formulated in this manner. When writers remark that Kurosawa is Japan's most Western director, the concept "Western" is never defined with precision. In fact, the concept "Western" is left implicit, as if Western modes were universally well defined and understood. They are not. Second, the question has not been so formulated because too many commentators approach Kurosawa without a sufficient knowledge of the language and literature of film. Those few who know Japanese culture with a certain thoroughness and possess a fair grasp of Japanese film history almost negate their utility by a lack of familiarity with regard to notions of filmic construction. On the other hand, we are also faced with critics who know little of Japanese culture and film history (and, unfortunately, little of American film history as well) and who choose to see in Kurosawa their own particular social, political, or sexual themes.

The third reason for a critical neglect of Kurosawa stems from the issue of cultural elitism. A disproportionate amount of critical attention has been paid to films like *Rashomon* and *Throne of Blood* at the expense of films like *Sanjuro* and *High and Low*. A possible explanation, of course, is the whole question of "popular" versus "high" art. While this question has been resolved with regards to the American cinema, as Western and Gangster genres have spawned whole libraries of books and articles, the same is not true of the Japanese cinema. The Samurai film and the *yakuza* film in particular remain relegated to the bottom rung of popular art. Kurosawa, let us remember, is, like Ford or Hawks, a great filmmaker not because he can turn a classic of literature into a great film, but because he can take a routine and highly codified formula story and turn that into a work of art.

This study attempts to alleviate some of these problems in Japanese film scholarship. First, this study takes the position that even though film is a cultural artifact whose political suprastructure and cultural climate must be known, it is also a formal-aesthetic system. An awareness of the nature of film language and the shape of film history on both sides of the Pacific Ocean must be brought to bear on the problem of Kurosawa's appeal in the West and his structural characteristics as a uniquely Japanese artist. This combination of film aesthetics, film history and Japanese cultural awareness, although not unique to this study, has rarely been applied to an understanding of the "genre impulse" in Kurosawa. As we have seen in certain studies of the Western and Gangster film[13] it is often the popular formulas which best reveal cultural tensions. It is the contention here that the same is true of Kurosawa's genre works. They show not only formally why Kurosawa is a major film talent, but also reveal the East/West dichotomy so important to his works and to the whole of modern Japanese society.

The study will define the true meaning of the statement that Kurosawa is Japan's most Western director by elucidating Noel Burch's correct but somewhat cryptic statement that "after thoroughly assimilating the Western mode of representation [Kurosawa] went on to build upon it."[14] This study attempts to break new ground not only by comparing specific American films to Kurosawa's, but by comparing specific filmic techniques as they appear in specific sequences. And it is the significance of such things as camera movement, framing, editing strategies and transitions that will be discussed, not simply their appearance as such. I want to go beyond a statement like "[Kurosawa is] Western in that he is a creator, in the pioneer sense of the word."[15] We must also go beyond the vague notions of "humanism" or "Dostoevskian"[16] (although they do apply) and go into the realm of filmic and cinematic codes and how they operate to make Kurosawa a Western and a Japanese film creator.

Along the way, if I can show how Kurosawa's traditional (or seemingly traditional) genre works must be taken seriously, perhaps I can inspire other critics to reconsider their attitudes toward the genres as a whole. That Donald Richie, the dean of Japanese film criticism in the West, can dismiss Kihachi Okamoto in one sentence, praising his little-seen *Age of Assassins* at the expense of "such ordinary films as *Kill* and unexceptional war dramas as *Human Bullet,*"[17] demonstrates an unfortunate lack of appreciation for the respective genres in which they fall. Although Richie certainly recognizes the major status of *Seven Samurai* and *Yojimbo,* he does not devote the space to them their popularity might warrant.

Andrew Sarris reminds us, in a brilliantly comparative listing of films, that "one of the fundamental correlations in *auteur* criticism is that between neglected directors and neglected genres. To resurrect Ford and Hawks, it is necessary to resurrect the Western."[18] Similarly, to recognize Kurosawa (he needs no resurrecting!), Kobayashi, Gosha, and Okamoto is to put an intrinsic worth on the Samurai film. And to this end, this study establishes the Samurai film as a major, important film genre, one in and of itself, worthy of study.

Kurosawa and American Film Motifs

This study proposes to answer the question posed earlier, namely, what is the nature of the themes, motifs, techniques and codes, that Akira Kurosawa adopts from the West? And when they are adopted, what is the significance of the resultant expression?

To begin to answer those questions, it first becomes necessary to work from a basic foundation that lays out Japanese traditions and forms. A corollary to the implicit recognition of Western codes in the statement that Kurosawa is Japan's most Western director, is the assumption of a "Japanese" mode of expression from which Kurosawa diverges. To this end, and in an effort to make a case for the value of the Samurai genre, I will undertake a structural explanation of the *jidai-geki,* isolating the "Samurai film" within its bounds. I will then examine the influence of Western popular formulas on Kurosawa's period films, with a particular emphasis on the Samurai films.

That I syphon off Kurosawa's period films from his other works (which in many ways are also generic) is neither arbitrary nor eccentric. To the Japanese audience and filmmaker, the genre or formula film holds an even fonder place than in the American industry. The Japanese film business, modeled quite specifically on America's, once relied almost exclusively on formula stories to attract and hold its audience(s). Whole studios became known for just one or two genres. More than in America, one knew beforehand what to expect of a film simply by its studio stamp. Even to this day this is quite true. Toei Studios, for example, produces exploitation films in the *yakuza* and "pinku" molds almost exclusively. (Without going into great detail, we can explain "pinku" as semi-pornographic, sexploitation films riddled with sado-masochism rather than hard-core pornography. It is worth noting, at least in passing, that there is a significant connection between the *yakuza* and *pinku* forms.) To the Japanese filmmaker himself the genre in which he works is of paramount importance.

> The non-Japanese film-maker thinks of his film as an entity, standing by itself.... The Japanese film-maker, on the other hand, is conscious not only that he is working in a given genre but also that within this genre he is specializing in a rigidly defined type, or *mono*....[19]

If the above statement is true, then Kurosawa's forays into the period film imply a deliberate eye on the past; not only on Japan's historical past, but, more importantly for my purposes, the past of the form. Tradition occupies a crucial place in all of Japanese culture, as true in poetry and prose as in cinema. If Kurosawa wishes to diverge, or add to, traditional Japanese modes he is thus making a significant statement.

Another important reason for isolating Kurosawa's Samurai films from the rest of his works is the often facile equation made between the Samurai film and the Western. Such an equation seems so common that to cite examples becomes almost arbitrary for it is undeniable that such an equation is made. And although the equation may be valid, the extent to which the Samurai film is indebted to the Western is questionable, just as the extent to which it diverges is relatively unspecified. By isolating Kurosawa's Samurai films and detailing the influences of American formulas upon them, I can elucidate the true nature of the East/West dichotomy as it is expressed in the films.

Chapter 2 is a structural analysis of the Samurai film. In it, I explore the idea of mythicization of history, an idea important to America as well as Japan. Then I make a case for the isolation of the Samurai film from within the broader cateogry of *jidai-geki*, or Period Drama. This is followed by a brief overview of the historical background in which the Samurai sagas are played out, pointing out along the way important differences between this genre and the Western. The last of my introductory remarks about the Samurai film concerns the idea of "sign systems" in Japan and the multiplicity of signifying systems the Japanese employ.

Chapter 2 introduces a structural conception of the genre, isolating four different sub-genre of Samurai film: (1) The Nostalgic Samurai Drama; (2) the Anti-Feudal Drama; (3) Zen Fighters; (4) the Sword Film. Basically, each of these four types has a different, specific function as regards the mythicization process they engage in. By isolating these four types I try to demonstrate that the Samurai film, like the Western, is a fairly amorphous form, one capable of permutation and evolution. Chapter 2 closes with an analysis of the function of the Samurai film in contemporary Japan.

Chapter 3 consists of my analysis of the influence of American popular formulas on the Samurai films of Akira Kurosawa. Following a brief biographical sketch solely from the point of view of Kurosawa's Western influences, I briefly analyze his non-Samurai period films. *Sanshiro Sugata, They Who Tread on the Tiger's Tail, Rashomon,* and *Throne of Blood* come under scrutiny for the ways they adhere to and diverge from traditional Japanese practices and the manner in which Western motifs are structured into their narratives.

Following that, I analyze in detail *Seven Samurai, The Hidden Fortress, Yojimbo, Sanjuro,* and *Kagemusha.* Although in one sense *Kagemusha* is more a *jidai-geki* than a Samurai film it can be seen as a summation of Kurosawa's themes and techniques and so I feel it requires a lengthy discussion.

Chapter 4 will discuss the implications for further study, going into some detail about the structure of the *yakuza* genre and the way in which Kurosawa's film *High and Low* might be analyzed.

I also suggest specific ways of understanding how Kurosawa has influenced Hollywood, especially the genre of the Western. Brief looks at important thematic borrowings from *Seven Samurai* on the part of John Sturges for *The Magnificent Seven* and, more importantly, Sam Peckinpah for *The Wild Bunch* suggest that Kurosawa's influence has been both more pervasive and more subtle than we might have thought.

A last implication I suggest involves the now-disgraced ideal of "humanism." Criticism since the mid-1970s has often used the Japanese cinema as a club against the dominant Hollywood mode (much as Francois Truffaut used the American cinema as a club against the French "tradition of quality" in his article inaugurating the "politiques des auteurs"). Certainly Noel Burch's *To the Distant Observer* is both the paradigm example of this and the most challenging one to come to terms with. This club, which we might call the "neoformalist club" (a pun on the latter term *is* implied) has greatly transformed the way we think, and write, about cinema. But Kurosawa has been excluded from the neoformalist pantheon (except for Burch, who tends to prize those films which manifest his vaunted "geometry" and to disgrace, or ignore, those which do not). And it is precisely Kurosawa's humanism, for which Donald Richie prized him, that has caused his elimination. I pose some questions about Kurosawa's humanism, while I call for a certain return to human values (without denying their problematic appearance).

Photo from *Shogun Assassin* (an American adaption of *The Sword of Vengeance, Part II*).

2

The Samurai Film

The Mythicization of History

In looking over the course of Japanese cinema, there is an immediate and striking similarity with the American cinema; a similarity, moreover, never commented upon to my knowledge. And this is that both major industrial powers (who are also major forces in international film) have consistently produced a body of work which has turned their respective histories into myth. Japan and America stand alone in this phenomenon. While certain European nations have had periods of this mythicization of history (e.g., Russia in the twenties, Germany under the Nazis) only the U.S. and Japan can trace an almost unbroken line of films dedicated to this transformation. And while India and China (Hong Kong) have similarly attempted a transformation of their pasts, their films remain too eccentrically formulaic to cross national boundaries into the world of serious film studies.

The crucial similarity between the two nations' mythologizing process is that both occurred in a free-enterprise economy. That is significant on more than one level and we will return to it. Suffice it to say now, that the free-enterprise system of film production-distribution created an ongoing dialectic between production and consumption so that producers could only release films that found a degree of popular success. To this end, both Japan and America found themselves the possessors of film industries whose backbone was formed by genre films. It is precisely in the consumption of genre films that the national image was mythologized.

When critics have compared the Japanese period film (or, more precisely, Samurai film) with the American Western, they were unknowingly more on the mark than it might seem. The obvious similarities of being set in the past, of having armed heroes who protect the weak or who seek bloody revenge, and the subscription to a codified set of behavioral norms like "The Code of the West" or the code of "Bushido," give the two forms an obvious affinity. Deeper, though, than the fact of historical setting or similar narrative patterns is the fact that both forms function as myth-makers. Both film genres gave rise to iconic archetypes; both formulas transformed historical figures or folk heroes into mythic heroes; both genres require that the societies understand them "structurally."

We can no longer make the mistake of seeing formula films as mere escapist entertainment. Nor can we understand the recurring hero-images as simple wish-fulfillment. Formulas, or genres, arise when they meet certain needs in a given culture. When the culture changes and the need disappears, the formulas die out. Regardless of the sometimes questionable aesthetic worth of many genre films, as cultural artifacts they possess extraordinary value. In some ways, it is not the unique works of genius that define a culture; genius easily crosses national boundaries. Rather, the routine, popular arts by their very natures have much to say about the culture that produced them.

Cawelti's "four hypotheses about the dialectic between formulaic literature and the culture that produces and enjoys it"[1] indicate an appropriate manner for the understanding of genre works. Cawelti proposes that (1) "Formula stories affirm existing interests and attitudes by presenting an imaginary world that is aligned with these interests and attitudes." (2) "Formulas resolve tensions and ambiguities resulting from the conflicting interest of different groups within a culture or from ambiguous attitudes toward particular values." (3) "Formulas enable the audience to explore in fantasy the boundary between the permitted and the forbidden...." (4) "... literary formulas assist in the process of assimilating changes in values to traditional imaginative constructs."[2] Formulaic works function in these ways on a kind of unconscious or semi-conscious level. Formulas, therefore, derived from historical situations and settings would speak clearly, if half consciously, to the contemporary audience. There would literally be a kind of eternal present occurring, one which is of significance when we turn now toward the theories of Claude Levi-Strauss.

In order to concentrate solely on structure, Levi-Strauss's analyses of myths were confined to oral tales. Problems of aesthetics or form never arose, nor did the structuralists' often thorny question, "Where is the structure to be found?" Moreover, the myths he analyzed for the most part, were the products of cultures which have no history. "... that is to say, on peoples... who think of their own society as changeless and conceive of time present as a straightforward perpetuation of the past."[3] The relationship between the myth-tales of ahistorical societies and the genre films of modern cultures is one of a functional nature. If Levi-Strauss is correct that these peoples do not distinguish between past and present, then it must follow that the myths themselves are the bonds between the then and the now. So too, it is my contention that the genre film, not simply by rewriting history, but by mythicizing it, makes the link between past and present simultaneously strong yet elusive. There comes to be no firm separation between the two, at the level of structure within the mind of the audience.

The Samurai Film

According to Levi-Strauss the myths of these synchronic societies function as synthesizers in ways not incompatible with Cawelti's four hypotheses, particularly point two. Levi-Strauss's (in)famous concluding remarks to his analysis of the Oedipal myths present his case at its more revealing.

> The myth has to do with the inability, for a culture which holds the belief that mankind is autochthonous, to find a satisfactory transition between this theory and the knowledge that human beings are actually born from the union of man and woman. Although the problem obviously cannot be solved, the Oedipus myth provides a kind of logical tool which relates the original—born from one or born from two?—to the derivative problem: born from different or born from same? By a correlation of this type, the overrating of blood relations is to the underrating of blood relations as the attempt to escape autochthony is to the impossibility to succeed it. Although experience contradicts theory, social life validates cosmology by its similarity of structure. Hence cosmology is true.[4]

Or, as he says thankfully somewhat more straightforwardly later in the same essay, "...the purpose of myth is to provide a logical model capable of overcoming a contradiction (an impossible achievement if, as it happens, the contradiction is real)...."[5]

There remains yet one more piece to the puzzle that Levi-Strauss can supply. It has its locus in his belief that the structure of myth resembles the structure of the mind. He sees the proof of this in the constant bundles of binary oppositions into which myths are structured; the linguistic theories of Jakobson and others support that contention as well. If the genre film has a mythic content/structure, it, too, must bear some resemblance to the structure of the mind. And it does this in the way it fits its mythic patterns into appropriate forms for a given society. The structures may stay the same—a syntagmatic chain of binary oppositions—but the paradigms used to deliver them change in accordance with a culture's changing degrees of sophistication. Forms arise when the society is ready for them in precisely the same way as the formula they contain. To separate them is indeed to destroy the formula's functioning ability. The formulaic pattern of pulp fiction, for instance, is literally inconceivable in verse form, just as the true epic has always presented filmmakers with an enormous aesthetic problem.

The cultures that produce and consume the myths analyzed by Levi-Strauss are reading them structurally at the level of the characteristics of their own minds. Although Levi-Strauss claims that the structure of the human mind is the same the world over, he underestimates the significance of language and, yes, myth to structure the mind according to its own characteristics. A proper understanding of myth, therefore, is not one which "reads" the structure but one which absorbs the tale at the level of its structure. We might wish to use a particular film genre as our example.

American forms like the Gangster, the Western, the Musical, and the Melodrama have found great favor at various times throughout Europe and Japan. On the one hand, we know for certain that the enjoyment of these films has been purely aesthetic; the French New Wave critics back in the early fifties were exposed to American films without sub-titles and they spoke almost no English. So too, the appreciation of Japanese films on the international scene has been almost strictly a formal appreciation. The rigorous stylistic of Ozu is always mentioned before the fact that he is a humanist with a warm and wise sense of humor. As a corollary, many French critics have undertaken structural readings of American films and film genres in much the same way Levi-Strauss has analyzed the myths of North and South American Indian tribes. The fact that it was the French who found a wealth of worth, both aesthetic and cultural, in our own formula films may be an index of their mythic functioning.

We can also understand the mythic/structural function of genre films when we compare genre works produced for the consuming culture with foreign imitations of them. The most obvious discussion would then be of the Italian, or "Spaghetti" Western. Although many of these films have achieved a degree of popular appeal, they are not appreciated at the level of "Western." Working almost exclusively in the iconic mode, they are, rather, Westerns about Westerns. The spaghetti Western uses only the signs of the true American Western: the gun, the landscape, the narrative syntagms. But without exception the Italian Western lacks the deep structural patterning. It is the difference here between the seeming artlessness of the classic Western and the artifice of the Italian. It is, then, a question of how the Italian Western uses the generic codes in different ways than its American counterpart. Thus it is the encoding of the myth that the genre film undertakes.

Both Japan and America, then, have produced a body of films by whose continual, repeated formulaic patterns have transformed their histories into myth. And they have done so by encoding, at the level of structure, certain basic patterns of motifs, themes, and settings. To understand how this works, however, necessitates not simply an understanding of myth-structure and mind-structure, but an understanding of how myths are actually encoded in the structure of films.

Levi-Strauss has stated that "myths are communications from a society to its members,"[6] while Roland Barthes has said that "myth is a type of speech."[7] This basic agreement between the two structuralists enables them to approach myth from a semiotic standpoint. But to Barthes, at least, myth is not just any type of speech and therefore requires a specific kind of semiotic approach. To begin such an approach requires, according to Barthes, the recognition that myth "is a second-order semiological system." Semiotic signs, which are the associative totals of given signifieds and signifiers, act in myth as mythical signifiers. "That which is a sign in the first system, becomes a mere signifier in the second... the materials of mythical speech (the language itself, photography, painting, posters, rituals, objects, etc.)...are reduced to a pure signifying function as soon as they are caught by myth."[8] To understand myth is to recognize the interplay between two levels of signifying functions.

According to Barthes, there are three ways in which myths can be deformed or deconstructed. One can focus on an empty signifier bereft of form. This is the mode of the producer of myth who begins with a concept and seeks a form for it. One can, alternately, focus on a full signifier in which case we "decipher" the myth by distinguishing the meaning and the form. Thirdly, we can examine the mythical signifier as being woven together by content and form so that the signification is both ambiguous and dynamic. According to Barthes, the first two modes of mythical analysis are static. They destroy the myth "either by making its intention obvious, or by unmasking.... The third type of focusing is dynamic, it consumes the myth according to the very ends built into its structure: the reader lives the myth as a story at once true and unreal."[9]

The significance of this for an understanding of film-myth, especially in terms of the genre film, is enormous. Film may be viewed most fruitfully as a second-order semiological system wherein a wide variety of sign systems interact to form a potentially more complex sign system. This new sign system of the cinema is able to embed myth into a complex of signifier/signified relationship the purpose of which is to disguise the original sign system. The mythic language of the cinema acts as spoken language which is able to take the aribtrary and transform it into the natural.

De Saussure's major contribution to linguistic studies (semiology) was the recognition of the arbitrary nature of language and the conventional relationship between the signifier and the signified. Peirce's tripartite division of the sign into icon, index, and symbol stressed the symbolic nature of spoken language. It is the nature of language to structure signs so that they become "natural"; by extension, mythic language is also able to perform the same function.

The genre film, especially here in the West, undertakes a similar task with regard to the naturalization of its signs. The myth is embedded in the structure of the film which is intent upon delivering a sign system devoted to structuring the conventional into the natural. The audience must deconstruct the film-myth, along the lines described by Barthes in his third mode, that of "reading" myths. It is the strength, and weakness, of the genre film that it rarely departs from the accepted codes, or "grammar" of film so that the entire experience is totally naturalized.

The relationship between myths of ahistorical societies and the myths produced and consumed by the genre films (and literature) of industrial societies is one of equivalence; an equivalence according to the same structural characteristics in which the societies receive and understand other types of communications. If a film appears that violates the accepted modes of communication it is unlikely to be well received. And it is absolutely unlikely to be received mythically. That is why, for instance, the myth tales of primitive cultures do not fulfill a similar function in the modern world as they do for the myth-producers. So, too, the myth-system created by the Chinese Kung Fu movies or the Indian cinema remains unappreciated. The mythicization of history, therefore, undertaken by America and Japan remains a particularized achievement and one whose origins provide a deeper understanding into the acceptance of filmic codes and myths.

There are two immediate preconditions for the mythicization of history. One is the industrial capability to mass-produce a substantial body of films; the other is the ability of the society to support their continued production. The two preconditions arise simultaneously. Industrial growth occurs such that the manufacture of the necessary raw materials exists in the marketplace and there are industrial models for a film industry to imitate. At the same time, an industry arises and creates a marketplace for its product. The dialectic of production/consumption is thus able to occur within national boundaries.

These two preconditions met, there needs to be a free-enterprise economy to foster the dialectic between producer and consumer. This dialectic also implies a degree of freedom on the part of the producer and the consumer. We can see how attempts at the mythicization of history by Russia and Nazi Germany failed when they denied this aspect of the process.

Both the Russians of the twenties and the Germans under the Nazis undertook the mythicization of history in a manner similar to that of Barthes's first mode of myth, namely, that of the producer. The failure of the Russians was one of the inappropriateness of the forms they chose to "fill" the mythic signifier. A number of films were produced giving them the potential to create a substantial body of myths which would rewrite history in their own image. Yet the films were not understood as myths in the dynamic mode of reading. The artificial continuation of the films could continue without the necessary response (financial reward) from its intended audience. The Germans, on the other hand, filled their mythic signifiers with forms which too obviously asked to be read mythically. The anti-Semitic films proved to be an embarrassment to their intended audience, yet the governmental support removed the need for audience acceptance. The Nazi film-myths would have died out almost immediately had they been left to the process of the consumer society.

Given the industrial capabilities and the lack of governmental interference (Japan under the Militarists and America held in the grip of McCarthyism are interludes with censorship; yet still a number of film genres survived with little change), there yet remains one more precondition to the mythicization of history. Something in the society, something within the national identity must feel the need for such a transformation. While many cultures routinely have produced formula literatures, only Japan and America have formularized so much of their past.

It is possible that the not dissimilar economic structures created by America and Japan indicate a similar predisposition toward remaking their images. America's film industry was shaped by the model established by earlier corporate formations. This was a model of cutthroat competition which eventually gave rise to monopoly capitalism. In the early years, attempts were made to streamline production, to mass-produce films to reduce costs and maximize profits. This was one of the unexpected benefits of the star system. The stars became the center of attention of a mini-assembly line of producers, directors, and writers. What initially arose as scientific tools or entertainment gimmicks, soon became a major industry. The economic status of its citizens enabled them to support massive film production while their educational and emotional status caused them to cry out for a star-system and formula stories.

For America, the creation of hero-images out of movie actors is an index of the American search for a national identity. A land without a history is a land without a national character. Genres and stars, associated with certain aspects of the culture, create images which reflexively define the culture that produced them.

Early in this century, Japanese filmmakers and would-be moguls took the American film industry as their model. Certain Japanese companies attempted to form a monopoly and, failing that, created their equivalent of the Patents Company.[10] Despite the moguls' best efforts the star-system arose as well in Japan (which included making stars out of the "benshi" which was not a development the industry would appreciate when sound technology came along).[11] When the Japanese industry found itself faced with the star-system, it also discovered the relationship between star and genre, thus turning formula films into the backbone of the industry. In this respect, it is significant to know that the Japanese cinema has been even more formulaic than the American. The importance of this similarity between America and Japan is not that the Japanese turned to America as their model, but that the model worked.

Yet why would the Japanese feel the impulse to use film as myth to transform their history? Though they possessed the first two preconditions to the process, so too, did Germany before the Nazis (and Germany today) and, perhaps, today's Italy as well. There is a further complicating factor, namely that the Japanese have traditionally held the director of films in higher regard than have Americans. It seems paradoxical that creative individuals should produce formulaic works to such a degree. And most surprising of all is the fact that the Japanese already possessed a substantial corpus of mythology.

Few societies are as aware of their past as the Japanese. They boast of an unbroken line of Emperors dating back to Jimmu at the dawn of recorded history. And more ancient than that is the religion of Shinto, the way of the gods, which is very much in evidence in today's Japan. The Shinto creation myths are quite similar to the creation myths of many non-European nations. The "kami" of the Shinto belief possess a high degree to anthropomorphism, for instance. The heroic literature of the Heian and Momoyama periods survives as myth-tales and folk tales while the tradition of oral narration of such stories is still prized as a genre in itself. However, we must realize that the formula stories, the genre films, that have arisen since the birth of the movies are not cinematic translations of the earlier tales. They mark an almost complete break with them; a "remythicization" if you will. To understand this remythicization, we need remember the significance of the Meiji Restoration.

We may understand the Meiji Restoration as a deliberate attempt to redefine Japan along Western lines. The slogan that became the rallying cry of the anti-Shogunate forces, "expel the barbarians, restore the Emperor," once the Shogunate was disbanded, quickly turned into "form a Western society before we get chewed alive by the superior Western technology." Consequently, a new mythology would be needed to remake the past in this new image. The new film industry at the turn of the century was in a unique position to take on this task given the Japanese fascination with the new medium. The early American film industry appealed primarily to the working class, but the Japanese films found a home among the middle and upper classes, precisely the people who would go on to work in the forms they were seeing. The wrench in Japanese society at the time of the American Occupation might have been even more severe than the changes at Meiji.[12] Accordingly, it comes as no surprise to see certain film genres, such as the Samurai film and the "Mother" film, reasserting themselves in the middle fifties. The older myth tales extant in the new Japan had been formulated to explain the then-contemporary society which felt a strong bond with the mythic past of the tale. The new Japan now needed to redefine, remythicize its image to make the past correspond to the present. In order to achieve this, films about the past became rigidly separated from films about the present. Formulas arose to fill the void created by this suddenly pastless society.

The Field of View

There are two broad categorical distinctions in the Japanese cinema. They are the *jidai-geki,* or period film, and the *gendai-mono,* or modern story. These are not genres as such, but rather handy references to describe the rather broad outlines of the narrative's placement. Basically, a *jidai-geki* is a film whose action takes place before 1868, the year of the Meiji Restoration. The modern story, then, is a film taking place after the time of the Restoration. (There is a small category of films known as *Meiji-mono* which revolve around the period of Restoration and the problems of restructuring the society on avowedly new principles.) In point of fact, the distinction between *jidai-geki* and *gendai-mono* is neater in theory than in practice. But the mere fact of the distinction is indicative of the Japanese feeling of the modern era beginning with the downfall of the Tokugawa Shogunate.

It is my contention, as indicated above, that the *jidai-geki,* per se, is not a genre. And yet too often we read critics who fail to distinguish one kind of period film from another. Even a priori, it should be clear that Mizoguchi's *Sansho the Bailiff* and Kurosawa's *Yojimbo* are two films of a different ilk. Though both are "period" films, their emphasis, narrative, stylistic, and themes have little in common except on the broadest of levels. Clearly, there must be a separation within the *jidai-geki* (and the *gendai-mono*); separate, distinguishable genres must exist and must be definable according to some defensible, logical boundaries.

The genre which I wish to subdivide out of the period film is the "Samurai Film." The Samurai film, in one sense, is more easily definable than the relatively more amorphous genre of the Western. The Samurai was an identifiable caste in feudal Japan distinguished by a certain status, mode of dress, and the like. There is no corresponding caste, or class, to which the Western can refer. The historical setting in "the Old West" is further no guarantee of generic bounds, as, for instance, *Gone With the Wind* is not considered a Western while *The Good, The Bad and The Ugly* at least qualifies as a Spaghetti Western, despite the fact that both films are set during the Civil War. The Samurai film, as a genre, becomes a bit more complex, when we begin to claim that those films which center on non-Samurai heroes yet whose focus is on men (or women) who wield swords in feudal Japan, is also a Samurai film. Anderson and Richie offer a generic definition which begins to distinguish the genre along narrative-structural lines.

> The hero in all these films was usually a samurai, masterless or not, or sometimes a sort of "chivalrous commoner" who is allowed to carry a sword—or again, he might be a gambler. The plot usually turns upon his receiving an obligation, usually accidentally which he must discharge by performing some dangerous or distasteful deed, often in conflict with other duties or obligations. Other plot movers are revenge and the protection of the innocent.[13]

Although Samurai, commoner, or gambler takes up a potentially broad range of the social spectrum, and the incurring of an obligation, the seeking of revenge or the protection of the innocent a large number of narrative possibilities, the above description is nonetheless an accurate assessment of the Samurai film. The only thing that should be added is the plot of conflict between two feudal clans, or between a Samurai and his lord.

Just as the genre of the Western takes shape when we understand it from the iconic standpoint, so too, the Samurai film can be defined along iconic lines. In addition to the historical setting, a key icon of the Samurai film is the Samurai sword. The wearing, in full view, of the long killing sword immediately places one in the genre of the Samurai. And it is the use of the sword to bring the narrative conflicts into resolution that basically completes the fundamental definition of the genre.

Naturally, the above is over-simplified. Some true Samurai films contain little killing, others seem devoted exclusively to the use of the sword (called in Japanese *chambara*, Sword Drama). Some Samurai films focus on feudal society and politics; others seem to ignore the historical setting. To this end, I have divided the Samurai genre into sub-genre which are descriptive rather than prescriptive. The forms I will discuss are to be considered ideal types. But before turning to those sub-genre some general comments about Japanese history, culture and language are necessary to understand the forms.

The Historical Background

The Samurai film is set in Japan's feudal past, which at its broadest can be considered from the years 1188-1868, encompassing the Kamakura, Momoyama, Muromachi, and Tokugawa eras. These years correspond to the rise of the warrior class and its assumption of power from the Emperor's court to the disbanding of the Samurai shortly after the Meiji Restoration. Yet, like the Western film, the Samurai film has chosen to situate itself only in a part of this broad spectrum. At its broadest, the period covered by the Western includes the years 1750-1917, yet most Westerns confine themselves to the years 1830-1890. So too, the Samurai film concentrates its attention only on the Tokugawa era from 1600-1868. And this is the great paradox of the Samurai film and what gives it its mythical foundations.

The Tokugawa era marked a period of virtual peace. After approximately three hundred years of Civil War, Japan was unified under the powerful Tokugawa *bakufu,* firmly ensconced in Edo. Unfortunately, virtual peace makes a warrior class obsolete. Trained in the ways of war and led to believe in Bushido, the way of the warrior, the Tokugawa Samurai were soldiers without a battle. Under the developing bureaucracy of the Tokugawa regime there was indeed a need for the Samurai, but not as fighters. Under the Confucian-style government modeled on the theories of the Chinese philosopher Chu Hsi, the reading, writing, and leadership skills of the Samurai could be put to use in administrative and governmental functions. The structuring of the Tokugawa society into four distinct classes placed the Samurai at the head of a formalized organization. They became not only the most likely, but literally the only candidates for bureaucratic posts. "In every castle-town there was a multitude of posts to be filled, their duties ranging from the formulation of policy to the government of rural districts, from control of finance or archives to service as attendants, guards and messengers. All were filled by Samurai...."[14] This is quite a different picture than armed men engaging in skilled and deadly contests! Bushido, under the Tokugawa, "...was as much a code of the bureaucrat as of the soldier."[15] The new bureaucrats received a salary, or stipend, in the form of *koku* of rice.

To consolidate their power and to preserve it, the Tokugawa Shogunate closed Japan to foreign trade and input and attempted to stratify the society in a stable manner. Moving from class to class in the form of upward mobility was difficult. Even climbing the bureaucratic ladder was hard, for in keeping with Japanese tradition, many posts became hereditary. The move toward stability by the Tokugawa extended to the economic plane. They tried to regulate growth by controlling the amount of new arable land that could be reclaimed. Unfortunately, the *bakufu* was soon left behind by a new class.

The rise of the merchant class begins concurrently with the stabilization of the country's political situation under the Tokugawa *bakufu*. The stagnation at the upper level of society could not stop the relative dynamism of the new merchant class. The Samurai may have been tied to a rice economy, but the merchants knew the power of money. We should note that the rise to economic power of the merchant class also gave birth to new cultural forms like the Kabuki, Bunraku, and the wood-block print. For the Samurai, the failure to change to the monetary system would prove disastrous. For one, the Tokugawa regime required the powerful Samurai lords to set up household in Edo and be in attendance for at least half of the year. This meant that many Samurai supported two households at great cost. Edo merchants rose to the challenge by supplying the sometimes pampered, sometimes perverse, and sometimes curious Samurai with luxuries and pleasures. But only for a price and only in cash. "The improvident [Samurai] soon found that their new habits had left no margin to meet the sort of unexpected expenditures or loss of income which were occasioned by fire or flood.... The merchant became moneylender, making advances against future income.... By 1700 the whole Samurai class was in a state of chronic debt."[16] As distasteful as the idea might have been to a class taught to despise money, the Samurai soon found themselves at its mercy.

The obsolescence of the Samurai as a warrior class during the Tokugawa era is one of the key structural underpinnings of the Samurai film. Filmmakers' seeming unwillingness to situate their Samurai dramas in the more violent Momoyama or Muromachi period indicates the function the Samurai genre fulfills to the Japanese mind. The audience must confront, at every moment the film is on screen, both the obsolescence and eventual destruction of the way of life of which the hero is a part. It puts the hero of the film in the curious position of being unable to succeed no matter what course of action he takes, a point to which I will return. For the meantime, it is worth examining the significance of situating the films during the Tokugawa era from the point of view of narrative tension.

If the Western finds enormous dramatic potential by situating itself at a frontier, the Samurai film seemingly has no similarity. The gunfighter in cinema exists at a moment of tension, at a moment when a nation is poised on the brink between savagery and civilization. The gunfighter is in the vanguard of a new culture spreading ever westward. It is the gunfighter who combines traits of the savage ways and traits of the civilized ways and who, through choice or otherwise, brings about a new society. The days of the gunfighter are known to be numbered, and often, as in *Shane* or *The Wild Bunch*, the gunman knows it too. However, the demise of the shootist implies the rise of a new civilization. He may ride off into the sunset, but the sun will rise on a new culture.

Japanese filmmakers have realized a very potent frontier precisely in that juncture between the Samurai class and its obsolescence. A tension exists because the Samurai warrior is born into a rigid society that extends back over a thousand years, but is soon doomed to extinction. The Samurai class will be abolished and the wake of World War II will leave his code in ruination. The frontier becomes a psychological one of a nation trying to hold back the inevitable, of a heroic, but ultimately futile struggle to preserve a way of life that will disappear and give rise not just to a new civilization, but one which will in many instances, repudiate its forebears. This difference in phenomenology between the Western and Samurai film can be understood as one of elegy versus criticism.

The classic Western film possesses an elegiac tone, a nostalgia for the wide-open spaces that seem to have disappeared. To a citified people, the landscape of the Western itself calls forth a wide variety of emotional responses. Primary among these responses is the relationship between the environment and the men who inhabit it. In one sense, it is very true that the Western is a man's genre. The "feminization of the American male"[17] calls forth a cinema in which the camaraderie of men in isolated outposts, in small professional groups, or alone struggling against wild men and the elements, is prized above the society of women. It is only after the Indians have been subdued, the bandits jailed, and the streets made safe for decent people that feminine-associated images like schools and churches arise. As Robert Warshow has noticed, the Western genre is an "adolescent" one in which the boys/men escape the women/mothers.[18]

This elegy for days gone by when men were men is missing from the Samurai film. Many of the Samurai films are overtly critical of the period in which they are situated. Those that are not call forth a very different kind of feeling, that known as "mono no aware" which is essentially quite distinct from nostalgia. I will discuss this later in some detail, but it is worth noting that for the Japanese the Samurai film calls forth a different sort of response.

We should note too, that the role of landscape in the two genres is wildly divergent. Once again, the Western's structuring principle of Desert/Garden is entirely missing from the Samurai film. The struggle to survive in a harsh environment that shapes the Westerner's character has no counterpart in Japan. If we Americans are proud to have conquered our wilderness, transformed it, in fact, the Japanese have always felt themselves blessed with nature's bounty. More than any people on earth, it seems, the Japanese are more conscious of nature's beauties. Typical Japanese activities are such things as flower arranging and flower viewing. Perhaps one of the greatest ironies one can point to is that despite the Japanese love of nature, Tokyo is plagued by pollution (although a cleanup effort is meeting with much success). Often Mt. Fuji cannot be seen through the smog.

The Samurai hero does not move through a landscape to be conquered and tamed. Although scenery, as such, is often prized in the films, the hero is shown to be in harmony with his environment. A film like *Jeremiah Johnson*, for instance, has no counterpart in the Japanese cinema. Once again, if the Western finds a natural source of drama in situating itself at the frontier of a hostile, forbidding environment, the Samurai film must look elsewhere for its conflicts.

In addition to a frontier of hopelessness, of a doomed struggle for the Samurai, the Samurai film finds a kind of interior frontier in the struggle between *giri* and *ninjo*. Usually and basically translated as "duty" and "human feelings," *giri* and *ninjo* occupy primary positions in the entire Japanese cinema. From the powerful anti-feudal dramas of Kobayashi to the gentle comedies of Ozu, from the humanism of Kurosawa to the dark sides of Oshima, the conflict between *giri* and *ninjo* is ever-present.

The Samurai hero, unlike his Western opposite, is born into a rigidly defined system which prizes its past. If the Code of the West evolved spontaneously (as much in cinema, one suspects, as on the real frontier), Bushido was actually codified. The non-conformist hero so prized in the Western was almost unknown in the Samurai film until Kurosawa introduced him to the form. It is not women who bring the code to the Samurai, but his past. Simply by being born into the caste, he inherits the code and all its myriad obligations. In the Western film, the true gunfighter is not born, he is forged by the harsh climate and the times in which he lives. The Samurai is not so much forged as molded so that when he grows older it is difficult to tell where training leaves off and humanity begins. To the modern Japanese this has great appeal, for despite the dissolution of feudalism, the *giri/ninjo* conflict continues. The Samurai film mythicizes the *giri/ninjo* conflict by placing it in historical situations and working out the conflict through heroic acts of violence.

Sign Systems

I discussed earlier the naturalizing function of genre films with regards to the signs employed. It becomes important now to understand the nature of signs and sign systems in Japan. And the first place to begin is with the morass of signs and structures which the Japanese have turned into their language.

Basically, the Japanese language consists of four "alphabets." There is the borrowed Chinese pronunciations and characters which when written are known as *kanji;* there is *hiragana* which are strictly phonetic symbols long ago adapted from the *kanji* but no longer related to them; there is *katakana,* another phonetic alphabet derived from the *kanji,* which has the same phonemes as *hiragana;* and there is *romaji,* the writing of Japanese in the Roman alphabet used in the United States.

As H. Paul Varley notes, the borrowing of Chinese characters by the Japanese in the Nara period is one of the most lamentable aspects of their language.[19] The utter dissimilarity between Chinese and Japanese, between monosyllabic and polysyllabic, has caused nothing but problems for Western and native scholars and speakers. The Chinese character is not simply a phonetic symbol. In and of itself it has a meaning in addition to a pronunciation. Initially, the Chinese alphabet was a pictorial rendering of the objects to be represented. Today one has to be sensitized to decipher that the character for "older brother" is formed by a union between two characters which render the concept into a "mouth with legs."

The first adaptation of the Chinese alphabet attempted to utilize the *kanji* as phonetic symbols. The classic poetry anthology, *The Man'yoshu,* is written in this fashion.[20] When that proved incompatible, it was decided to keep both the meaning and pronunciation from the Chinese, while the strictly phonetic use remained in the rendering of proper names. Today, even with the *kanji* limited for the most part to 1,850 different characters, written Japanese is a complex problem.

A typical Japanese sentence consists of *kanji* and *hiragana* (and sometimes *katakana* as well). The *kanji* become verb stems, proper nouns, impersonal nouns, and adjectival stems. Basically, one must be able to speak Japanese before one can read it.

The Japanese educational system devotes much time to the teaching of *kanji,* with an expected mastery of a certain number at the end of elementary, junior, and senior high school. The use of *kanji* may also be seen as a status symbol or an index of one's educational attainments. The *kanji* are necessary to avoid a potential source of confusion that could arise if *hiragana* were the sole source of written information. Many words have a similar pronunciation (such as "kami" for paper or for the Shinto gods, "hashi" for bridge and chopsticks) but their *kanji* are different. Although it is possible to write all of spoken Japanese in *hiragana,* the *kanji* eliminate confusion.

The use of both *katakana* and *romaji* might be good indexes of the pervasiveness of foreign influence. *Katakana* is used today for the phonetic rendering of foreign words. This is not to be confused with foreign words which have become a part of the native vocabulary, such as the Portuguese word "pan" for bread. Western names, for instance, would be written in *katakana,* although again, one must have a sufficient familiarity with spoken Japanese to recognize the original source. Just as one can theoretically write all of Japanese in *hiragana,* so too, with *romaji* (although similar confusing incidents would arise). At one time in post-war Japan a movement arose to transform all of written Japanese into *romaji,* but many thought that was carrying the penchant for things Western a bit too far.

Another important feature of the Japanese language, and one with great psycho-sociological significance, is the levels, or degrees, of politeness which appear. These levels are social codes which betray education, social standing, maturity, and the expected self-effacement the mature Japanese person is expected to manifest. One level of politeness is a kind of neutral level which is appropriate for any occasion. Still, even speaking with these forms the mature Japanese person and the adult Westerner speaking Japanese are expected to use certain humble/honorific forms such as the two pronunciations for "father" corresponding to one's own father and the other's. Using the wrong word for father or mother would be a total and complete mistake. A Westerner could perhaps be excused for using the wrong form, but he would be looked down upon. For a native speaker, such an occurrence is almost impossible. For adult speakers of Japanese, there is a more complicated humble/honorific system which consists of different verb stems used to honor the other and humble onself. What these do to the native speaker is to foster a respect for others while building up a corresponding denigration of self.

Another important characteristic of the Japanese language is the so-called "gender-based" forms that appear in certain kinds of prefixes and sentence endings only appropriate for a specific gender. Women are taught to honor, through the language, kitchen utensils, for instance. These gender-based forms not only add a subtlety to the language almost impossible to translate, they also create different world-views in the native speakers.

It is important to note that, despite the complexity of the language, or perhaps because of it, the Japanese have a basic mistrust of words. They have no tradition of rhetoric, of great oratory. Rather, they are appreciative of understatement and subtlety, a trait which extends to much of their artistic tastes as well. As a corollary perhaps to the mistrust of words, there is a great emphasis on para-linguistic codes, such as the dress of school children, the amount of food one should eat at a meal, the proper time, place and manner of expressing emotions and the like. Truly, the Japanese have a multiplicity of codes and a great awareness of them.

The significance of the Japanese language in relation to their traditions and appreciations of art, including film, is found precisely in this multiplicity of codes. The variety of alphabets in the language, the number of para-linguistic and dress codes, give the Japanese people a built-in sensitivity to the arbitrary nature of the sign. However, if the function of language is to naturalize the conventional, the Japanese language might be said to have naturalized the idea of the arbitrary.

Scholars have noted the traditional willingness of the Japanese artist to call attention to the signs of the art it utilizes.[21] Indeed, this aesthetic mode has made Japanese art so popular with modernists. It is typical, for instance, for Japanese wood sculpture to use the textures of the wood as an integral part of the design. So too, traditional Japanese architecture is designed to blend in with the surroundings. An examination of Japan's major theatrical genres will also demonstrate their use of aesthetic signs.

The Nō theatre of Japan, though never a popular theatre in the true sense of the term, is a highly influential art form. Begun around the twelfth century, the Nō theatre emerged as a highly esoteric presentational form which relies on dance, music, masks, and declamatory narrative to relate traditional folk tales. The narrative, as such, is both minimal and known to its audience. What little story is told is a function of the declamatory narrative combined with the precise and subtle movements of the dancer-protagonists. Each gesture performed has a specific meaning which must be learned by the audience that seeks to understand it. The encoding and decoding of the Nō presentation is thus dependant upon exclusively arbitrary sign systems; sign systems, which unlike much of Western aesthetic presentations, are designed to call attention to themselves. In Nō, one decodes the gestures, the masks, the music, and not the narrative being related.

More popular theatres like the Bunraku and the Kabuki move the Japanese theatrical tradition a little closer toward representational modes, but, as Burch points out, "towards (but only towards) a representational theatre."[22] The Bunraku and the Kabuki plays were rather complexly plotted works involving many of the themes and concerns which appealed to the burgeoning middle-class which patronized them. Yet compared to the Western bourgeois theatre which strove ever closer toward Naturalism until it reached absurd proportions in the 1930s for instance, the Bunraku and the Kabuki are extremely stylized forms.

Perhaps the most striking instance of their non-Naturalistic approach, and their willingness to call attention to the play as *play,* can be found in the figure of the "kuroko," the black-clothed stage hands who change sets in full view of the audience. In one sense, they are regarded as "invisible," a convention, like the closing of the curtain in the Western theatre. But the curtains never do close in Japan. The *kuroko* operate in full view of the audience. And how invisible can they truly be if Shinoda can utilize their very presence to such an extent that they take on a positive character in his film *Double Suicide?*

The whole mode of presentation of the Bunraku theatre, itself, can be taken as an index of the aesthetic mode in Japanese art. As Barthes notes,[23] the Bunraku play operates on three levels of signs simultaneously. There is the level of the puppets themselves, their action and costumes. There is also the level of the puppet-operators. And there is the level of the half-declaimed, half-sung narration, which can further be broken down into the words spoken and the stylization in which they are delivered. Such a compendium of sign systems which constantly call attention to themselves, allegedly while delivering a narrative, is totally alien to the West.

There is yet another theatrical convention that separates East and West and that is the use of stage scenery. The Kabuki, with its live actors, is content to use a painted back-drop stretched horizontally across the stage. Depth, both on the stage and in the painted back-drop, is eschewed. Indeed, although I will return to this issue, horizontal versus in-depth composition seems to be an interesting way of distinguishing East from West.

I have saved perhaps the most revealing and distinguishing argument about the nature of signs for last. And that is the convention of the *oyama*. The portrayal of women by men is, of course, not specific to Japan, or even to the Orient. And both Eastern and Western utilizations of male in female roles arose for the same reason: governmental edict. It was precisely the drive and demands of naturalism that demolished the practice in Europe. In China and Japan, the same call for reality was not apparent. Yet even during Europe's phase of male substitution, the actual performances were not mannered, or "signed" in the way the *oyama* had been trained. The use of males in women's roles in Europe was indeed strictly conventional. In Japan, it was turned into an art, with the male actually embodying the signs of femininity. The appreciation of the *oyama* roles requires a subtle dialectic between the obvious felicity of the actor as a woman and the fact of maleness. The *oyama* goes beyond female impersonation, for the actor does not imitate the characteristics of a particular woman in a kind of caricature. He adopts femininity, transforming himself from the outside in, in a kind of reverse method-acting style. The *oyama* is stylization taken to its limit and it too was eventually replaced by the demands of naturalism made by the cinema. As late as the 1920s, however, even in film, the *oyama* could be seen.

The language of the Japanese and their use of the aesthetic mode in virtually all their arts translates into a cinema in some ways equally as willing to forego naturalism and the naturalizing of conventional signs. The various kinds of traditional Japanese painting (e.g., landscape painting in the so-called Chinese style or the Japanese style, calligraphy, Zen brush painting, etc.) has led to a highly pictorial sense in the Japanese cinema. The fact, too, that directors like Ozu and Kurosawa were actually trained as painters, has encouraged directors to explore the pictorial side of the motion picture.

The extensive use of icons to define roles, character and setting bespeaks a sensitivity to the pictorial elements. The icons of the Samurai film, even more so than the heavily iconic Western genre, define and delimit the form. From head to toe, the Samurai is a walking sign-system. From his well-groomed hair tied in a top knot to his silken kimono which bears the family crest to the two swords worn in their carved scabbards, the Samurai defines himself. And should we see a man walking a dusty trail in a colorless and dirty kimono with its obi still containing the two swords, we are immediately confronted by a *ronin* who has little left but pride in himself and his code of Bushido. Iconography, at this level, formed an important part of the early, silent Westerns. The good guy in white and the bad guy in black were shorthand, pictorial ways of defining who was who. As conventions they kept in force, extending to the classic *Shane* in which a buckskin-clad Alan Ladd confronts a villainous, black-clad Jack Palance.

The great complexity of signs extends often into the narrative as well. Indeed, failure to comply with certain codes is all that drives the classic Japanese revenge tragedy, *The Loyal 47 Ronin*. Or take a scene in *The Sword of Vengeance Part I (Lone Wolf With Child)* where the hero, Ogami Itto, cannot be struck with a sword so long as he wears his kimono with the Shogunate crest. The sign equals the status; there is no separation. I will show later, how Kurosawa himself builds a whole film around this idea of signs in *Kagemusha*.

Pictorial signs within the narrative are combined with a sense of graphic design and pictorial composition that also distinguishes the Samurai film from the Western. Although both film genres early on adapted CinemaScope, the uses of the process differ widely. As we know, 'Scope was adopted in America in order to compete with television which had robbed the motion picture industry of much of its audience. The Western also coupled 'Scope, and other wide-screen processes such as VistaVision, with color to further separate films from televison. In Japan, on the other hand, 'Scope was often separate from color, and Samurai films made in black and white continued to proliferate into the sixties. Many American directors forced to shoot in 'Scope often circumvented the wide screen by masking off the frame with props. In Japan, 'Scope was adopted for its wide-ranging pictorial possibilities. When adopting 'Scope, the Japanese filmmaker demonstrated his willingness to work with horizontal staging while ignoring, many times, the demands of composition in depth. Significantly, while declining to work in depth, the typical Japanese director of Samurai films also made no effort to define off-screen space. Simply put, the Japanese filmmaker in this genre, was most definitely not working in the "realist mode." It was Kurosawa, unsurprisingly, who introduced both depth and off-screen space into the form as we will see.

Another Japanese tendency in the Samurai form is the emphasis on graphics that "dehumanize" the human characters. This reduction to graphic design is an index of the Oriental attitude toward the idea of the individual. In the West, the individual is sacrosanct. To the Oriental mind he is not. In "the way of the warrior" the life of the individual Samurai is worthless. He is willing to take his own life at any time as symbolized by the short sword he always wears. Pictorial compositions which place the characters in a two-dimensional scheme symbolize this relative worthlessness.

The Samurai Film

Another reduction of the value of human life may be seen in the sheer number of deaths which many sword films deliver. It is not unusual for the Samurai hero to dispatch dozens of swordsmen to their death. Or, again, using *The Sword of Vengeance* series for my example, people are literally only the sum of their parts, as piece by piece, antagonists are chopped apart—an arm here, a leg there, a hand yonder. Even Kurosawa finds this to be true in the famous shot from *Yojimbo* in which a dog crosses the screen carrying a human hand.

Pictorial, or graphic concerns, become then, one of an equal series of signs and sign systems which the Japanese filmmaker utilizes simultaneously. Like cinema everywhere, the signs are encoded in a complex chain of events which are decoded by audience members who possess various levels of sophistication. It is the hallmark of the Japanese cinema that the very multiplicity of sign systems throughout the culture makes their audience more receptive to the multiplicity of sign systems within films. This multiplicity, however, has led to a complexity in the Samurai genre, whereby simultaneous, and often conflicting, "messages" are delivered. To understand these messages I have isolated four traits—"types" or sub-genres—which can explain how the mythicization of history has come about through the use of the Samurai film.

Genre Types

The genre types I have isolated stand more as paradigms than hard-and-fast sub-genres within the Samurai film. Although the lines between the sub-genres are not always clear-cut, there are nevertheless certain tendencies that are specific to the individual types. Although they may overlap in terms of production, these varieties have emerged more or less over a given period of time in chronological order. To a great extent the sub-genres emerge as the culture changes. This simply reflects the relationship between popular formulas and the culture which gives them their origin. For instance, the sub-genre of the aviation film was once an important sub-genre of the Adventure formula. Around this same period we also saw a heavy reliance on the stock character of the newsman. Both the aviation film and the newsman are mostly extinct (noticing that the success of *All the President's Men, Lou Grant,* and *The Great Santini* have not spawned a wave of formula imitators). So too, the Samurai film has reflected Japan's changing attitudes towards its past and its present.

At one point during the thirties, Sword dramas were the most popular films in Japan. Richie and Anderson, looking back on that period, have little to say about many of the individual works, isolating only those that either stray from the norm or define the norm.[24] Such popularity was not to continue into the immediate post-war period. The occupation army (SCAP) put forth a list of regulations with regard to film content which certainly seemed to eliminate the possibility of making Samurai films. It prohibited, for instance, films "favoring or approving feudal loyalty [and] direct or indirect approval of suicide."[25] SCAP also prohibited the showing of Kurosawa's maiden directorial effort *Sanshiro Sugata* and Inagaki's original tackling of the story of Musashi Miyamoto in a film of the same name. Under such conditions the Samurai was unlikely to prosper.

An early period film produced under SCAP's watchful eye was Mizoguchi's "democratic" interpretation of the life of the wood-block artist Utamaro, *Utamaro and His 5 Women*. Although the film was well received in Japan, it did nothing to encourage further efforts in the field of period dramas. Sensitive Japanese directors were both encouraged and inclined to produce contemporary social documents that explored the almost constant crisis conditions which then prevailed. The incredible success abroad of Kurosawa's *Rashomon* was not only the breakthrough in terms of Western appreciation of Japan's filmic treasures, but also began a flurry of interest in period dramas. Although not a Samurai film, *Rashomon* spawned films like *Gate of Hell* and Mizoguchi's *New Tales of the Taira Clan* which moved tentatively toward dramas concerning Samurai. And when in 1954 Kurosawa proved to his contemporaries in Japan that it was possible to deal with true fighting men in a dramatic fashion as *Seven Samurai* so clearly did, the drought was ended. Inagaki's *Samurai Trilogy* was produced and a host of inferior films followed.

By the years 1959-61, the Samurai film once again became a staple of the Japanese cinema. Much of this output is clearly "B" features produced and released by the Toei company. These "B" features were enormously successful and they in turn spawned bigger-budgeted pictures which chose to deal with swordsmen and sword fighting in similar fashion. By the time the mid-sixties rolled around, all the major studios were making Samurai films of a like nature. And we should note, by the mid-seventies, the Samurai film, like the American Western, was basically dead. However, unlike the American Western, the Samurai film survives quite comfortably on television with little content or formal change.

The growth, development and change of the Samurai genre corresponds to the sub-genres I have isolated. The initial wave of Samurai films which began with *Seven Samurai* belong to what I call the sub-genre of the Nostalgic Samurai Drama.

The Nostalgic Samurai Drama

The Nostalgic Samurai Drama begins, as I have said, with *Seven Samurai*. These films, although they may be action-packed, as *Seven Samurai* itself, or more contemplative as the work of Inagaki, the paradigmatic director of the form, reveal the special Japanese propensity for what they call *"mono no aware."*[26] This feeling of "sweet sadness," or an almost inexpressible nostalgia which is pleasantly painful, runs throughout the work of Ozu and so seems at first glance surprising in the Samurai form. And yet, it should not be thought so strange.

Ozu achieves his effects partly by juxtaposing the cares of the individual against the stillness of nature or his surroundings. Ozu's people struggle for happiness and rarely achieve their true heart's desire. When Ozu's people reflect on their past, as they so frequently do, they discover as much pain and dissatisfaction as they do pleasure. And yet they rarely grieve outright. Rather, they savor the combined feelings. So too, the protagonists of the Nostalgic Samurai Drama rarely achieve a total victory. Their achievements invariably are mixed. The director may show this in a number of ways, the most common of which is to have the hero die. Although he may have reached his goal, he is not around to savor the fruits of victory. Examples may be found in Inagaki's *Bandits on the Wind* or his version of The Loyal Ronin tale, *Chushingura*.

The Nostalgic Samurai Drama usually focuses on a *ronin*, a masterless Samurai. The term *ronin* itself means "wave man," an index of the status he now possesses. He rides the waves of fate helpless to battle against wherever it may take him. A *ronin* is not likely to find employment as a true Samurai, for these films are situated during the Tokugawa era, and in times of peace, a lord *(daimyo)* is not likely to need his services. It was true of most *ronin* that they were unlikely to seek another kind of gainful employment as say, a craftsman, an artist, or a priest which might have been logical options. One simply did not give up one's Samurai status for mere money. The *ronin* then, becomes a wanderer, a doer of good deeds in exchange for food and gratitude. He rarely has enemies of his own; his enemies become the enemies of those on whom he would bestow his beneficence. And when the *ronin* has dispatched these doers of evil, he sets off again to wander.

Mono no aware arises on a number of levels in this sub-genre. One stems from the fact that the *ronin* hero does not forge a new society. He never questions the moral right of the system which has given rise to his existence. He sets off on the path of righteousness out of a sense of obligation. Trapped in the ways of *giri/ninjo* he can do little but serve. He can, at least, follow some of the dictates of *ninjo* even though he still feels the pull of *giri*. The *ronin* might try to sever his links with his feudal past in order to cut ties that bind by changing his name. As a sign which links him with the past, his name calls forth all of his obligations; by changing it the *ronin* attempts to recreate himself. He never can, of course, and so becomes a tragic figure.

The tragic figure of the *ronin* in the Nostalgic Samurai Drama is also found in the Anti-Feudal Drama interestingly enough. Both sub-genres play upon the Japanese penchant for "The Nobility of Failure."[27] To the Japanese mind the self-sacrificing hero is the most admirable hero of all, as witness the innumerable versions of The Loyal 47 *Ronin* tale. The man willing to give his life for the cause is held in the highest esteem. The Samurai retainer who commits *seppuku* to convince the lord to hear his plea is a self-sacrificing figure that the West is hard pressed to duplicate. The Western hero may be willing to give his life to the cause, as for instance, the man stepping in front of a bullet to save the life of another, but we in the West prefer a live hero to a dead one. Hollywood formula stories almost always demand that the hero be left alive at the end.

However, the nobiity of failure extends well beyond this conception of living or dead. It is not just the dying that the Japanese admire, it is the hero who struggles for a doomed cause. The hero of many Nostalgic Samurai Dramas (and Anti-Feudal Dramas) fights and sides with the inevitable loser. Even when the cause is clearly lost, or *especially* when the cause is lost, the hero can be seen proudly fighting to the bitter end.

We might take note, for instance, of the many instances in which Japanese audiences admire the men fighting on the Shogunate side around the time of the Meiji Restoration. While most Japanese today would side with the Meiji forces they nevertheless admire the Samurai fighting to keep the Shogun in power. It stems not from any nostalgia for the feudal past, for few Japanese would advocate a return of feudalism, but from the perception of the nobility of failure. The very inevitability of the hero's defeat gives rise to *mono no aware* for it combines the admiration of purely heroic deeds with the knowledge of their uselessness. The Nostalgic Samurai Drama is nostalgic, then, not because it desires to call forth positive memories of the middle ages, if such a thing were possible, but because it gives rise to *mono no aware*.

The feeling of *mono no aware* is a very special Japanese sensibility, treasured in much of Japan's artistic genres and it arises mainly from purely formal means. *Mono no aware* is produced in art by a combination of the seen and the unseen, the written and the unwritten. As an aesthetic principle it arose in the Heian period (e.g., *The Tale of Genji*) but was soon replaced by the notion of *miyabi,* the courtly refinement which was not at all intended to produce the sweet sadness or the "sensitivity to things" of *mono no aware*. The aesthetic of *mono no aware* is best represented by the *haiku* which in three lines captures a scene which holds in its boundaries both life and death, timeliness and timelessness. Although many feel that *sabi* ("old," specifically taking pleasure in antiquity) communicates the feeling of the *haiku,* the finest of them contain that ambivalence, a tugging and twisting that causes exquisite sadness that is pleasurable, best defined as *mono no aware*.

Another Japanese artistic form which is prized because it gives rise to *mono no aware* is the *haiku* equivalent of painting—water-color brush painting. A few broad strokes of the brush conjure up a whole scene, which, like the *haiku,* is denotatively simple yet connotatively rich.

So too, there is a formalistic approach in the Nostalgic Samurai Drama which elicits *mono no aware*. The analysis of *Seven Samurai* in chapter 3 will demonstrate in detail the filmic foundations of this approach. A discussion now of one of Hiroshi Inagaki's more unified (and overlooked) films can also elucidate the formal basis of the sub-genre.

Filmed in black and white, *Bandits on the Wind* is one of Inagaki's most artistically satisfying films, perhaps because it elicits *mono no aware* so completely. The plot line of *Bandits on the Wind* could just as easily have served to create an Anti-Feudal Drama, yet Inagaki's handling of the material puts it firmly in the Nostalgic Samurai sub-genre. The film focuses on a small village forced to accede to the unreasonable demands of a feudal overlord. Into this volatile situation ride three *ronin* who quickly get involved with the villagers against the specific advice of the *daimyo's* retainers. At the end of the film all are killed in a fierce battle, but they have, in this case, won their cause.

Inagaki's treatment of the heroes is both gentle and slightly mocking. Moreover, they are not superb fighters (unlike the three *ronin* in Gosha's *Three Outlaw Samurai*). These men grow into the role of hero as they become involved in the plight of the villagers. The villagers come to love them so that their deaths take on slightly tragic/pathetic proportions.

Yet it is not simply in the tragic death of the likable heroes that we find the feeling of *mono no aware*. Inagaki has the ability to use his camera (whether shooting black and white or color) and art direction to reflect characterization. Although his treatment of action is grossly inferior to directors like Kurosawa and Gosha, his graceful camera movements imbue his films with a great deal of sensitivity so long as the narrative justifies it. (He is capable of using this same style in the service of wildly improbable scripts.) In *Bandits on the Wind* we must first take note of the use of black and white cinematography, for Inagaki himself had used color to marvelous effect in *Samurai Trilogy* and *Rickshaw Man*. The black and white becomes an aesthetic device which in this case reflects the Japanese ideal of *wabi* ("poverty"; the prizing of that which looks simple). Like a monochrome painting, *Bandits on the Wind* tries to capture a landscape without coloring in its details, details which might detract from the purity of its vision and the feelings its hopes to arouse. Too, the camera movements tend toward horizontal tracking which deemphasizes the depth of the screen. The relatively long takes combined with this movement tend to link the surrounding natural landscape with the village itself, calling forth an association between nature and the villagers. Nature, per se, is a common artistic image which alone seems to be sufficient to call forth *mono no aware*. Too, the final death scene of the film recalls the shot that closes *Ugetsu* wherein a gentle crane-up of the camera reminds one of the timelessness of nature compared to the mortality of the human body.

The structuring of the *giri/ninjo* conflict and its ultimate resolution is also a distinguishing feature of the Nostalgic Samurai Drama. To the Japanese of a very confusing modern world, the period film in general offers a clear picture of good and evil, right and wrong. Doubtless today many Japanese are caught up in the kinds of existential crises previously unknown to the Japanese of an earlier age. Whether or not the hero succeeds, and he usually does not, he moves in a world of clear-cut moral choices. When confronted by the *giri/ninjo* dichotomy, the hero of the Nostalgic Drama chooses the one or the other, knowing full well the price to be paid. When he chooses *giri* he duplicates the socialization process whereby the Japanese are asked to suppress a part of themselves. If and when he chooses *ninjo* he breaks out of the powerful codes which rule Japanese life.

What remains fascinating and crucial to our understanding of the Samurai form is that, of course, the *giri/ninjo* conflict is unresolvable. The mythology created by the Samurai film which structures this conflict into the narrative of its tales, never resolves it but in true mythic fashion disperses the feelings. By bringing the *giri/ninjo* dichotomy to the surface, and by choosing the one over the other, the *ronin*-hero recreates the crisis for the audience and resolves it ritualistically. The climax of virtually every Samurai film (as in the Western) is a violent one. The choice the *ronin* has made leads inevitably to violence and usually his own death. The cathartic nature of the violence helps to resolve, temporarily, the anxiety created by the realization of the problem's ultimate irresolution. The hero becomes a kind of sacrifice in the ritual of repeated formula stories. In the Nostalgic Samurai Drama, this sacrificial hero becomes associated with the lower classes on the narrative plane and with nature on the formal level, so that the viewer is left savoring life's ironies and its impermanence. He is reminded of the bittersweet nature of existence and treasures that feeling.

The Anti-Feudal Samurai Drama

Following close on the heels of the first wave of Nostalgic Samurai Dramas were the Anti-Feudal Samurai Dramas. This sub-genre has produced, outside of Kurosawa's works, the best-known and critically respected films in the Samurai field. This is mainly due to the films of Masaki Kobayashi and Hideo Gosha. Kobayashi's *Hara-Kiri* (1962) and *Rebellion* (1967), in particular, stand as extremely popular films both in Japan and here in America and as paradigms of the sub-genre.

It is surprising to note, considering the kinds of virulent anti-feudal films with modern settings produced in the fifties, that the forceful Anti-Feudal Samurai film did not arise earlier in the post-war era. It is difficult to explain why. One possible reason might be the unwillingness of filmmakers with an anti-feudal theme even to work in the feudal setting so soon after the repressions of the militarists who glorified Bushido. Another reason might have to do with the turmoil which arose in Japan starting in 1960.

The Japanese became a divided people over the issue of the renewal of the Mutual Security Pact with the U.S. in 1960. Actual rioting broke out over debates and in the ensuing violence hundreds of student protestors were injured.[28] These mass demonstrations arose when the Socialists boycotted the Diet debates over renewal and the government party ratified the Pact in their absence. Students, labor union members, and civil servants took to the streets, their virulence causing President Eisenhower to cancel his scheduled visit to Japan in honor of the new Pact. Although the Pact remained in force, Prime Minister Kishi resigned.[29]

Under these conditions, filmmakers were reminded of the militarist past and of the possibility, at least, of becoming involved in militarist politics. The Mutual Defense Pact called for an increase in Japan's visibility in world politics and their implicit siding with America in the still-sensitive Cold War. To the left wing such an alliance was cause for bitter disagreement with the more conservative Liberal-Democrats. Filmmakers in the intellectual forefront, like many of their intellectual counterparts in other media, have typically sided with left-wing tendencies[30] so that a seeming return to militarism, even at this low level, was cause for concern.

The Anti-Feudal Samurai Drama arose in the early sixties as a possible filmic reminder of the dangers of feudalism, of putting the system before the welfare of the individual. This sub-genre seems to have no formulaic counterpart in the Western genre. The so-called strain of "demythological" Westerns tend, as many Westerns do, to concentrate on individual character. A film like *Dirty Little Billy* (Stan Dragoti, 1972), a fairly unpleasant attempt to tell the "truth" about Billy the Kid, savors the demythification of the legend. Films like *Soldier Blue* (Ralph Nelson, 1970) and *Heaven's Gate* (Michael Cimino, 1980) tend to be more critical of institutionalized policy but they are by no means a part of a cycle. This demythological impulse is a strain of the Western that is both intermittent and reactionary in the true sense of the term. It responds to other films in a deliberate reversal of the prevailing mythos. The Anti-Feudal Samurai drama is more complex, responding both to earlier portraits of the era while at the same time responding to contemporary issues and concerns.

The Anti-Feudal Samurai Drama is complicated further by the filmmakers' seeming inability to overcome the archetypal mythos of "the nobility of failure." For while these films may denigrate a whole system with a staunch virulence, they almost inevitably juxtapose the system with a truly tragic-heroic figure. Succumbing to this temptation tends to take the sting out of the indictments. Works like *Hara-Kiri* and *Tenchu* (Gosha, 1969) are powerful anti-feudal works, yet their tendency toward sentiment at worst or *mono no aware* at least undercuts their intent. Kon Ichikawa, unsurprisingly, has come closest to achieving this aim with his part-Samurai, part-*yakuza* black comedy, *The Wanderers* (1973).

The Anti-Feudal sub-genre can be distinguished by its structuring of the *giri/ninjo* conflict. As we have seen in regards to the Nostalgic Dramas, the conflict, basically unresolvable in reality, is structured so as to cause *mono no aware* in the viewer. The hero is torn between the impulses of *giri* and *ninjo* and can never quite choose the one or the other. In the Anti-Feudal Samurai film, the hero inevitably opts for *ninjo*, for humanity over the system. Taught from birth to obey the feudal laws, the hero will be confronted with a situation in which obedience becomes impossible.

The heroes of the Anti-Feudal Drama are almost invariably men of position, men (and women) who respect the code of Bushido and who serve their feudal lords faithfully. The heroes are rarely at the top of the societal rung; rather, they are ordinary Samurai who have been born with a certain status which they expect to maintain by playing by the rules. The society demands and expects something from these men, and they likewise expect something in return.

The hero of these films has been born into a pre-existing situation; the pathos arises when we realize that the situation is stagnant. If the Western film celebrates the imminent changes to be made on the Frontier, such as the coming of the railroad, the building of churches and schools with all of their symbolic intent, the Anti-Feudal Drama revels in the impossibility of gradual, orderly social change. Historically, the audience knows that a social change will indeed come about, but it will come at the almost total expense of its predecessor. When the Samurai hero, through no fault of his own, loses his status, there is virtually no way he can regain it. Becoming a *ronin*, a wave man, is inherently more painful and pathetic for him than his Nostalgic counterpart. The hero remains bound by *giri* but can look forward to no corresponding *on*, the obligations met by his superiors. His choice of options at this point is bleak.

The extreme bleakness of the *ronin's* alternatives inevitably puts him in contact with his repressed *ninjo*. Yet whatever he does spells his doom, for he can work to bring about the destruction of the system which has mistreated him, in which case the Samurai as a class are eliminated, or he can accept his fate with a whimper and struggle to eke out a living in some other fashion. Such a bleak view of the human condition seems unique to the Japanese cinema and might be one reason why Western critics, including Donald Richie and Joan Mellen, tend to regard this sub-genre with the highest respect of all the Samurai films.

There is another reason that the Anti-Feudal Samurai Drama has found favor in the West. (Many of them have found favor in Japan as well. *Hara-Kiri* was named Kinema Jumpo #3, while *Rebellion* won the coveted "Best One" for 1967.) The Anti-Feudal film is a deliberate attempt by modern filmmakers to address contemporary issues in the period setting. We in the West prize a film like *High Noon*, even though it seems to me to be an inferior Western, because it addresses issues like courage in the face of pressures to conform. In one sense, it would be pointless for filmmakers to castigate a society that no longer exists; hence it is clear that the Anti-Feudal film speaks to today's Japanese. And the virulence with which they rail against the filmic societies which they portray is an anger unmatched by any other native film genre. The Japanese tendency toward self-hate is rather extreme, matching, paradoxically, their tendency toward feelings of cultural superiority.

Because the Anti-Feudal films so clearly address contemporary issues, Western critics respond to them as serious films as opposed to the action-oriented *chambara* which they either ignore or misinterpret. In order to attract the native audience, however, the Anti-Feudal Drama is obliged to present at least one scene of sword-fighting action. In this manner, it achieves its genre or "exploitation" status while delivering its political/social message. However, the blaze of violence which climaxes the films also serves a cathartic function, just as in the Nostalgic Drama. The now-disenfranchised hero may die a pathetic death, but it is one possessing the nobility of failure. He would rather die fighting, knowing he cannot succeed, than live a life of poverty, of ignoble deeds and actions. Yet in the Anti-Feudal Drama the violence is more graphic; the climactic conflict bloodier. The hero himself tends to be a better swordsman than the Nostalgic Drama's *ronin* as if to demonstrate the point that all his training and skills are ironically what caused his violent death.

The Anti-Feudal Drama, then, relies heavily upon the juxtaposition of a trapped individual existing within a rigid social structure. Formally, the films lean toward 'Scope framing which emphasizes the space around the individual, as if to deemphasize him. Too, there is a greater tendency toward working in depth in this sub-genre which further puts the individual in some kind of context. Certainly, we cannot compare the formal strategies with those of Italian Neo-Realism or even the French New Wave, for virtually no Samurai film is "realist" according to any Western aesthetic system. It is a question of degree. The lyricism and the linkage to nature found in the Nostalgic film here give way to a camera style which, while it may be graceful, is also forceful while society (in the form of buildings, streets, formal gardens, tea rooms and the like) replaces nature. In short, humanity is beaten down by society.

Zen Fighters

It is axiomatic by now that there is a close relationship between Zen and the military classes of Japan. All histories of Japan note the rise of Zen concurrent with the rise of the Hojo regents of the Kamakura Shogunate (1185-1338). Yet it is worth exploring briefly the interconnectedness of Zen and swordsmanship, for the ideals make their way into the films of Kurosawa as well as form the foundation of a sub-genre of the Samurai film, which I have termed "Zen Fighters."

"We have the saying in Japan: 'The Tendai is for the royal family, the Shingon for the nobility, the Zen for the warrior classes and the Jodo for the masses.'"[31] With Zen's belief in intuition over intellect, in seeking a path and following it without hesitation and the denial of both life and death, it was a natural philosophy for the warrior seeking glory to adopt. Zen caught the fancy of the Kamakura Shogunate due in part to its greater simplicity compared to the esoteric Buddhism practiced by the decadent Fujiwara courtiers in Kyoto. It is worth noting as well the implicit political basis upon which Zen was first adopted by the warrior class. The landed aristocracy, including many ex-emperors, had infiltrated the higher echelons of the Buddhist temples. The close political ties between the Buddhist church and the Kyoto court made esoteric Buddhism a volatile system for the Kamakura Shogunate to deal with while attempting to unify its power. Zen was adopted not only for its freedom from esoteric practices and texts, but from the influence of the established Buddhist temples.

As the Muromachi and Momoyama periods wore on, Zen more firmly attached itself to the warrior class due to the nature of the teaching methods it came to adopt. Zen stories abound with legends of fighting monks who challenge, and defeat, master-swordsmen. The idea of questioning a priest and receiving a sharp blow from a stick in lieu of an answer must have exhibited a certain attraction to fighting men. The spirit and teaching of Zen also appealed to the native mistrust of the rhetorical and the facile. Although the Japanese Samurai tended to be reasonably well educated, he would still have preferred the subtle, the mysterious, and the arational to the more dogmatic forms of Buddhism. Too, Zen's tendency toward self-reliance and self-enlightenment would have appealed to him more than the simple "Amidaism" which raged across Japan from time to time, especially among the peasantry.

The sub-genre of the Samurai film which I call Zen Fighters deals with warriors of ancient legend or modern creation who explicitly invoke and evoke Zen Swordsmanship. This sub-genre both precedes and post-dates the Nostalgic Drama, especially when dealing with that most famous of Japanese Swordsmen, Miyamoto Musashi. We should note, however, as a point of interest, that Inagaki's *Samurai Trilogy* which deals with Musashi tends more toward the Nostalgic than the Zen Fighter sub-genre. The reason, of course, lies in the treatment of its subject.

There are a number of film versions of the life of Musashi, with much agreement as to the facts of his exploits. Musashi was born around 1584 under the name of Shinmen Takizo, and he fought on the losing side at the battle of Sekigahara. A desire for fame and a wild temper landed him in constant trouble until he fell under the sway of the Zen priest Takuan. Under the tutelage of this highly influential figure, Musashi was transformed from a young ruffian into a disciplined fencer. In addition, he became well known as a skilled calligrapher and artist working in ink. Although Musashi died in 1645 in the service of the *daimyo* Tadatoshi Hosokawa, most of his adult life was spent seeking duels to test the perfection of his swordsmanship.[32] In this quest, the legend of Musashi comes literally head-to-head with another legendary Zen fighter, Sasaki Kojiro, also the subject of numerous films. What we must note here is the

Japanese acceptance of the idea of perfection removed from morality. Perhaps an example from Musashi's legendary exploits will demonstrate this.

There is the famous story told about Musashi of how the family and students of a swordsman Musashi had defeated challenged him to a duel. They secreted themselves at the appointed spot in a wooded field, placing their eight-year-old family head in the middle of their ring of warriors. Musashi, suspecting their scheme, contrived to fight them anyway by killing the young boy, which he did. Never is the moral rightness of Musashi's actions questioned.

The sub-genre of the Zen Fighters ignores, or perhaps, transcends the social context of its times. The *giri/ninjo* conflict is transposed into a more Zen-like conflict, which can be expressed in Buddhist terms as between the forces of Samsara and Nirvana. That is, the struggle between the illusionary world of everyday reality and the release from the cycle of death and rebirth. What Zen has done is to find a way to use the things of our own existence as the way to a transcendence of it. Rather than the need to lock oneself away in a monastery (although there are certainly Zen temples of this sort), there is the Zen of real life which allows the artist, the poet, the street cleaner, the teacher, and the swordsman, to practice his craft. Zen encourages the practitioner to attain the state of *mushin* (nomindedness) so that his actions may flow freely, unencumbered by conscious thought and intervention. *Satori*, the sudden enlightenment of Zen, can come at any time, but only after the conscious mind dissolves itself. To the swordsman, such a view was needed to encourage him to remove his ego from the contest; to practice his art in combat without concern for its eventual outcome.

Although Zen philosophy has it that the best swordsman never uses his sword (recall a remark to that effect in *Sanjuro*), for cinematic purposes, that would be quite impractical. What Zen has encouraged in the Zen Fighter sub-genre is the focus on swordsmen who remove themselves from the constraints of Bushido in order to achieve perfection in the art of swordsmanship. In this manner, filmmakers can pay lip service to the ideal of the "sheathed sword" while delivering a startling and often frightening array of terrific sword fights.

The usual screen portrayal of Musashi has him as a man obsessed with testing his skill as a swordsman. A more typical example than Inagaki's *Samurai Trilogy* is Tomu Uchida's six-part *Zen and Sword* (1962-64). Each feature barely longer than a television episode, details another duel in Musashi's bloody career. It is, however, precisely in the deliverance of the blood and gore that the Zen Fighter sub-genre distinguishes itself. More so than the climax of the Anti-Feudal film, the Zen Fighter picture offers extremely graphic images of death. The removal of the social context from the films tends to make its heroes, including Musashi, stand outside of time and transforms them into mythical warriors who are beyond the bounds of society and morality. Zen translates into nihilism quite easily in this sub-genre.

To the modern Japanese, bound by the notions of *giri* and *ninjo,* the Zen Fighter offers an image of a man who has transcended entirely *both* forces. The hero shows his disdain for life by constantly engaging in fights to the finish; he shows his disdain for common morality when he shows himself willing to kill women and children. This latter ideal would virtually never appear as an attitude in the hero of the Western genre. It is the Gangster form in the West which fulfills this kind of function, yet though the main protagonist engages in this kind of activity, few could call him a "hero."

Certainly, there is in the Western an equivalence of the Zen ideal of worldly detachment combined with supreme confidence. A remark made by John Wayne in *Rio Bravo* is indicative of the Zen ideal of the sheathed sword when he says a gunman is so good he does not have to prove it. The difference is that while the gunman has arrived at this state through a kind of natural grace, the Japanese swordsman strives to attain it.

Another possible way to understand the essential difference between Eastern and Western in this case is to understand the difference between existentialism and Zen. The two philosophies are concerned with the ways of living one's daily existence. The difference is in the issue of transcendence. To the existentialist, there is nothing to transcend. Each day is a struggle, but ultimately there is only defeat. In Zen, each day is not a struggle because essentially there is no "I" struggling and there is therefore neither victory nor defeat. In both the Western and the Zen Fighter film, the heroes often engage in "pure struggles" with only their skill with their respective weapons acting as the margin between life and death. The Western existentialist and the Eastern Zen believer each look upon the fight with calm and dispatch. To the Westerner if this fight does not end in his death, the next one might. To the Easterner, here is a chance to lose himself in the purity of combat.

The setting of the Western film enables it to achieve its purity of vision. The awesome and desolate vistas literally remove the hero from a social context. Many Westerns make this use of landscape both explicit and symbolic, particularly those of Anthony Mann and Budd Boetticher. The Zen Fighter lives in a landscape of the mind, moving through cities, towns, and fields which seem timeless and permanent. Years and the passage of time have little relevance to this sub-genre. Formally, the works in this sub-genre lean more toward the use of dynamic montage than either the Nostalgic (which uses almost none) and the Anti-Feudal (which also rarely utilizes this technique). The montage, as is the nature of editing, breaks up space and reconstructs it. Although Noel Burch makes much of the Japanese tendency to ignore certain "rules" of decoupage, the Samurai film tends to obey them, so that the cutting patterns of eye-line matches, direction matches, etc., are adhered to. Basically, since the outcome of the typical contest is well known to the audience, particularly when Musashi is fighting, the cutting is employed to generate suspense and tension physiologically. The key element in the genre is the fact of the hero's transcendence of the social codes. The next important point to realize now is that the hero usually survives.

The Sword Film

Commercial appeal, both in Japan and in America, combined with critical deprecation mark the last of the sub-genres in the Samurai film. I call this group the Sword Film and see it containing many of the films that the Japanese call *chambara*. Literally translated as "sword play" films, *chambara* is often used interchangeably with what I call the Samurai film. To avoid this confusion then, I call the sub-genre the Sword Film as I will outline its structural elements below.

First we should recognize some of the economic, cultural, and societal forces which gave rise to what is in many ways the most interesting and revealing of all the sub-genres of the Samurai film. The Sword Film as I define it begins with Kurosawa's *Yojimbo*, hits its stride in 1962 with the first "Zato Ichi" film and reaches its zenith in 1972 as the first *Sword of Vengeance* is released. Structurally, if not stylistically, these films have much in common with American films, especially the Western and the Gangster forms.

By the late fifties, Japan had absorbed American culture to the extent that it could partially be called a "Western nation." And if Japan made American culture its own, it also developed American problems and concerns. Japan, once neatly divided between its urban and agrarian societies, became like America, a primarily urban culture. In redeveloping its industrial capabilities, Japan found itself dependent upon maintaining a favorable balance of trade and upon relying on the international marketplace to dispose of its manufactured goods. It could neither feed its own on the food it could grow, nor handle its own industrial output within its national boundaries. Once fairly insular with regards its own film production and exhibition, Japan was suddenly faced with the fact that foreign films, particularly American ones, were often more popular.

In order to compete with the imported American films, Japanese filmmakers went the route of either big-budget (by Japanese standards) spectaculars or lower-budget exploitation pictures. Taking the latter course meant attracting a certain audience who would guarantee a profit for each film. In this fashion, Japan developed the modern "B" feature along much the same lines as America did during the same period. The success of "B" features which were completely formulaic encouraged others to try the "A" feature approach, figuring that the bigger budgets and stars might lead to bigger box-office. It was in this fashion that the Sword Film arose, beginning with "B" features from Toei studios in imitation of *Yojimbo*. Soon studios like Daiei, Shochiku, and Toho all got into the marketplace with these new kinds of Samurai films.

To attract an audience obviously supportive of American films, these genre pictures were obligated to deliver the kind of action and pacing that are hallmarks of Hollywood's style. Since the stylistics employed by many of the American films appealed to this new mass audience, there was reason to believe that Western-style heroes and villains would as well. The heroes of these Sword Films soon came to take on many of the attributes of their Western counterparts. Yet, the Sword Film did not entirely reject the past. Rather, it borrowed elements from all three sub-genres and neatly added the more Westernized traits.

The Sword Film, like the Nostalgic Samurai genre, usually uses a *ronin* as its hero. More rarely, the hero will begin as a clansman, but will lose his status. Like the Anti-Feudal Drama, the films are situated in the Tokugawa era, but like the Zen Fighter films, the society is pretty much laid aside. Like the Zen Fighter, the hero of the Sword Film is a master swordsman, but he does not live merely for perfection of his art. Like the Zen Fighter films, and like the Western, the hero of the Sword Film lives—he is a survivor. So much a survivor in fact, that the sub-genre of the Sword Film is dominated by multi-part series or heroes recurring in film after film. (There are twenty-three "Zato Ichi" films, for instance.)

There are two crucial borrowings from the Western, both of which distinguish this sub-genre. One is the element of "sword for hire"; the other is the pivotal role of the villain.

The hired gun is a popular formula character in both Westerns and Gangster films. It is a reflection, no doubt, of the mythos of capitalism. One perfects one's skills not in a Zen quest for transcendence through the action, but in order to be competitive in the marketplace. His fast draw and deadly aim become negotiable skills available to the highest bidder. There is a proviso here, however, and that is that the hero will reject the offer of money if the cause is unjust. Typically, he will sell his gun but join the other side once he realizes the criminal or immoral aims of his employer. Many Westerns use the structure of hero and villain linked by their deadly skills and separated only by the one's higher moral ethics. The hero will switch allegiances; the villain will stay on the payroll. Eventually, the two will come face to face in battle.

The "sword for hire" appears, of course, in the Nostalgic Samurai drama, but the element of "hire" per se, becomes deemphasized through narrative linkage of the hero with those whom he comes to rescue. In the Sword Film it is not unusual for the hero to require a large sum of money first and inquire about the cause second. If the Western hero seems an altruist with a gun, the Sword Film hero will kill anybody as long as his price is met. The "sword for hire," and for an extremely high price, reflects Japan's changing attitudes toward merchant capitalism. Bushido, as I have mentioned, disdains money. For the hero of the Sword Film to sell his sword arm, as it were, becomes a kind of perversion of the code.

The function of the antagonist in this sub-genre is also a distinguishing feature. In the earlier sub-genres, the structuring is one of the individual versus the society, as personified by the *giri/ninjo* conflict. The actual villain is depersonalized into a system in both the Nostaglic and Anti-Feudal Dramas. In the Zen film, the antagonist is important for his skill as a swordsman, but he is sought out by the hero. That is, the antagonist does not manipulate the plot.

In many Western films, the hero takes on significance in direct proportion to the villain he opposes. The greater a man's enemies, the greater a man he is. If the villain is weak and ineffectual, the hero's task does not seem especially heroic. There must be a sense that the hero can lose but that he will not. In the remarkable Westerns of Anthony Mann and Budd Boetticher, the villains and heroes are linked, either by family as in Mann, or by paired oppositions as in Boetticher. Hero and villain can be seen as two sides of the same coin or as the anima and animus.[33]

In the Sword Film a similar pattern of matching oppositions occurs. For the first time, the villains are personified as viable, powerful enemies. For the first time, the hero struggles against a man (or men) and not a depersonalized system. Such a tactic enables the Sword film to dispense with the *giri/ninjo* conflict and move into the realm of a kind of "pure struggle" played out against a timeless landscape. Remember, although the Sword Film takes place during the Tokugawa era, it is a vague conception at best.

The Sword Film also offers up non-Samurai heroes. These men (and women) are highly skilled swordsmen, of course, but are not, and never were, members of the Samurai caste. In this sense, they can be perceived as more ordinary people who possess a certain skill rather than a certain social rank. It is as if anyone can become a hero in this kind of sword drama. Two of the more popular heroes in the form are the blind masseur, "Zato Ichi," and the blind woman "The Crimson Bat." The possibility of women heroes, in specific, offers up the chance for the individual audience member to perceive of himself as a possible hero. If one of the key factors in the Western is that virtually anyone can shoot a gun and so become a hero, so too, the Sword Film claims that swordsmanship is not the province of a special class. It brings the Samurai film to the level of a merchant society.

Unlike the Western hero, the hero of the Sword Film tends to revel in the death and destruction he causes. He often acknowledges that he "treads the path to hell," engaging in a virtual slaughter-fest at least once in every film.

The underlying philosophy of the Sword Film, which many critics have noted,[34] is a kind of nihilism. The rigid moral codes of Confucianism here give way to a world of death and destruction brought about by personal considerations; by greed, jealousy, revenge. The Sword Film offers up a world of violence and chaos, a world in which people are mere objects for the cutting edge of a sword. Indeed, one of the most striking characteristics of the Sword Film is the "anti-valuation of the object."

Photo from *Shogun Assassin*.

The Sword Film is extremely violent both in regard to the number of deaths and the methods of death. The sight, in color, of fountains of blood emerging from headless bodies, of severed limbs flying through the air, is a common, and expected, sight in the sub-genre. People are reduced to their components. They become mere patterns of color and shapes. But the very extremity of the violence where people do not bleed but gush, removes it from the plane of reality. People seem more cartoon-like than anything else. It is significant that the paradigmatic Sword Film, *The Sword of Vengeance* series, was adapted from a popular newspaper comic strip. Comics, are, after all, simply drawings which emphasize line and form. The characters in comic books are not real people, but "essential people," people reduced to their defining essence. In a sense, they are archetypes, both physical and mythical. It is worth noting that the image of the "superhero" like Superman or Wonder Woman, arises in comic books and not films. Filmic heroes, even Douglas Fairbanks, tended to have at least one foothold in the real world. It was always the purpose of cinema in the twenties through the sixties to make the fantastic seem real. It is the purpose of comic books to make the fantastic seem incredible. The Sword Film, especially as it progresses into the seventies, begins to lose all its realistic ties, becoming a virtual *tour de force* of flying shapes and actions.

An index of the ever-increasing sense of fantasy, or at least far-fetched extensions of reality, is the number of antagonists the hero is able to dispatch in a single battle. Ogami Itto, in *The Sword of Vengeance* series, kills perhaps two dozen combatants in the first film but by the fifth or sixth entry is killing over a hundred, all by himself.

Given the reduction of characters to graphic elements, the extra-prowess of the hero and the removal of the historico-social context, the Sword Film begins to take shape as a sub-genre which operates on a slightly different order from the rest of the Samurai genre. The comparison with comic books, while important, does not go far enough to explain the genre's functioning. We must remain aware of the fact that, though the Sword Film is highly removed from reality, it still has a correspondence to it. And this correspondence is similar to the relationship of a myth-tale to the reality it tries to explain.

The hero of folklore or of tribal myths is often an idealized extension of certain features of a given culture. The mythic qualities of a Paul Bunyan or a Johnny Appleseed are an index of America's admiration of the staunch individualist who nevertheless makes a contribution to his fellow man. Folk heroes out of history like Jesse James or Robin Hood reflect our rebellious spirit which is tempered by ethical righteousness. Folk heroes tend simply to be just bigger, stronger, smarter and tougher than the rest of us. It becomes valuable then, to extract the character traits of the hero in the Sword Film to see just what kind of idealized image Japan, or a certain segment of her society, has of itself. The hero is a phenomenally great swordsman who does not hesitate to kill, who is not above killing for money and will even kill women and children for pay. He has abandoned all notions of societal responsibility, of family and friends. He deliberately treads the path to hell and seems to enjoy it.

Yet there is more to be said as to why the Sword Film can be understood as a kind of folk tale or myth-tale even more so than other kinds of genre films. Taken as a body of work, the Sword Film betrays a remarkable consistency of structure on the level of narrative. The films of this type seem to be Levi-Straussian variants of the same myth. If this is so we can perhaps isolate a "morphology" of the Sword Film along similar lines to Propp's *Morphology of the Folk-Tale*.[35] This "morphology" is reduced to its barest essentials, only to demonstrate the consistency of narrative patterns and character relations in the form. I do not wish to exhaust the Sword Film here but only indicate a possible method of analysis. This then is a schematic of how the films are put together.

(1) A scene of violence is underway
    (a) a battle in progress
    (b) a duel in progress
    (c) a quarrel in progress
    (d) a violent ritual in progress

(2) The hero is identified
    (a) the hero carries a sword which he uses successfully
    (b) the hero carries a sword which he deigns to use
    (c) the hero uses some other weapon

(3) The hero's circumstances are detailed
    (a) the hero is a *ronin*
    (b) the hero is a clansman
    (c) the hero is a non-Samurai wanderer who carries a sword

(4) The victim is introduced
    (a) a clan in need
    (b) a peasant in need
    (c) an errant child uncovered
    (d) a town in need
    (e) the hero is the victim

(5) The villain is introduced
    (a) a clan leader
    (b) a clan schemer
    (c) an *oyabun* (gang boss)

(6) The hero comes in contact with the victim
    (a) the wanderer-hero travels the countryside and gets involved
    (b) the victim seeks out the hero because of his reputation
    (c) the villain engineers the hero's destruction

(7) The villain's henchman is introduced
    (a) henchman is given a separate narrative segment
    (b) henchman is literally introduced by the villain

These first seven functions are what I call the standard Basic Situation. The Basic Situation is structured according to the following lined patterns:

```
(1)—(2)
(3)         or
(3)—(4)
(5)         or
(4)—(5)
(6)
(7)
```

In detail, it is organized according to the following sequence.

(1)—(2). Most of the films begin on a note of confusion with a scene of violence into whose midst we are plunged. It sets the tone of action to follow; it is a dynamic plunge into the filmic world, letting us know that anything can happen. The hero is perceived due to his superior abilities and attitudes.

(3) The heroes' circumstances are revealed indexically by the quality of his kimono, how many swords he carries (one or two), how he wears his hair, where he lives, etc. Often we get a glimpse of his circumstances in (1)—(2) wherein the hero walks a country road only to be attacked or to intervene in a quarrel.

(4) Sometimes the hero is the victim, in which case (3) and (4) are linked. Otherwise, a separate syntagmatic section will detail the victim, or the hero will witness the victim's treatment at the hands of the villain.

(5) The villain usually receives his own little syntagm in which he will reveal his aims, e.g., the hero's destruction or his victim's intended plight. Alternately, if he is an *oyabun,* we might not see him until later. This section will detail the villain through a third party.

(6) If the hero is not the victim he will now come into intimate contact with him/them.

(7) The villain's henchman will often get his own syntagm by way of dynamic introduction. Or he will be asked by the villain or a more minor henchman to show his skill.

Once the Basic Situation is under way, the Sword Film proceeds on its way toward the eventual meeting of hero and villain according to functions like this:

(8) The hero and henchman sound each other out

(9) The hero and victim form an intimate relationship
   (a) romance
   (b) romance with a member of the victim's family
   (c) extreme sympathy and pity for each other's circumstances

(10) The villain sends minor henchman to attack the hero

(11) The hero has an interlude
   (a) the hero engages in comic by-play and defeats the villain comically
   (b) the hero remembers his past life—relates to (3)
   (c) the hero comes into contact with a reminder of past life

(12) The hero engages in a slaughterfest of the villain's minions

(13) The hero defeats the chief henchman
   (a) a spectacular duel
   (b) the henchman decides not to fight

(14) The hero kills the villain

The relationships in the sub-genre can also be schematized in this fashion:

$$\begin{matrix} \text{hero} \\ \text{victim} \end{matrix} : \begin{matrix} \text{henchman} \\ \text{villain} \end{matrix}$$

The relationships here are to be understood both horizontally and diagonally. Often there is, as I have said, a linkage between hero and villain, but in the Sword Film the real bonded pair is hero and henchman. Many times, when the hero is the victim, there is no corresponding henchman so that the relationship is one to one.

The hero:henchman relationship helps us understand the kind of self-contained nihilism within the genre. The hero relies only on himself and attempts to be the master of his own fate. The fact that he helps others is secondary to his inner journey to the gates of hell, his quest for revenge. The henchman, on the other hand, has subjugated his desires to the villain. In some way, the henchman still subscribes to Bushido and is still involved in society, even if on the criminal side. The hero repudiates all society.

The nihilistic foundation of the Sword Film can also be seen by understanding the relationship between the individual and society in all of the sub-genres. The relationships expressed in the Nostalgic Samurai film and the Anti-Feudal Drama can be expressed in the following manner: *undervaluation of the individual : overvaluation of society*. Naturally, as we have seen, these two sub-genres are after very different emotional effects, yet they both are based upon societal superiority over the individual self.

The Zen Fighter sub-genre is quite the opposite: *overvaluation of the individual : undervaluation of society*. But the Sword Film is quite different still: *undervaluation of the individual : undervaluation of society*. Neither *giri* nor *ninjo* is to be prized. On every level the Sword Film emerges as a bleak, though very stylized and stylish view of the human condition.

The Mythicization of History and the Samurai Film

The rather extraordinary differences between the Sword Film and its filmic forebears bring up the question of how and why the myth is transformed. What this implies, among other things, is the presence of a "mythical signified"; or at least a kind of sub-structure which might be called a mythical signified. This sub-structure can be isolated according to various perspectives, as Levi-Strauss might have it, e.g., economic, political, cosmological. To understand the mythical signified would be it seems to isolate any given perspective. But that would, in a sense, defeat the purpose of myth as we have seen above in Barthes's analysis of the "reading" of the myths. In other words, the mythical signified can be said to be the process of signification itself. Understanding myth in the truest sense of the term is both instinctual and circular. Levi-Strauss's symphonic analyses of myths notwithstanding, myth is read only in the act of reading.

A complication with regard to cinema is precisely in the area of myth production and consumption. The deliberate creation of myth is not myth.[36] It is an elaboration of a myth; the use of a mythic motif; or the demythicization of myth, but it is not myth. To understand this we can look at the phenomenon of the *"auteur."* Myths are authorless; they are communications from society to its members, not from one member to his peers. Analyzing the films of Howard Hawks or John Ford at this point, becomes a kind of "chicken or the egg" controversy. We can isolate the mythic structures of Ford or Hawks but then cannot separate them from the creator known as "Ford" or "Hawks." Regardless of personality or intentionality, the attribution of a myth to an author negates its mythic capabilities.

The Nostalgic Samurai Film, the Anti-Feudal Drama and to a lesser extent, the Zen Fighter sub-genres, all attracted powerful *auteurs* to the form. Kurosawa's transformation of the Samurai film is a given; Kobayashi's anti-feudal themes extend to his war trilogy *The Human Condition;* Gosha's *yakuza* film *The Wolves* examines the *giri/ninjo* relationship in the same manner as his period pieces. Turning, however, to the Sword Film, we find (outside of Kurosawa himself, but he is a special case) many great stylists such as Kenji Misumi and Kazuo Ikehiro, yet in no way are they the "authors" of these films. The Sword Film is a formula tale of anonymity like myth. The very lack of authors enables the films to function on the myth-ritual level without interference and hence without being "read."

Still, it remains to be asked why the myth or myth-structure of the Samurai film should undergo so many peregrinations. Our discussion earlier of the bond between the formula film and the society which nurtures it implies that as the society changes, so too, the formulas. But it does not explain the transformation, if indeed one has taken place, of the mythos embodied within the formula. Levi-Strauss discussed "How Myths Die," although his analysis is over space and not time. Yet, it might be worthwhile to examine his thesis.

> Two paths... remain open (to a myth which is exhausted): that of fictional elaboration, and that of reactivation with a view to legitimizing history. This history, in its turn, may be of two types: retrospective, to found a traditional order on a distant past; or prospective, to make this past the beginning of a future which is starting to take shape.[37]

Obviously, one reason that he does not analyze how myths die in time is that the societies he focuses upon are, as we have seen, ahistorical; the implication being that the myths of these cultures do not, in fact, change. Recognizing, however, that modern societies do change, we must still admit that societal differences over time in our rapidly changing world equate with the changes that occur over space. The passing away of myth, or the disintegration of a myth's function can be understood to occur similarly. We can point to studies of Western film genres which take this view.[38]

Therefore, we can see that it is possible for certain of the sub-genre to lose their mythic utility and so become "mere dramas." Let us point to the Spaghetti Western and see the transformation over space equates to a transformation over time when America itself begins producing Westerns in the "Italian style" (e.g., *Hang 'Em High, High Plains Drifter*).

Fictional elaboration, however, dismisses myth entirely. "Reactivation" requires a subtle distribution between the myth and the "reactified" myth. Reactivation implies a conscious control, that is, "myth creator" at some level since the myth has ceased to function mythically. Whether forward looking or backward looking, the reactivator of myth must be part of a ruling-class in order to guarantee the means of myth-production.

The "ruling class" aspect of myth production returns us to the discussion of the mythical signified as the process of signification. It is, as we have seen above, the function of language to turn the arbitrary into the natural. According to Barthes, it is the purpose of bourgeois ideology to transform "the reality of the world into an image of the world, History into Nature."³⁹ The process whereby this occurs is in myth-making for "myth has the task of giving an historical intention a natural justification...."⁴⁰ In terms of bourgeois ideology and the sub-structure of the mythos of the bourgeoisie we cannot point to a single author and given the perpetuation of the status quo, the myths soon lose their point of origin. "... myth is constituted by the loss of the historical quality of things: in it, things lose the memory that they once were made."⁴¹ Films then, are built upon a mythic structure whose origin remains obscure and whose authorship is never questioned. Further, filmmakers who work within the status quo are liable to build their films on the very structures that have been ingrained into them as members of that society. It is only when a filmmaker rebels against the mythic strictures can the myth be isolated. And this occurrence corresponds to the "fictional elaboration" or deliberate "reactivation" discussed earlier.

One possible reason for the decline of the Nostaglic Samurai film can be laid at the feet of filmmakers who chose to focus on the "empty signifier" of myth. They began with concepts and sought forms, forms which would give rise to the feeling *mono no aware*. More complicated is the decline of the Anti-Feudal Drama *as a mythical functionary*. As a dramatic form, this sub-genre may have lost its popularity (due in part to its lack of the mythic function) but as an effective tool for aesthetic production it remains viable. To understand its mythic decline we must recall the close association between filmmakers in this sub-genre and the Japanese Left Wing. We have seen how left-wing politics infused these films and now we must again turn to Barthes to understand how myth works on the political left.

> ... myth exists on the Left but it does not at all have there the same qualities as bourgeois myth. *Left-wing myth is inessential*....It is an incidental myth, its use is not part of a strategy... but only of a tactics, or, at worst, of a deviation; if it occurs, it is as a myth suited to a convenience not a necessity.⁴²

Its lack of true mythic content springs from the fact that "the Left always defines itself in relation to the oppressed..."⁴³ So the Anti-Feudal film structures itself around the situation of *giri/ninjo* as expressed by the Tokugawa's societal repression of its individual members. The creator of Anti-Feudal dramas focuses on the "full signifier" of the myth and so requires a conscious mythic reading of his work. Too, the authorial presence, the knowledge and awareness that there is a creator behind the artifact, interferes with any mythic transmission that the film might possess. The discovery of *"auteurs"* in the Western, although this has never been pointed out to my knowledge, was a powerful weapon against the mythos they had been thought to embody. The personality structures of Ford, Hawks, Mann, and Boetticher removed the deeply mythic content of their films so that what had once been perceived as mythic artifact, as communications from society to its members by means of the ruling class, now became the products of recognizable personalities.

The Zen Fighter film managed to preserve its mythos while we can also say that it gave way rather quickly to the more violent, action-filled Sword Films. The Sword Film has, for the moment, retained its status as myth by remaining strictly generic, by not encouraging *auteurs*, and by not stretching the bounds of each new entry. The repetitive narrative patterns according to a similar morphology further equate the films with mythic tales. Thus far, this sub-genre has managed to avoid getting caught in a societal flux which would deprive the formula of its validity while it has not encouraged any powerful authors to demythicize its content.

But what is the mythic sub-structure which underlies the Sword Film? Is the nihilism, the violence, the seeming misanthropy to be read as the image of Japan's self? Or is there a mythic code that unlocks a very different kind of image? We have seen that one of the basic functions of the Samurai film was the mythic presentation of the *giri/ninjo* conflict. But we have not seen the way in which this conflict "mythicizes history." It does so by rewriting history as the struggle between man's society and man's humanity.

It becomes important again to recognize the key role that Confucian philosophy has played in shaping Japan's cultural heritage. The tenets of Confucianism, which were, remember, cosmological as much as philosophical, put forth a rigid social order based upon a divine decree. The individual was devalued at the expense of society. At every level of interpersonal dynamics, the individual was confronted by a need to relegate his status. From emperor worship, to ancestor worship, to filial piety, the single individual was always deemphasized. In attempting to mythicize history, the Samurai genre structures the *giri/ninjo* conflict toward a resolution on the side of *ninjo*. The breakdown of the Samurai class is both inevitable and natural, recalling that *ninjo* is literally, "natural human feeling." The oppression of the individual is thus seen as inevitably leading up to the present which prizes the right of the individual to pursue his own desires.

There was, perhaps accidentally, perhaps as a response to the militarism of the thirties, or perhaps as a response to Westernization, the introduction of a certain Marxist historical dialectic into the genre. In a sense, the Samurai film can be seen as a Marxist formulation wherein the proletariat are inevitably to triumph after a series of dialectical struggles against various ruling classes. What we see in the Samurai genre is the explicit, or sometimes implicit, opposition to the status quo. The Samurai is seen defending the farmers or the merchants whom he sees as "the only winners" of his violent struggle. Such a view of the past was not quite satisfactory, of course, to Japan's form of capitalism which has its roots in feudalism, if of a more benign sort. The prevailing mythos of the new Samurai film, the Sword Film, mythicized history ns the struggle for the arrival of the true individual, but it was to take place *outside* of society.

Thus we might say that the seeming nihilism of the Sword Film is, besides cathartic, mythic in the sense of bringing together the forces of capitalism and individualism. Couched in terms of extremely self-contained, often actually psychopathic heroes, the mythos of the Sword Film maintained that history was an evolution toward personal freedom to be attained outside of society, within the confines of the individual's own world. These films mythicized history by ignoring history. It turned the actual past into an iconic past devoid of actual indexes. Given the fact that modern Japanese society is not ahistorical, the Sword Film did the best it could to contradict that. "Myth deprives the object of which it speaks of all History. In it, history evaporates."[44] The sometimes glorious, sometimes shameful, sometimes disturbing Japanese past disappeared as a culture, giving way to men with swords roaming a land of violence and heroism.

Photo from *Seven Samurai*.

3

The Samurai Films of Akira Kurosawa

Kurosawa and the West

It would not necessarily affect my study's validity if Akira Kurosawa had never seen, read, or heard about a single Western artistic text. This study concerns a director named "Kurosawa," not a man who is called Kurosawa. In *Signs and Meaning in the Cinema*, Peter Wollen discusses the potential "biographical fallacy" with regard to Howard Hawks. He states that the study is concerned with a director who is called "Hawks" and is less concerned with the man behind the name.[1] The same is true here as well. I am not writing a biography. I say that my study concerns a director—Kurosawa—and that this director is not simply the man but the totality of his filmic texts. The contention, then, is that this director "Kurosawa" has been influenced by Western, specifically American, popular formulas, and that this "Kurosawa" has utilized these formulas to create works of art meaningful to both Japanese and American audiences. It might be useful to consider, however, the possibility that Kurosawa consciously adopted these Western formulas. In order to consider this possibility, biography might be necessary.

In 1927, Akira Kurosawa, the son of a middle-school Physical Education instructor, enrolled in the Doshusha School of Western painting.[2] The traditional Japanese penchant for classification naturally extends to painting such that various styles are studied separately. For instance, throughout the Muromachi, Momoyama, and early Tokugawa periods, landscape painting was divided into the Chinese and the Native *("Yamato")* styles. By the late Tokugawa period, Western art had made such an impact that it became fashionable to study and work in the new Western mold.[3] It is significant, in and of itself, that the future film director should come from a background which includes training in the visual arts, but it is obviously doubly significant that Western painting should have attracted him.

At this same time Kurosawa joined a Communist group called the "Japan Proletariat Artists' Group." "We [Keinosuke Uegusa and Kurosawa] signed up not because we were in love with Marxist theory, but because we felt such a strong resistance against things as they were...we were both [also] much interested in nineteenth-century Russian Literature."[4]

Again we can see the seeds of the concerns that will occupy the film director. First, the dissatisfaction he feels for "things as they are" will express itself initially in a desire to change the course of Japanese cinema and later to influence the whole of Japanese society. And secondly, we see the crucial, in some ways fundamental, attraction for Russian literature.

Another all-important influence on Japan's most Western director was his older brother Heigo. Heigo, who committed suicide in the early 1930s, was a popular *benshi* who specialized in foreign silent films.[5] Although Kurosawa was not a film buff by any means, his devotion for his brother inclined him to take note of the films which most attracted him.

Elsewhere, Kurosawa overtly acknowledges the influences upon him. "From the very beginning I respected John Ford. I have always paid close attention to his films and they've influenced me I think....Other influences...well, the first film that really impressed me was *La roue* of Abel Gance, and the pictures of Howard Hawks and George Stevens."[6] It is gratifying personally to learn of Kurosawa's respect for both Hawks and Stevens for, as I hope to show later on, both directors' works appear in altered forms in Kurosawa's own.

Interest in the West in these and other kinds of explorations might have given Kurosawa an extra sensitivity toward experimentation by introducing him to alternate ways of "seeing." The differences between Japanese (and Oriental) painting and Western painting is not simply one of brush strokes or the use of color, although these too lead the imagination into different directions. Rather, as developed earlier, such ideas as the centrality of the individual, symmetrical framing, perspective, etc., place the human subject in a different relationship with his universe. As the Meiji leaders discovered, the adoption of Western ways brings with it the adoption of Western cosmology. The slogan "Eastern ethics and Western science"[7] was an admirable attempt to create a new orientation for Japanese society, but new science (and literature and art) brought new ethics, morality and religions with it.

Kurosawa, confronted all his life with the idea of "Eastern ways in Western dress," found the film industry similarly structured by this dialectic. On the one hand, he found an industry modeled on the American system of studios, stars and genres. Yet, as traditional Japanese school-based aesthetics (i.e., an aesthetics based upon the idea of a "master" who passes the traditions on) found its way into the movie industry, Japanese directors became intimidated by the codified formulas that became law.

Examining the history of the Japanese film, one is impressed by the relatively few *"auteurs"* that can be discovered. There are indeed a large number of brilliant film stylists, but even stretching the bounds of authorial personality, one can point to many, many more in the Hollywood cinema. The paradox that explains this lack of *auteurs* in what is expressly considered a "director's cinema" is that by giving directors a free hand they discourage *auteurs*. The dialectic that gave rise to the noticeable hand of an author in the Hollywood cinema was the struggle between impersonal material and a personal stamp.[8] The director in Hollywood was considered a cog in a machine; nevertheless, the *auteur* director managed to impose his personality on whatever project he was given. The Japanese director, given a free hand, was nonetheless made conscious of working not just within a system, but a tradition. This tradition nurtured him and gave him a chance to work. It was difficult to break out of it, difficult more often than not because he also felt no compelling need to try.

Kurosawa's willingness to try and break away from the Japanese traditions through experimentation, in contradistinction to his compatriots, has led Richie and others to call him "Western."[9] Of course, we must distinguish Kurosawa-as-*auteur* from the *auteurs* of the Golden Age of Hollywood in that Kurosawa was not obliged to leave his mark on impersonal material; given his status as a director, he could pick and choose his subjects almost from the start. It is worth noting, however, that Kurosawa's cinematic experiments have been undertaken not only on formal levels but narrative levels as well. To a certain extent, this distinguishes him from great American creators who pushed the bounds of the cinema in only one direction. Griffith, for instance, virtually coded the cinematic language while working in the prevailing narrative mode of nineteenth-century melodrama. The dazzling *mise-en-scene* on Josef von Sternberg cannot be said to reveal a particularly rich narrative pattern. Even Ford, Hawks, and Hitchcock worked within the bounds of formula without ever quite exploding them. There is no need to press this much further. I am not trying to "elevate" Kurosawa above artists like Ford or Hawks. Rather, it is important to note how few American critics yet appreciate Kurosawa's bold attempts to twist the cinema to ever new shapes.

Another trait of Kurosawa's that seems to Westernize him, in the eyes of Western critics at any rate, is his humanism. ". . . it is Kurosawa's concentration on character and his belief in the value of individual action that reflects his occidental outlook."[10] Very different attitudes toward the individual and his relationship to his society do indeed distinguish the Orient from the Occident, and Kurosawa's primacy of the individual in his films does seem to Westernize him. Yet we must not forget the "Americanization" of Japan wherein the new generation, what the Japanese call *"apres guerre"* from the French, are as much Western as Eastern. American culture in the form of dress, sports, and movies has made an everlasting change in Japan so that today's young Japanese would no doubt feel right at home in Los Angeles (yet the reverse would not be true). Kurosawa himself is very much aware of this fact, for he says, "Perhaps it is because I am making films for today's young Japanese that I should find a Western-looking format the most practical."[11] This last statement implies that Kurosawa has made a deliberate choice in seeking Western influences.

Yet to ignore the fact that other Japanese artists have similarly discovered the Western notion of the individual would be doing a disservice to Kurosawa's place in the Japanese avant-garde. The "interior" novel of Henry James, James Joyce, and Virginia Woolf found its way to Japan in the 1920s and early 1930s.[12] At this time, i.e., just prior to the rise of militarists, Marxism had reached its pre-war height in Japan. Notions of individual consciousness and action as well as the idea of the individual as a member of a social class, a potentially revolutionary social class, replaced the idea of the individual as subordinated to a culture. The relationship, alluded to earlier, between Japanese writers and artists and the left wing led to a reexamination of the individual's function in Japanese society. Kurosawa's combination of an awareness of social class combined with the interiorized feelings of his characters put him in a different position with respect to Marxists or Feminists. Unlike Mizoguchi, for instance, Kurosawa's politics are not gender-based or class-based. Unlike a Marxist artist, Kurosawa utilizes characters suffering from psychological alienation, as the works of Dostoevsky exert a powerful influence on his conception of individual character. "A deeply ingrained nineteenth-century Russian literary cast can be seen in many of [his] characterizations...."[13] There is a quality of haunted obsession in Kurosawa's heroes as well as a tragic sense of fate overhanging them. Perhaps their sense of introspection makes them "Western" heroes, giving them a self-consciousness that to this day remains almost unique in the Japanese film. Perhaps only Oshima, the most radical modernist to emerge from Japan, shares this trait with Kurosawa. As such, we must recognize Kurosawa's affinities with the Japanese avant-garde.

Though Kurosawa has undeniable affinities with the Japanese avant-garde, he also worked within the realm of traditional film genres. There can be seen in his career an alternation between experimental works, such as the adaptations of Western literary classics, and generic, formulaic films. Yet, as any true experimental artist, Kurosawa does not simply take a routine approach to potentially routine projects. If *Seven Samurai, The Hidden Fortress,* and *Sanjuro* are not as obviously experimental or revolutionary as *Rashomon, Throne of Blood,* or *Yojimbo,* they are far from routine. In fact, given the nature of movie consumption/appreciation in Japan and in the West, one could say that the genre-based films occupy a more central, crucial place in the Kurosawa canon. We can use, to demonstrate this, the example of his adaptation of Dostoevsky's *The Idiot.*

The "recognized" degree of failure regarding *The Idiot,* or its "artistic inferiority to his best works,"[14] demonstrates once again the problems in overstepping the bounds of accepted convention. If it is true that "the fact remains that no other Japanese director has ever attempted to bring Shakespeare or Russian literature to a Japanese setting for a Japanese viewing public,"[15] it is also true that two out of the three such filmic transformations are among Kurosawa's least appreciated or revived works. *The Idiot* and *The Lower Depths* received the worst reception from the magazine *Kinema Jumpo* of any Kurosawa film since 1947. *The Idiot* did not even place in the "Best Ten" list, while *The Lower Depths* placed tenth. Every other Kurosawa film of the late forties, fifties and sixties fared far better on the rankings. Similarly, here in the West, *The Idiot* is infrequently revived while *The Lower Depths* is virtually never screened. Only *Throne of Blood* fared well.

Although I do not necessarily agree that *The Idiot* is artistically inferior or flawed, in fact, I think rather the opposite, as does Burch,[16] it is important to note the relative critical and commercial failure of this cross-cultural adaptation. What we are faced with is the fact that Kurosawa's genius is most appreciated by critics and audiences alike in films whose origins can be traced to traditional intra-cultural sources. His most famous films, outside of *Rashomon* and *Throne of Blood*, are genre works with affinities with both Japanese and American formulaic structures. Even those films adapted from the West, like *Throne of Blood* and *High and Low,* maintain a traditional narrative pattern revolving around a series of rising climaxes. Kurosawa, in these and other films, may introduce new structural tensions which virtually explode the old formulas, but at least he provides his audience with a comfortable and familiar means of entry into his work.

Although there may be a conscious imposition of the East/West dialectic on Kurosawa's part, it is still possible to pursue the line of enquiry on which I will embark even if there were not. The method of analysis employed here is structural and basically structure is unconscious. Even if Kurosawa explicitly adapted Ed McBain's *King's Ransom* for *High and Low* and implicitly adapted *Shane* in creating *Sanjuro,* the isolation of structural motifs would be unaffected. In some sense Kurosawa cannot help but be subject to the tensions of Western culture, and therefore similar formulaic patterns would likely arise in his films (Cf. Chapter 2).

The Period Films of Akira Kurosawa

Just as Kurosawa utilizes a dialectical tension between East and West in his films, and just as his films show other stylistic alternations, so too his whole career may be seen as a series of shifts. Just as Wollen claims that Hawks is a richer filmmaker for the dialectical alternation between the adventure dramas and the comedies,[17] so too Kurosawa's career might be fruitfully examined. An alternation between period and modern stories, between films of social protest and fanciful excursions, and between adaptations of Western works and reworking of traditional Japanese themes immeasurably enrich his *oeuvre*.

Once his career is firmly under way, Kurosawa may fairly be said to divide his time equally between the two sides of this *"auteur*ist dialectic." Such a pattern is in keeping with Kurosawa's stated intention to make films in the Western style for Japanese audiences. We notice for instance that *Scandal* (1950) is followed by *Rashomon* (1950), and that *The Hidden Fortress* (1957) is followed by *The Bad Sleep Well* (1958). Eventually, Kurosawa will find a way to combine virtually all of his concerns within the same film, as he does so brilliantly in *Red Beard* (1965) and *Dodeskaden* (1970).

This study, however, is not concerned with the entire *oeuvre;* yet, although I am most interested in the true Samurai films that Kurosawa made, I wish first to examine his non-Samurai *jidai-geki*. There are a number of reasons why I propose to do this. First, many of these films owe much of their strength to Western sources and motifs. Second, I may be able to clarify further the differences between the Samurai films and the non-Samurai *jidai-geki*. Third, many of the techniques and motifs appear in the Samurai films themselves. Fourth, these period films are too interesting to ignore simply because they do not happen to focus on Samurai.

The first film of any great director seems in retrospect to be fascinating. Sometimes, one is surprised at how ordinary a first effort from a soon-to-be-great director can be. At other times, one can immediately spot the signs of greatness. In the case of Kurosawa, his first film, *Sanshiro Sugata,* is not exactly the *Citizen Kane* of Japan; on the other hand, neither is it merely a routine piece of work.

Akira Kurosawa came up through the ranks as an Assistant Director, having first successfully competed in a placement examination for the position. As all other Assistant Directors in the Japanese industry, he was constantly given scenarios to write. His training in this area, and his natural adeptness with scripts, stood him in good stead with the man who would become his mentor, Kajiro Yamamoto. It is significant that Kurosawa had a major hand in shaping one of Yamamoto's finest films, *Horse* (1941), for the horse becomes in Kurosawa a frequent symbol of naturalness and power. Before directing his first feature, two of his scripts had been printed and one had even received an award. Neither was produced, however, as apparently they were not appropriate for war-time needs. "It was said that the reason none of his early scripts were filmed (until after the war) was that they showed too much American influence."[18] In *Sanshiro Sugata,* Kurosawa found a project that appealed to him and would likely meet the propaganda requirements of the Japanese militarist government. The film was based on a novel of the same name published in 1943. Although the novel was a great critical success, Japanese reviewers found Kurosawa's adaptation wanting in its portrayal of the spirit of judo.[19]

From our point of view, it is significant not that Kurosawa decided to make a film about judo, or the spirit of Zen in judo, but that he chose to film a story situated in the Meiji period. Kurosawa begins his career with a film about the junction of the old Japan and the new. The struggle in *Sanshiro Sugata* is between ju-jitsu and judo, which comes to stand for the struggle between the old ways of traditionalism and feudalism and the new ways of competitive individualism.

Historically, judo arose in the Meiji period as the sport form of ju-jitsu. Judo was the invention of a Japanese physical education professor who intended that it be used to teach the martial spirit in the schools. For many years, due to being the official sport of Japan, Japan dominated the judo matches at every Olympic games. Judo soon became, before karate, one of their most popular sports exports.

What *Sanshiro Sugata* presents, then, is the struggle between tradition and innovation within a strictly Japanese context. A natural extension of this implied message is that Japan, to survive, must adapt. Japan may build on the past but she must move into the future. From a propagandistic standpoint, such a portrayal of judo should have pleased the militarists. However, Kurosawa could not simply make that film. His eponymous hero here is much like his young protagonist in another Meiji-era masterpiece of his, *Red Beard*. (That young protagonist in the latter film was played by Yuzo Kayama and Red Beard himself by Toshiro Mifune. Interestingly, both actors appeared in the remake of *Sanshiro Sugata*, with Kayama playing the young judo student.) Kurosawa's film version of this "judo saga" as the film is also known, maintains that both the martial spirit and the egocentric spirit must be held in check. However, they should be repressed not by *giri*, which might have pleased the militarists, but by a synthesis of the *giri/ninjo* dichotomy. To be a judo master is to be free of ego, vanity, and the need for glory. The true way of Judo is non-violent. (This same idea is put forth in *Sanjuro* and in the Zen Fighters sub-genre of the Samurai film.)

Sanshiro Sugata is a formal triumph, especially considering it is a first film and considering the conditions under which it was made. Oddly enough, this film seems stylistically more assured, more finely tuned, than any Kurosawa film until *Stray Dog*. The camera and the editing are character-centered. The actual environments are minimized so that individuals can be examined. Although the film as it exists today is some eighteen minutes shorter than its original running time (due to censorship by the Americans), individual sequences remain intact. There is, for instance, one bravura sequence that would have impressed Don Siegel, then making his justly-famous montages at Warner Brothers. Kurosawa shows the passage of time by following the path of an abandoned *geta* (sandal) of Sugata's. The *geta* sits in the middle of a road as pedestrians, traffic, and the seasons pass it by. Eventually, the sandal makes its way downstream, there to head for the sea. Although the various cuts are indices of the passage of time, the scene is more subtle than that. The *geta* continues its association with Sanshiro so that we know that time is affecting him as well. The associations established between the citizens, animals, the street, the river, and the seasons indicate a certain harmony has been achieved by Sanshiro and that there is a timelessness in what Sanshiro is doing, as well.

Ultimately the film is resolved formulaically with Sugata winning the girl (that romance even enters into the film should be noted) and defeating the villain. However, the formulaic resolution should not disguise the unique layers of meaning Kurosawa has nevertheless built in. To a Western director, having Sanshiro fall in love with the daughter of the ju-jitsu master he must fight would simply be ironic or melodramatic; to Kurosawa it becomes an ethical dilemma. On the one hand, Sanshiro knows he can simply lose the contest and thus save the girl's father from disgrace (and possibly death, for the decision in a fight often goes to the one who survives) and probably save his relationship. On the other hand, there are obligations he must live up to, such as his master, the sport of judo, and the spirit of judo which now lives in him. What might then, in the hands of a Japanese director, turn into a tragedy of *giri* versus *ninjo,* is redeemed by Kurosawa as he finds a solution in which all can live happily ever after, which means they can remain true to both duty and humanity. Kurosawa, to put it another way, has resolved the film according to ideals, a solution which can be appreciated in both the East and the West.

If Kurosawa could adapt a modern Japanese novel like *Sanshiro Sugata* and find a way to structure it around the junction of past and present, he could also take one of the classics of Japanese tradition and structure it similarly. Kurosawa's 1945 film *They Who Tread on the Tiger's Tail* was an adaptation of the story which forms the basis of the Nō play *Ataka* and the Kabuki classic *Kanjincho.* Both are based on the historical figure of Yoshitsune, tragic brother of Yoritomo, a figure dealt with in a Japanese literary classic of the middle-ages and also examined in Morris's *The Nobility of Failure.*[20] *They Who Tread on the Tiger's Tail* came about according to Richie because Kurosawa "had wanted to make a costume picture, but horses were not available...."[21]

Kurosawa did not simply adapt the episode in which Yoshitsune and his retainers escape out of hostile territory disguised as monks. Kurosawa added one figure which changes the focus of the tale. He "added one character, an extra porter, and gave the part to comedian Kenichi Enomoto, better known as Enoken—a bit like adding Jerry Lewis to the cast of Hamlet."[22] This addition did not go unnoticed in 1945. "Such near sacrilege had never been dared before, and the film is so funny and unpropagandistic that it was not released."[23] It is ironic that the American censors banned the film as well after the war.

The addition of Enoken brings the film in dialectical opposition to the feudal epoch. As Richie points out, Enoken's character was that of an "ordinary, neurotic Japanese who over-reacts to everything—including the war."[24] The ordinary, neurotic Japanese character, added by Kurosawa, bereft of some of its comic acts, might owe something to Dostoevsky. Enoken becomes the object with whom we identify so that the immediacy of the feudal era is removed. An identification with Enoken enables the audience to be dispassionate about the "feudal" subject matter while at the same time, the era can be examined from a modernistic perspective. Further, Kurosawa can structure the old and new in dramatic terms, bringing this structure to life. Of course, at forty-five minutes in length, the film emerges as more of an interlude. Yet, the obvious humanism and the relationships are clearly present.

They Who Tread on a Tiger's Tail serves as a prelude to both The Hidden Fortress and Sanjuro. Its comparisons with The Hidden Fortress also look forward to the way the dialectic of old versus new, East versus West is structured in the mature films. Modern versus feudal appears in the narratives by the juxtaposition of modernist characters in feudal societies. In both Tiger's Tail and The Hidden Fortress there emerges an ultimate incompatibility. In the former Enoken is revealed to be simply too neurotic to live in a world of rigidified codes; in the latter the peasants are similarly unable to comprehend the actions of men who place the good of the clan before wealth. Enoken, although he perceives the nobility and sacrifice of the warriors with whom he travels, cannot understand their ability and need to suppress their natural desires and inclinations. In other words, while he gives in to his feelings, fears, and doubts, they repress theirs.

Kurosawa mediates the pressures of *giri* through Enoken; his responses to the code of duty, obligation and the hierarchy become ours. What emerges from Enoken's confusion and neurosis is a statement about life lived under rigid conditions on the order of, "He who gives in to his natural feelings is better off not treading on tigers' tails."

If Kurosawa's first film, *Sanshiro Sugata,* is not the *Citizen Kane* of his career, or of Japan, *Rashomon* might be. Although I agree with Noel Burch's assessment that

> It is tempting to see the Western discovery of *Rashomon* as something of an accident, considering both the scale and quality of the Japanese production over the previous three decades on the one hand, and, on the other, the film's minor importance in the eyes of Japanese and (today) many Western critics . . .[25]

we must still recognize that *Rashomon* remains in the West the most famous film produced in Japan. Nevertheless, we must also recognize that its place in Japanese film history is marginal for it is resolutely outside of the mainstream.

Rashomon does indeed have much in common with Welles' stylistic tour de force. Both films are essentially metaphysical mystery stories about the impossibility of certainty and the relativity of truth. Both films proceed from the notion of filmic space-time as "mindscreen" as Bruce Kawin defines it.[26] But whereas *Citizen Kane* is at bottom a quintessentially American film, *Rashomon* is most assuredly not Japan's hidden idea of itself.

fashioned

For *Rashomon*, Kurosawa again turned toward Japanese sources for inspiration and again lays claim to his essential precept that he makes films first for Japan and only secondarily for the West. *Rashomon* is based on two stories by Ryunosuke Akutagawa, a modern writer who killed himself at the age of twenty-seven. Akutagawa utilized something of the dialectic between old and new as he entered the arena of avant-garde art.[27] There is much in his tales that implies the idea of truth's vagaries, a cosmogony basically foreign to the non-relativistic Japanese. Yet, Kurosawa's additions to Akutagawa can be seen as more fundamentally revealing than his attraction for the stories themselves.

To the combination of two stories, "In a Grove" and "At the Rasho Gate," Kurosawa added a climactic sequence in which a baby is discovered in the confines of the ruined gate. Analyses of this scene claim that the poor woodcutter who adopts the baby is Kurosawa's way of easing the pain, as it were, of the preceding narrative; that this act of human kindness betrays the potential good in mankind after we have been confronted with the bad. The adoption of the baby is, perhaps, Kurosawa's vaunted "humanism" shining forth.

Curiously, this ending, so seemingly pat and sentimental, brings forth cries of derision in the West, yet this very sequence is perhaps the most "Japanese" touch in the film. Doubtless, the initial attraction to *Rashomon* overseas was its exoticism—the vague period setting, the costumes, and the acting styles. The bravura techniques, which, while they found a receptive audience, were also "Japanese" to Western eyes. However, it is the completely non-intellectual, egoless, and selfless act of the woodcutter which establishes the film's only thematic bond with typical Japanese characteristics.

The genius of *Rashomon*, however, is surely not in its theme, but, like *Citizen Kane*, in the barrage of cinematic techniques brought to bear. That the intellectual weight of both *Citizen Kane* and *Rashomon* can support their stylistic bravura is, I suspect, almost incidental to both Welles and Kurosawa. Kurosawa chooses substantial works to adapt so that the intellectual substructure will be sufficient to carry the weight of his formal experimentation. Kurosawa's primary interest in the cinema, despite his humanism and all that implies, is a formal one. He explores the nature of his medium, communicating through formal devices. That is why, for instance, a work like *Throne of Blood* and *Rashomon* to a lesser extent, can originate from a filmmaker seemingly working within the (Western) tradition of psychological realism. These films are almost entirely formal exeperiments. Kurosawa's penchant for long films is another index of this concern. Masterworks like *Ikiru, Seven Samurai, Red Beard, High and Low,* and *Dodeskaden* (as well as Kurosawa's original versions of *The Idiot* and *Kagemusha*) are examples of a cinema not only of space but of *duration*.

Rashomon, although it is a metaphysical mystery, uses much of the Classic Detective Story formula. "The classical story begins with an unsolved crime and moves toward the elucidation of its mystery."[28] In *Rashomon* we are presented with a crime, a crime whose solution seems at first straightforward. However, it is quickly revealed that the "solution" is riddled with contradiction. Through a variety of stories told by the protagonists involved, we gather that there are some facts which are "true," or, at least, agreed upon by all. A bandit has tricked a Samurai, tied him up, and raped his wife. The Samurai's death followed soon after. The major points of contention are the woman's duplicity in the event following the rape and the manner in which the Samurai-husband met his death. The unsolved crime leans not toward who did it, but *how*. The "how" of a murder forms an important part of the classical detective story as well. The works of Agatha Christie, for instance, find their true glory in the revelation of the manner in which the murder was committed.

In the classical detective story these events would be straightened out, revealed that is, by a detective with particular powers and abilities. Further, this detective tends to have a certain kind of relationship to the crime which is mainly one of detachment. The outside world "intrudes" upon the detective with its request for a "solution" to the crime.[29] In *Rashomon* the figure of the detective (not to mention the idea of a solution) is lacking. However, we soon gather that we, the audience, are thrust into the role. The figure with whom one identifies in the classical detective story, is, of course, the detective rather than the victim or the criminal (although it is also worth noting the relationship between the narrator and the detective and one's own similarities to the "detective's friend," i.e., the narrator of the tale). Kurosawa simply literalizes this identification by forcing us into the structure of the film.

The use of "mindscreen" to present the crime is related to an important sub-genre of the classical detective story, "...the story told by a number of narrators, each of whom moves a step closer to the solution of the crime."[30] The stories related in *Rashomon* reproduce this pattern, each story building on the information of the previous one so that some of the facts become accepted while the essential ones become distorted. There is, upon first viewing, every indication that a solution will be forthcoming either within the narrative or by a perceptive member of the audience. Cawelti isolates a structural "problem" of this wrinkle in the formula, a problem which Kurosawa puts to good use. "The problem [multiple narrators] pose... lies in the way it necessarily fragments the process of investigation and the role of the detective."[31] The fragmentation of the narrative is indicative of the fragmentation of reality that rests within the mindscreens of each character; we as detectives are then fragmented in the same fashion. The reality about which we are so sure is suddenly called into question. How can we ever solve the mystery of *Rashomon*?

Rashomon is commonly thought of as being divided into two sections: the action at the ruined gate and the tales told by the protagonists/suspects. There are however, three sections to the film, each photographed and edited uniquely and each posing different questions about the nature of reality, both the pro-filmic "real" and what Brian De Palma has one of his characters say in *Phantom of the Paradise,* "real real."

The first section of the film is the framing story which takes place at the ruined Rasho Gate in twelfth-century Kyoto. Three men seek shelter from the pouring rain and huddle together amidst the crumbling ruins. Kurosawa imbues the rainfall with a texture and feel all of its own, capturing the special character of the Japanese rain. As with horses, Kurosawa can communicate the sensation of nature and have it signify both itself and a kind of essential idea of "nature." The graphics of the rain combine with the sensation of the rain, which, when combined with the image of the ruined gate places the nature/culture dichotomy on an emotional plane. The combination of images and sensations is a *haiku* producing *mono no aware* as the things of man give way to the timelessness of nature. There is as well, in the image of the surviving gate, a sense of antiquity, of the past continuing into the present. The origination of *mono no aware* in the first shot forms a dialectic with the theme of the stories related in flashback. Man's inhumanity to man, his inability to perceive the world outside of his own mental construct, is juxtaposed against the purity of nature. *Mono no aware,* that special Japanese feeling, will soon give way to an existential *angst,* a most un-Japanese idea.

The feeling of *mono no aware* is further reinforced in this opening sequence by the metonymical character of the three men who meet at this gate. The three travelers who seek respite are a microcosm of society. The woodcutter stands for the common man, the traditional Japanese idea of the common man at that; the priest is religious, aesthetic man, taught to believe in certain cosmological, metaphysical realities. As Kurosawa did in *Tiger's Tail,* he introduces a modernist figure into a (seemingly) feudal tale, here that of the con man who is cynical and nihilistic. Fate has thrown the three of them together, a fact emphasized by Kurosawa's framing strategy which places them together in a series of medium-long shots. As the narrative proceeds with the strange and disturbing events affecting the men differently, Kurosawa splits them up with a series of one or two shots emphasizing their fragmentation. This fragmentation comes to represent the existential crisis wherein man feels himself to be alone in the universe. Then again, at the film's sentimental-humanist conclusion, he returns to a series of long shots, except now the con man has departed. Only the priest and the woodcutter remain, but at least they occupy the same frame.

The second section of the film is a mindscreen, a flashback which is an (allegedly) factual account of the inquiry into the crime as related to the con man by the woodcutter and the priest. Space in this section is compressed, consisting merely of foreground and background. Harsh light further compresses the space here as well. Those on the witness stand sit in the foreground facing the camera, looking directly into it. In this case, this technique does not violate the rule of the camera's invisibility, for we soon

Photo from *Rashomon*.

realize that we are the "judge" (detective) to whom the witnesses are speaking. The fact that this sequence is a mindscreen develops into a dialectical relationship with the idea of the camera's fealty to reality. The single-take technique of this sequence combines with the direct-address of the witnesses to give the feel of reality. This sequence serves merely as a means of introducing the third section, that of the crime. Therefore, we are not expected to call the "truth" of this section into question, just as we are never expected to doubt the veracity of the framing story of the men at the gate. However, if the stories-within-the-flashbacks are called into doubt, we are left uncertain about whose mindscreen is relating the supposedly real story at the gate.

This second section is denatured as well. The very flat feel of space, a long horizontal white wall against which witnesses awaiting their turn sit, and the harsh white light, place this section in a nebulous context.

The third (and most famous) section of the film is more obviously mindscreen, four of them in fact: the bandit, the wife, the husband, and the woodcutter. This section is filmed in still a third cinematic style, one of bravura techniques. Nature in this section, even more than the first, occupies a primary place. As the bandit himself says, if it had not been for a cool breeze the whole thing never would have happened.

The bandit's own tale is the most frenetic, but also the one in which nature is allowed to dominate. The bandit is thus linked most clearly with nature and his actions, instinctual, undisciplined and energetic, underscore this. This link with nature is made explicit in Kurosawa's famous story in which he relates how he told Mifune to imitate the actions of a caged tiger. The bandit, in his own mindscreen, is first seen lying under a tree in a densely wooded forest. As a Samurai and his new bride ride by, a breeze awakens the bandit in time to see this same breeze stir the bridal veils around the woman's face. He then quickly plots a way to have her.

In order to get his way he decides to trick the samurai into following him through the woods, thus putting the samurai on the bandit's home ground. The bandit lures the samurai away from his journey with the promise of treasure, i.e., valuable cultural artifacts. To get to the treasure, though, requires, without wishing to stretch the analogy too far, a journey through a "heart of darkness." As they walk, the sun's rays come pouring through the dense overgrowth; the camera tracks with them as their pace quickens. A sense of disorientation overcomes the samurai in this combination of speed, shifting graphic patterns and winding woods. Kurosawa's camera movements and editing patterns, or as Burch calls it, his "rough hewn geometry,"[32] dehumanize his subjects. Paradoxically, both nature, in the form of the lush, overgrown forest, and culture, in the form of Kurosawa's cinematic tools, overwhelm the situation. Man is here at the mercy of both nature and culture, an uncomfortable position but not one unfamiliar to avant-garde artists in America and Europe.

Kurosawa fragments the manner in which the three stories are related to the audience. The three men meet at the gate; we shift to the trial in flashback; we shift to the "mindscreens" of the witnesses in a flashback-within-a-flashback; we return to the gate and begin the process again. The dialectic between *mono no aware* and existential *angst,* between objectivity and subjectivity, between fact and fabulation, are thus constantly reintroduced and reinforced. The differentiation between the cinematic styles used to relate the three planes of action further deny us any certainty. We never know "the truth" of the crime; but we do learn the truth about human nature in the final sequence. You take what you can get in an uncertain world.

There is a great paradox about Kurosawa's "masterpiece" *Throne of Blood.* On the one hand, it is unique in the Japanese cinema, standing outside of Japan's mainstream even more forthrightly than *Rashomon.* If the Japanese mainstream is a relatively amorphous mass, it still reveals a constancy, and that is that its stories are grounded in social contexts. From the feminist tracts of Mizoguchi, to the family comedies of Ozu, to the anti-feudal exposes of Kobayashi, even to the seemingly eccentric and unique *Woman in the Dunes,* the Japanese cinema proceeds from a structure of Man in a context. *Throne of Blood* does not.

On the other hand, *Throne of Blood* is a film that clearly only a Japanese director could have fashioned. Its insistent emphasis on graphic patterning, the deliberate foregrounding of its artifice, its bold intermingling of cinematic styles, all bespeak of a consciousness rooted in Japanese aesthetics.

Throne of Blood is, in my opinion, disproportionately studied compared to other films in Kurosawa's *oeuvre.* Much of this critical over-attention relates back to a statement made earlier (in Chapter 1), namely, that much of the attraction of the Japanese cinema in the West is formal. Indeed, Noel Burch claims that *Throne of Blood* is Kurosawa's best film solely on formalistic evidence when he says, "*Cobweb Castle* [i.e., *Throne of Blood*]... is indisputably Kurosawa's finest achievement, largely because it carries furthest the rationalization process of his geometry."[33] Yet one wonders if that is what contributes to greatness. Although Burch's statement is underlaid by an attempt to redress the emphasis placed upon narrative by the preceding generation of film critics, it leads to further problems. What Burch has done here is to carry the implicit argument which structures his book a bit too far. In trying to liberate film from its ties to an anterior reality, Burch may have strayed too far on the formalistic side, for if film does possess a strictly formal dimension, one culturally derived and understood, it also possesses a humanistic plane, more universal in appeal. *Throne of Blood* may be an example of film functioning spectacularly on a purely formal plane, but the human element is lacking.

The formalistic elements of *Throne of Blood* stem from its roots in the stylistic of the Nō theatre. In fact, the film owes as much to the Nō as it does to *Macbeth*. The use of many devices traditional in the Nō is a good index of Kurosawa's willingness to ground his film on the aesthetic plane. As Kurosawa has said, "I like the Nō drama. I like it because it is the real heart, the core of all Japanese drama. Its degree of compression is extreme, and it is full of symbols...."[34] The Nō is indeed a paradigmatic case of a Japanese aesthetic system which, as we have seen, does not begin from a "representational" or mimetic impulse. The Nō theatre is a presentational, deliberately theatrical mode; a mode of metaphor, poetry, and ellipsis. The clearest (and most frequently noted) influence from the Nō can be seen in the character of Lady Asaji, with the stark white make-up on her face and her ritualistically-oriented movements. However, *Throne of Blood* has even more fundamental links to the form.

The narrative of *Throne of Blood* is similar to the "narrative" of the Nō. The Nō theatre presents the relation of events, not their reproduction. The Nō theatre offers us a *fait accompli* in the sense that there is no mystery to the unfolding of the plot. *Throne of Blood* similarly offers up a relation of a tale not its unfolding. The film opens on an image of a gravestone with a ruined castle in the background. A chorus of voices chants, in the style of the Nō, the events we are about to witness. And if the Nō theatre relates action through the medium of the chants, so too, as Burch points out, much of the action of the film takes place offscreen.[35]

What one is presented with in the Nō theatre, and in *Throne of Blood*, is a symbolic reaction to events. The highly formalized, stylized movements of the Nō *replace* action. So too in the film. For instance, the planning of Miki's murder is followed by a cut to a horse neighing. The next time Miki appears he is a ghost. The horse's neigh meant the murder; it did not foreshadow its presentation, it was its presentation.

The narrative mode employed by *Throne of Blood* combined with its presentational mode of action points up what is, at heart, the problem with the film. If Nō is an abstract form, a form of symbols which substitute for action, the cinema is concrete. If Nō shows the essence of allusion, "film shows the substance, it cannot *show* the essence...."[36] Whether or not film is tied, as Bazin might wish, to an anterior reality, there is a certain *phenomenological* ontology to the film image. Nō tries to remove the concrete from its presentation through a variety of formal means. Although Nō uses human actors, these actors are abstracted by the wearing of symbolic masks. Nō relies on specific dance movements to substitute for action while a variety of chants and music accompanies the presentation, not as a background but literally in the foreground. Kurosawa tries to use the concrete nature of the cinema in similarly abstract ways.

Kurosawa attempts, in *Throne of Blood*, to duplicate the symbology of the Nō theatre through a substitution of nature for humanity. In the film, Nature and Man are not simply linked; rather a metonymical substitution occurs. There is a constant attempt to let Nature make all the statements here, to let the action occur in Nature. Nature associations are primary to the film beginning with the Japanese title "*Kumonosu-Jo,*" or "Castle of the Spider's Web." This title is understood denotatively as well. The castle is a spider's web; it is a confusing yet beautiful maze which arises naturally.

The links with nature are typically more formal than metaphorical, however. The first shot in the film combines a gravestone, which is man-made, with mist and mountain (Mt. Fuji, in fact). The things of man are conjoined, inseparably on the formal plane, with the things of nature. This occurs again in the second sequence of the film. Two mounted warriors, Washizu and Miki, ride through a dense forest. Their first introduction is therefore an introduction with nature-associations (a pattern which continues throughout the film as for instance, Miki's horse connoting Miki's murder). The two riders come upon a spirit which can easily be construed to mean the "spirit of the forest," so that it is nature which clouds their minds through a combination of mystery and awe. Too, the textural handling of the horses and the forest imbues the nature with greater life than the human beings in the film. The stiff and formal performance delivered by Toshiro Mifune in the lead role is in marked contrast to his lively efforts in the rest of the Kurosawa canon.

In point of fact, all of the significant action of the film, except for the rebellion of Washizu's men, utilizes this metonymical substitution. Crows invade the castle portending doom; when the situation is hopeless, rats flee the castle. The most significant action in the film, the "Birnham Wood" scene, is a literal transformation of men into a forest. These substitutions, we must constantly remember, are not metaphorical as in a work like *Animal Farm*. They are metonymical on the level of function. Human interaction is eliminated. The humans become equal to any other "object," for other objects take on meaning on the human plane. When this occurs, humanity is deemphasized; form is all.

In the final sequence, people are allowed, finally, to act, and act on the literal level. However, the handling of the scene, the extremity of its violence and the obvious cinematic "trick," still reduce the central figure to an object. Washizu's men rebel and turn on him, firing their arrows with deadly accuracy. Washizu becomes little more than a semi-mobile pincushion, with dozens of arrows sticking out of him. Finally, in a shot surpassed in Kurosawa's works only by the incredible "fountain of blood" in *Sanjuro* (a shot whose graphic implications are far different), Washizu is halted as an arrow passes through his throat. Whatever irony such a shot might have possessed in an English-language version of *Macbeth* is denied, for Washizu,

Photo from *Throne of Blood*.

in keeping with his animal-like links, has surely not been a man of words. The arrow though his throat is striking and memorable only on the formal level.

On the narrative level, there is a similar deemphasis of humanity via the removal of free will. If a fundamental paradox of Greek tragedy is the illusion of free will in a universe ruled by fate, the fundamental problem with *Throne of Blood* is the total absence of even this illusion. It is important to note that this is not a specific structuring of the *giri/ninjo* conflict. Free will, either in the form of choosing to obey a feudal lord or choosing to obey the spirit within the human soul is for the most part absent. In *Throne of Blood,* mankind does not seem to exist in communities, at least not established communities with specific laws. There is no central authority, nor is there a narrative movement to form one. Washizu's ambitions are not quite so specific. Indeed, to speak of "ambition" as the driving force behind his character would be entirely stretching things.

The lack of humanity, especially vis-a-vis the *giri/ninjo* conflict is essentially why *Throne of Blood* is not at its core a Japanese film. The lack of societal references prevents the film from taking on structural meaning beyond its admittedly impressive formal patterning. Although the film begins promisingly with its pictorially rich and seemingly significant opening shot, by the time the events have played out we have received only what we have been told we would.

We might compare, for instance, the opening and closing shots of *Throne of Blood* with those of *Hara-Kiri,* Masaki Kobayashi's masterpiece of antifeudal passion. Both films open with a tracking shot accompanied by voice-over; both films close with the same shot with which they open. Yet in *Throne of Blood* the final shot serves as a formal closure, nothing more. The events we have been told we will witness have played out in the manner in which we were forewarned. The final shot gives the impression merely that the events will somehow always play out in this fashion. In *Hara-Kiri,* on the other hand, the closing shot functions as irony, as a bitter conclusion to a filmed narrative that contradicts the information the shot delivers. Certain Japanese beliefs and traditions have been revealed to be hollow and false in *Hara-Kiri* as the events related between the opening and closing shots reveal. By implication, Kobayashi explores the nature of myth and legend and the manner in which cinema aids their construction. Kurosawa, in this case, does not offer contradictory evidence, but rather formal revelation of known events. He relates myth and legend without either elucidating the manner in which it arose or the way it may be redefined. (He will do just that in *Kagemusha.*)

The feeling of *mono no aware* engendered in the opening shot of *Hira-Kiri,* by virtue of the sonorous chanting, the gracefully mobile camera and the appeal to antiquity, lull us into a certain frame of mind. This feeling will be rudely and ruthlessly destroyed, slowly but surely, until all traces are obliterated by the climactic battle. When the shot is then repeated at the end, what initially produced *mono no aware* now produces irony and bitterness.

The opening shot of *Throne of Blood* similarly calls forth the feeling of *mono no aware* through its formal linking of timelessness (the mountains and the mist) with the mortality of man (the grave-stone implying that quite clearly). The second time the shot appears, similarly following a spectacular, action-filled climax, it may still call forth *mono no aware*, but this time it will be free of greater associations.

Ultimately, *Throne of Blood* may be seen as not so much adaptation of *Macbeth*, but a transliteration of its basic narrative pattern. If *Macbeth* is separated from its roots in formula by its poetry (with all that the term "poetry" implies), *Throne of Blood* is divorced from genre by its form. But in borrowing the narrative pattern without a corresponding thematic enrichment (even through the formal plane), Kurosawa has borrowed the bones of tragedy without the heart. Humanity has not simply been undervalued, it has been put aside. *Throne of Blood,* a film Kurosawa did not initially intend to direct,[37] marks the last time he would forget that the heart of the cinema is the revelation of the human condition.

The Samurai Films

The films I will be dealing with in this section are the true Samurai films. These are the films most typically thought of as "Western," a statement not without much justification but one which demands close examination. These are Kurosawa's genre films, films which despite their Western influence have their roots firmly within the Japanese *Jidai-geki* and *chambara* traditions. For Kurosawa to transcend genre, as he so clearly has, to explode the formula (or to implode them as well) he begins with generic patterns. In this manner, Kurosawa truly shares a commonality with Americans John Ford and Howard Hawks. And like these American masters Kurosawa has made his most personal and revealing statements while trying to hide behind the mask of formula.

Working within formula boundaries, Kurosawa has also found the paradoxical freedom to experiment. He has used this freedom much like Samuel Fuller; his influence can similarly be seen on Sam Peckinpah and many of the various "New Wave" directors of France and Germany. This "modernist" aspect of Kurosawa, alluded to in *Rashomon* (which is, after all, a fairly obvious example) distinguishes him from virtually all of the directors who have worked in the period drama, just as his work in the period form distinguishes him from Japan's own New Wave. Only Masahiro Shinoda, the most "conservative" New Wave director, has produced formula films which work as genre and transcend genre simultaneously. (Kon Ichikawa produced one film, *The Wanderers,* which is also a modernist film, but which is never intended to be taken as a genre work. His recent forays into formula are curiously non-modernist.)

The Samurai films of Akira Kurosawa are all concerned with swordsmen who exist in an ambiguous moral universe. Theirs is a world of uncertainty. There is no established authority in these films; it has yet to arise or it is in the process of breaking down. Of the four true Samurai films, two—*Seven Samurai* and *The Hidden Fortress*—are situated in the pre-Tokugawa era, the era of civil wars, and two—*Yojimbo* and *Sanjuro,* although the era is not crucial—are stated to take place in the late Tokugawa era, the time of the *bakufu*'s decline. Kurosawa's Samurai films thus take place at a frontier, a frontier whose boundaries are not so much physical as moral.

The lack of a traditional authority places the moral/ethical stance within the realm of the individual. The individual in Kurosawa's films is faced with choices, a responsibility that places the individual consciousness at the center of the film's "moral universe," a reversal of the traditional Japanese film. The typical Japanese film finds the individual to be a social product, taught a set of social codes. The schism that arises between these social codes and the individual's developing sense of a human-self, determines the drama. When the individual resigns himself to the split, we find the Nostalgic Samurai drama; when the split causes a reexamination of the feudal foundations, we have the Anti-Feudal Drama, and when the split is transformed into a religious quest which ignores the society, we have the Zen Swordsman. Society in Kurosawa, however, is a social compact that does not exist a priori. Ethics and morals are not imposed *upon* but are established *between* individuals. The *giri/ninjo* conflict is in this manner elevated beyond society and its impositions upon the individual. Goodness is a product of the individual self, a much more existential position.

When this existential positing combines with certain of the motifs and characters introduced in *They Who Tread on the Tiger's Tail* and *Rashomon,* we can understand Kurosawa's transcendence of genre into the realm of modernity. Modernist figures and techniques which appear in *The Hidden Fortress, Yojimbo,* and *Sanjuro* must be related to both the traditional formulas and Western influences. A self-reflexive stance demands acknowledgment, so that Kurosawa speaks through formula and beyond it. There is another dialectic thus apparent, that of a combination of tradition with the avant-garde.

Basically, Kurosawa works in two of the four sub-genres isolated in Chapter 2. The films produced in the 1950s are basically Nostalgic Samurai Dramas; the two of the early 1960s are Sword Films. Naturally, each of the films works perfectly well within these bounds, yet each transcends them. Like the films of any great filmmaker, Kurosawa's works are deceptively simple and royally entertaining. He offers enjoyment to the audience seekng escapism and the audience seeking substance; he speaks to the Japanese and to the West. Most importantly, through a dialectical combination of the two, he speaks to both about each other.

Seven Samurai

Kurosawa is a "dialectical" filmmaker. There are numerous seemingly contradictory patterns that can be, and have been isolated in his films. We have already noticed a tension between montage and stasis in *Throne of Blood* and *Rashomon*. I have alluded to a tension between tradition and avant-garde, and there is also the fundamental structure of East versus West.

In order to demonstrate this dialectical process at work, I will analyze *Seven Samurai* by breaking the film down into significant bits of action. This sequential approach isolates the dialectical oppositions as they arise in the filmic text. This also duplicates the film viewing process, a process Kurosawa understands. He structures his films dialectically so that we constantly evaluate and re-evaluate. He presents information that will later be contradicted. His cinema is like a mystery story, not simply on the level of plot but on the level of signification, of shifting syntagms and paradigms. The richness of his films stems partly from this re-evaluative approach. It also stems from his dialectics within the frame whereby he presents information that is self-contradictory on the level of cinematic codes.

Seven Samurai has been understood to be a "classical" text, an epic in the best Western tradition. As such, it will be instructive to take a sequential approach in order to see how the film *means* as a simultaneity, how numerous codes are impacted into the text so that when they are separated out this classical work is shown to be both conservative and radical; both a reaffirmation and a subversion. In other words, Kurosawa's dialectics extend to the mythos of the film as well.

Seven Samurai is situated, as I have noted, in the era of constant civil war so that the need for "situational" ethics arises. In this manner, Kurosawa implies that all members of the various social classes which he will examine must make ethical choices. It is not just the three-hour-plus running time, but the look at a whole culture that makes the film an epic.

Seven Samurai can be divided into either three or four sections; I have chosen four only for the sake of convenience, for the real division is three: the gathering of the heroes; the training of the farmers; the battle and its aftermath. My fourth section arises by dividing the first into the introduction of the farmers and the finding of the samurai. The other two remain the same. An examination of each section as a unit will show how Kurosawa introduces a new theme and how these themes are not drawn together until the final section. Dialectical oppositions arise between sections as well as within sections.

Detailings of Western influence will be noted within the discussion, again, to duplicate the way in which the film is understood and to show more clearly the manner in which they are structured into the film.

One more point before beginning, a point of some importance. A significant dialectic within Kurosawa's career and within his films is that between the formalist and the humanist. In this manner, Kurosawa synthesizes his influences from George Stevens and William Wyler on the one hand, and John Ford on the other. Naturally, this is not to imply that Stevens and Wyler are not humanists (they are, at certain points), nor that Ford is not a master of the cinematic medium (!), but rather to acknowledge the primacy of their intent. Kurosawa is both a formalist and a humanist; sometimes this dialectic is established between films (*Scandal* versus *Rashomon*; *Throne of Blood* versus *The Bad Sleep Well*) but most often, it occurs within the same film, most spectacularly in *Ikiru, Red Beard, Dodeskaden,* and *Seven Samurai.* This struggle between formalism and humanism manifests itself as well in Kurosawa's interest in historical accuracy (the castle's construction in *Throne of Blood*, the firearms in *Seven Samurai*, the surgical techniques employed in *Red Beard*, the mode of battle in *Kagemusha*) as well as in processes (the search for the gun in *Stray Dog*, the running of the bureaucratic maze in *Ikiru*, the police-procedure in *High and Low*, the demonstration of how Shingen Takeda was shot in *Kagemusha*). These interests do not detract from the humanistic slant but they do indicate a willingness to sacrifice one kind of attention and replace it with another, perhaps reminiscent of Meville's explanations of whales and whaling in *Moby Dick*. This pattern of formalism and humanism will similarly structure *Seven Samurai.*

The opening shot of *Seven Samurai* is of title cards which tell us we are in the era of constant civil war. Brigands roam the country plundering villages. The next shot shows us a stormy sky which establishes a formal link between the *mise-en-scene* and the thematic thrust of the film. Into this stormy environment ride mounted brigands. Their horses are at the gallop, their expressions fierce. Although we do not yet know precisely what is happening, we feel a strong sense of energy and dynamism. Kurosawa's textural handling of the horses combined with the other formal elements within the frame (and including the camera position and movement) communicates the sense of chaos and of drama. We already feel that these are the brigands. Then, through their conversation, we learn the essential details that will drive the plot: they have plundered and robbed a village earlier in the year and will return later.

The brigands' conversation carries them to a spot overlooking a little village. The village sits under sunny skies, so that its seeming peacefulness and bucolic look is undercut by the events taking place above them. This shot literalizes the sense of powerlessness that the farmers will feel. Just as they are unable to control such forces as the weather, so too, they cannot control other forces which come from above and beyond their little world.

Photo from *Seven Samurai*.

Finally, in this opening sequence which introduces the brigands, we note that they are conversing in front of a pile of wood which stands at the top of the hill overlooking the village. As the brigands ride away, silence and peace remain in the frame they have vacated. The wood pile slowly begins to move and a man, with a pile of wood strapped on his back, arises. The surprise we feel at seeing a man spring up out of the inanimate woodpile, combined with the comic/pathetic expression on his face, makes us laugh. Our laughter is a function of surprise, but also of relief from the tension and dynamism of the preceding sequence. With this action, Kurosawa has also now linked the brigands' conversation with its human counterpart. Kurosawa shows us the human side of war. Like Griffith in *Birth of a Nation,* where a single shot shows us an army on the march and then a mother holding her baby, Kurosawa shifts from formalism to humanism. He has quickly and brilliantly shifted attention from the brigands as dynamic actors with whom we are uninvolved to the more passive and static farmers with whom we become involved.

The next sequence introduces us to the farmers—their situation vis-a-vis the brigands and their attitudes toward them. The farmers are confused, torn between rebellion and giving in to despair. As an old woman speaks and bemoans her situation, Kurosawa presents her with a curious and disturbing (if amusing) low-angle shot of her rear end. The juxtaposition of the camera angle with the content of her speech undercuts the seriousness of the issue, a hint of the ambivalent attitude that emerges toward the farmers.

We should note at this point that such an ambivalence creates a dialectical tension between the audience and the farmers. The ambivalence manifested by the director is communicated to us so that we tend to question, now and throughout the film, the degree to which these farmers are "worth saving." That is, there is some doubt about the mission to save the farmers. The Western film for the most part cannot afford such doubts. The society that is in the process of emerging is worth whatever efforts it takes to help it along. The true Western (unlike say, *High Noon* which repudiates the hero's task to save the ungrateful, unworthy town) must see the town as the repository of civilization. On the other hand, it is precisely because the farmer/villagers are often weak, insecure, and ungrateful that the Samurai's heroic defense of them takes on added heroism, pathos, and tragedy. It is because they are flawed and imperfect that the Samurai become noble; it is because they are flawed that they should be saved.

The farmers seek the advice of the village elder who suggests that if they cannot defend themselves they should hire men who can. When they maintain they could only pay their defenders in food, the village elder offers them a piece of perfect Zen-like advice: "Then find hungry Samurai."

Despite the ambivalent attitude manifested toward the farmers, we do side with them. Our sympathy, if not our admiration, has been won over. The sage advice, moreover, offered by the village elder, is both clever and humorous, showing us another side of the farmers, a side we can appreciate.

The farmers select a few representatives to go to "town" and hire some Samurai, figuring they can afford four. With the farmers' departure to the town, the introductory section comes to an end, and the second section begins.

When the farmers come to town in search of swordsmen, they find a baffling array of confusing circumstances. This town bears more than a surface resemblance to a wild-west town. Lawlessness and banditry seems rampant as swordsmen of all sorts swarm about. Paradoxically, there is an abundance of *ronin* (masterless Samurai) about. One would think if ever an era was filled with the potential for the would-be hero to make his mark, this would be it. For instance, Mizoguchi's *Ugetsu* is situated in this era and indeed one of the central figures runs away from his family to seek fame as a Samurai warrior. (A fame he tragically achieves.) Yet here in Kurosawa's village we find *ronin* at virtually every turn. The dream of fame for the Samurai is undercut by the reality of the situation.

The farmers have not the faintest idea of whom to approach for help. They are, that is, ill-equipped to understand and judge the men they see. Their only standard thus far is the carrying of a weapon, but, as we soon see, even that is suspect. Approaching one fierce looking warrior, they are rebuked in the strongest terms for suggesting that a proud (though unemployed) warrior would ever work for them.

The farmers begin to despair about ever finding rescuers. Kurosawa juxtaposes their confusion and timidity with the brashness and carefree attitudes of townsmen with whom they share lodging at a run-down inn. These townsmen, though they are poor, reflect how they would never want to be farmers. These men are confident as they laugh at the poor farmers' condition, although we know that their laughter is only to make themselves feel better. At this point our sympathy with the farmers is perhaps at its height, for their confusion and helplessness seems indeed pitiable. Further, as Kurosawa soon introduces the Samurai themselves, our allegiance and identification will shift, so that at this point we must be won over to their cause.

The idea of role-confusion, of being unable to judge men by their dress because the usual codes of status have broken down in this "wild-west town," structures the introduction of the first Samurai enlisted by the farmers: Kembei. A child has been kidnapped by a bandit who has taken shelter in a barn. The farmers see a man, apparently a *ronin,* having his head shaved, which is, as the Japanese audience knows, the sign of a priest. Sure enough, once the *ronin*'s head is shaved he dons a Buddhist robe. With this "disguise" now complete the *ronin* gets two rice balls which he takes into the barn. The *ronin*-priest enters the barn; the camera remains outside. A scream is heard and then the bandit comes rushing out of the barn. After he freezes for a moment, he then, in slow motion, falls down dead. The *ronin* comes out with the baby and then returns the robe to the monk. The farmers have found their man.

This incident, we should note, is drawn from the annals of Zen legends. D.T. Suzuki relates this story about Kami-idzumi Ise no Kami who founded the *Shinkageryu* school of swordsmanship. He was traveling the countryside when he came to a small village. An outlaw had kidnapped a small boy and taken refuge in a deserted house. Ise no Kami had his head shaved, borrowed a robe and went in with two lunch boxes and captured the bandit.[38] One suspects that the average Japanese would recognize, if not the specifics, the roots of Kurosawa's scene. In this manner, the introduction of the first Samurai starts to transform *Seven Samurai* into the realm of legend. The association has been clearly made between the hero and a figure out of Japan's glorious past.

This introduction of Kambei sets the tone for the gathering of the rest of the Samurai. Kambei will not rely on icons to make his decision. Just as he fooled a bandit by adopting the clothes of a priest, Kambei knows that the wearing of a sword does not guarantee Samurai status or ability. For instance, Kambei is confronted by a wild and energetic young man (Toshiro Mifune) following the killing of the bandit. When Kambei asks the boy if he is a Samurai, the boy says that he is. Kambei mutters, half to himself, "I wonder." One gets the feeling about Kambei that if he had been introduced to the shadow warrior in *Kagemusha* he would have spotted the imposter immediately.

From this point on until the Samurai arrive in the farmers' village, Kurosawa combines his penchant for process with insights into character. If part I sets up the basic situation which both attracts us to and repels us from the farmers, part II shifts our allegiance toward the Samurai. Our identification with the Samurai changes, to a certain extent, our perspective toward the farmers. We tend to be more objective. We are also, in this section, fascinated, as is Kurosawa, with the means by which Kambei gathers together his little army. Kambei's methods not only provide insight into his own character, but into the characters of the other Samurai. These character traits are of prime importance having significant reverberations later on.

Kambei is enlisted to the farmers' cause on two levels, tactically (intellectually) and humanistically. His first reaction upon hearing their situation is to question them about the lay of the land and to figure out that he needs seven men, one to guard each direction of the compass, two in reserve and himself. At this point, even before he has committed himself to the task, he wonders where he could find so many good men, another paradox in a time of constant warfare. He also wonders whether he wants to fight again. When he learns from the laborers that while he eats their rice the farmers eat millet, Kambei's involvement shifts from the intellectual to the emotional. Kambei implicitly recognizes their sacrifice and so decides to help them. Courage and sacrifice are relative. Kambei's recognition of that, his skill as a fighter combined with his humanity make him the perfect leader.

The first recruit to the cause is the youth Katsushiro. Katsushiro had witnessed Kambei's rescue of the child and was taken by Kambei's skill, modesty, and compassion. Katsushiro already worships the older warrior. Kurosawa has in this manner introduced another figure with whom we identify. If we were asked initially to identify with the farmers, we now identify with Katsushiro as well, and it is sometimes through his eyes that we view Kambei. The phenomenological link between a young protagonist in the film and the audience is a common pattern in the Western as well. My discussion of *Sanjuro* will explicate this link in detail. Suffice it to say for the moment, that as much as we would like to identify with Kambei, we tend to have more in common with Katsushiro. Kurosawa's treatment of Kambei duplicates Katsushiro's point of view on numerous occasions.

Although Katsushiro seems to be a young Samurai, for some reason he is on his own. From a Samurai family obviously, based upon his dress, his manners, and his speech, he is a young *ronin* looking to learn Bushido. He has chosen Kambei to be his teacher. Katsushiro is attracted to the farmers' cause by his admiration for Kambei, yet he too has a natural sympathy for the farmers. (A sympathy that will appear more obvious when he becomes involved with a young girl of the village.)

Kambei begins Katsushiro's training by way of aiding him in the enlistment of other warriors in the cause. Kambei sits facing the open door of an inn while Katsushiro waits beside it holding a heavy wooden stick over his head to strike the Samurai who walk through. The first Samurai tested passes with flying colors. As Katsushiro brings the stick down, the Samurai catches Katsushiro by the wrists and easily flings him across the room. Kambei apologizes to the Samurai and explains why he did it. The Samurai is intrigued until he learns that his employers will be a group of farmers. He refuses.

The farmers, Kambei and Katsushiro, then sit and watch as a variety of Samurai pass by. Then Kambei spots a likely one and they prepare to duplicate the test procedure. This time the *ronin*, Gorobei, stops before crossing the threshold. He senses something amiss and smiles saying, "I see. It's a joke!" Kambei is immensely pleased by Gorobei's actions and finds Gorobei easier to placate with the explanation. Gorobei agrees to join the cause, not, however, because of the farmers' plight, but because he is intrigued by Kambei's personality. Kurosawa has now finalized Kambei's personality to the extent that we recognize that he is a charismatic leader, though a modest and humane one. His cause is followed not because he is a clan leader or because he badgers people into following him, but because of the strength of his beliefs and attitudes.

The next recruit is Shichiroji, an old friend of Kambei's. They had fought together before, apparently on the losing side, and each is pleased to discover his old friend alive and well. The two reunite to fight again.

The fourth recruit is gathered by Gorobei. In talking to a stall keeper, Gorobei remarks that he is suprised at how hard it is to find good Samurai. The stall keeper tells Gorobei that there is a Samurai cutting wood behind the shed, but says that he is probably not a good one, for he is cutting wood in exchange for food. Gorobei relates the Samurai's condition to his own and is not discouraged from talking to him. Gorobei finds his way to the Samurai because of the shouts he hears coming from behind the shed. There he sees the *ronin*, Heihachi, chopping wood, exhaling in a shout as the ax meets wood. Heihachi cuts wood as if he were engaged in a *kendo* match, a nice touch on Kurosawa's part, indicating that Heihachi is a kind of "Zen fool," putting himself wholeheartedly and amusingly into his work, chopping wood with the same spirit he would fight a match. Gorobei sits down to enjoy the show when he gets to the back of the wood shed. In another little amusing touch, Heihachi slowly and deliberately moves his sword away from Gorobei when this happens.

Gorobei comments to Heihachi how much he admires the latter's skill and dedication. Heihachi thinks chopping wood is harder than killing enemies. When asked how many enemies he has killed, Heihachi answers, in a very Zen-like manner, that since it is impossible to kill them all he usually runs away. Gorobei laughs at that answer and, while Heihachi resumes chopping, asks him if he would like to kill twenty or thirty bandits; the question causes Heihachi to miss his target completely.

From this comic scene Kurosawa cuts to a more tense and dramatic confrontation (again indicating his typical pattern of dialectical editing). This scene introduces Kyuzo, the master swordsman. Kyuzo duels another man with bamboo swords; both men claim victory. When the man then challenges Kyuzo to a fight with real swords, Kambei, standing with Katsushiro and watching, comments, "How senseless; it is obvious what will happen." It does not seem to be obvious to Katsushiro however, again indicating Kambei's perceptivity.

Kyuzo kills his opponent quite easily. Kurosawa's handling of the scene is significant. The death is shown in slow-motion, with an extreme long shot. The slow-motion shot recalls Kambei's killing of the outlaw, but the camera distance here literally distances us from the action. Kambei killed a man to save the life of a child; Kyuzo has killed a man to prove his skill, a very different ethical situation. Thus, the long shot to distance us.

Kyuzo, we learn, is not much interested in joining the cause, for it does not offer him much chance to perfect his skill. Kyuzo is thus a figure out of the Zen Swordsman Drama and through his attitudes, Kurosawa demonstrates the moral/ethical problem with that kind of stance: humanity takes second place in such an attitude.

Kyuzo, however, does eventually come around and join, at which point Kambei decides that time is of the essence and will not seek out a seventh member. This serves as the reintroduction of Toshiro Mifune as Kikuchiyo. Kambei is told by the laborers that they know of a fierce fighter who would join their cause, a fighter who turns out to be the Kikuchiyo who had earlier accosted Kambei. Kambei decides to test Kikuchiyo as he had Gorobei and Katsushiro assumes his place beside the door. The laborers insist that the test is not fair, for Kikuchiyo is drunk. Kambei tells them that a true Samurai would never get that drunk. When Kikuchiyo comes through the door Katsushiro's stick lands with a resounding "thwack!" The Samurai all laugh at the drunk and hurt young man staggering around the room. He insists, however, that he is a Samurai and produces a scroll to prove it. But scrolls are meaningless in this chaotic world where people are not what they seem and this scroll is even more meaningless, for it says that its bearer is thirteen years old. Kikuchiyo had been taken in by the officialness of the scroll, but he could not read it, just as the farmers found it difficult to "read" the Samurai of the town. The Samurai leave town, leaving Kikuchiyo behind.

The third section begins with the Samurai and the farmers traveling together to the village. However, before the Samurai arrive in the little town, Kurosawa cuts back to the village itself. Manzo, one of the farmers, grabs his daughter Shino and insists that she cut her hair. He wants her to look like a boy. "Samurai are coming. They are dangerous." Manzo and the rest of the farmers fear their protectors, a fear and distrust that will never be entirely overcome, an important motif in the film. There is a tragic gap between farmers and Samurai, a gap that will never close.

As the Samurai and the farmers walk to the village, Kikuchiyo acts his way into the Samurai's affections. He is determined to be one of them. If his skill as a warrior is questionable, Kurosawa shows us his natural abilities when he has Kikuchiyo catch fish with his bare hands, no mean feat!

When the Samurai first see the farming village they are singularly uninspired. Kikuchiyo utters the prophetic sentence, "I'd hate to die in a dung heap like that." When the Samurai enter the village they are further dismayed when no one comes out to greet them. Kambei and the other Samurai are angered at this display but Kikuchiyo finds the villagers' actions amusing. Finally, Rikichi, one of the farmers, decides they should all go see the village elder. Gisaku, the elder, tells the Samurai what we already have learned, that the farmers are afraid. Part of the dynamics of this film arises because, despite everything, we see a part of ourselves in the farmers as well. As much as we would like to be Samurai, and identify with the Samurai, we are closer to the farmers in being powerless to control events outside of our own little "village." The ambivalence we (and Kurosawa) feel toward the farmers stems from the implicit recognition of the similarity of our own "existential" situation and that of the farmers.

While the Samurai speak with Gisaku, the village alarm rings out. This rouses the villagers, while the Samurai, swords drawn, come hurrying to the rescue. The alarm is a false alarm, for Kikuchiyo sounded it merely to call the villagers out. Kikuchiyo berates the farmers for hiding from them, pointing out correctly that when they thought they were in danger they turned immediately to the Samurai for help. Kikuchiyo's speech inspires Heihachi to proclaim, "Now we are seven."

Kikuchiyo's actions have already given us a clue to his real identity. His familiarity with the village's alarm system and his willingness to berate them so forthrightly demonstrate his links with farmers, links further established by his peculiar fishing ability.

The seven Samurai and their relationship with the farmers forms the core of the third section of the film, but, here too, Kurosawa maintains his fascination with process. The organization of the village's defense and the training of the farmers is as detailed and as interesting as Kambei's gathering of the Samurai.

The relationship between fighters and farmers begins through the mediation of weaponry. In particular, Kyuzo, Heihachi, and Kikuchiyo undertake to train the villagers in the ways of war. At this point we should note that the character traits established in section two reappear here in the interpersonal dynamics between the warriors and the farmers, and though we do not quite realize it yet, the Samurai who are killed are "flawed" in some manner. The three Samurai who train the farmers will all die in the battle.

Kyuzo and Heihachi train the farmers by virtue of their superior skill, as Heihachi also becomes emotionally attached to the farmers. Kikuchiyo has the natural ability to win over the farmers with his clown-trickster behavior. More importantly, this wayward youth wins over the children. Kikuchiyo also wins us over for a variety of reasons, one of the most significant of which is his embodiment by Mifune. Certainly the most compelling actor on the screen (although we should never overlook Takashi Shimura as Kambei), he is all energy and motion. He is the most human, given to fits of anger and laughter. If most of the Samurai are flawed in some manner, he is deeply flawed. But if there is to be a union, a synthesis between Samurai and farmer, Kikuchiyo will be the one to bring it about. (As we will see, he manages this union on the literal level, as well.)

Kikuchiyo's relationship with the farmers transcends the medium of weaponry by which the other Samurai must communicate. He is the "natural" one. On this level we see that the important distinction between farmer and Samurai is not simply a matter of status or class, it is a question of technology, i.e., culture.

The first significant closing of the cultural gap between Samurai and farmer is brought about by Kikuchiyo. He has discovered a secret cache of weapons. When he presents his discovery to the other Samurai, they are shocked, particularly when they realize that the farmers came by these weapons by hunting down wounded Samurai and killing them, then stripping the bodies. Shichiroji is scandalized by Kikuchiyo's flippancy in the matter, but Kambei calmly reminds him that Kikuchiyo doubtless never experienced the terror of being hunted "by bamboo spears," i.e., by farmers seeking to rob them.

Kyuzo, in a rare moment of emotion, exclaims that he would like to kill every one of the farmers for their betrayal of Bushido, a code to which they can certainly not afford to subscribe. Kyuzo's anger is literally absurd, but understandable in these circumstances. Kikuchiyo berates the Samurai now, just as earlier he had berated the farmers. Kikuchiyo begins by saying that farmers are not saints, indeed they are the most cunning animals on earth. They hunt the wounded and the defeated, they hide food, and they lie. But who, he asks, made them that way? And with bitterness he supplies the answer: Samurai.

Kambei now realizes the Kikuchiyo is a farmer's son, and it is Kambei who is the most deeply affected by Kikuchiyo's tirade.

Meanwhile, if Kikuchiyo now is the literal synthesis of farmer and fighter, Katsushiro has been doing a little closing of the gap himself. Wandering through the woods he encounters Shino, but does not initially realize that she is a girl. When she tries to run away from him, he wrestles her to the ground and makes the crucial discovery about her gender. These two youths, both similarly untrained in the ways of their respective social classes, the girl not yet married and a mother, the boy not yet a true warrior, are brought together by their natural inclinations. They are the only real mediators between the two groups.

The fourth section of the film begins when the Samurai kill the three scouts of the brigands. It is Kyuzo, Kikuchiyo, and Katsushiro who accomplish this, with the latter as observer. It is important that the two youths be together in this scene, for they represent the two sides of youth in general: the brash, confident, playful side and the shy, quiet, and scholarly type. We identify with each of them and also get a slightly different perspective on the Samurai by our identification with them. Just as our impression of the farmers is constantly shifted by our shifting allegiance between farmer and Samurai, so too, our attitudes about the Samurai change as our perspective shifts between Katsushiro and Kikuchiyo. In this, the first battle of the film, Kikuchiyo is carefree and reckless, Katshushiro admiring and obedient.

One of the scouts is taken prisoner by the Samurai who insist on treating him as if he were a prisoner of war. The farmers, however, decide that an old woman who has lost her son at the brigands' hands be allowed to take revenge. The Samurai walk away in shame as the woman staggers forth with a large sickle in her hands.

Kambei decides to even up the odds by staging a raid on the brigands' hideout. For this he selects Kyuzo the Zen Swordsman, Heihachi the Zen Woodcutter, and Kikuchiyo the clown, the three men who had been assigned the task of training the farmers. Rikichi, one of the most intense and mysterious of the farmers, leads the way. It is important to recall a scene earlier in which the Samurai help the farmers harvest their crop. Heihachi jokes with Rikichi that Rikichi should get married. Rikichi reacts strangely to this joke. This scene established two things: Rikichi's disturbance over not having a wife, and Heihachi's emotional attachment to Rikichi. In typical Kurosawa fashion, the journey to the brigands' camp is handled comically, for it will be followed by a scene of drama and tragedy.

The scene in which the Samurai and Rikichi peer into the brigands' hut is one of the most extraordinary and brilliant in a film filled with brilliance. Utterly without dialogue, Kurosawa tells us everything not only about the Samurai and the young, beautiful woman they see, but about the attitudes behind the actions. The Samurai peer into the hut and decide to set it on fire and kill the bandits when they come out (a tactic that will reappear in *Yojimbo*). They set their fire and look back inside. From their point of view, Kurosawa pans around the hut revealing the sleeping bandits and their women in various stages of disarray. The Samurai's attention is drawn to one woman in particular, an extremely pretty woman who has just begun to stir. The woman's sensuality stirs the men and they look at each other in surprise, trying to establish her reality in this strange surrounding. Suddenly, the woman sees the smoke. Her first reaction is fright, then a sudden flash of enlightenment reveals a tired and resigned smile. In that one moment we realize her whole history. She went with the brigands willingly perhaps; or unwillingly, it does not matter. She gave in to her life with them but now that it seems to be coming to an end, she accepts her death (and theirs) without giving out a cry.

The brigands stir and panic when they realize what is happening. They come rushing out where they are met by the flashing swords of Kyuzo, Heihachi, and Kikuchiyo (although he is not as skilled). The brigands rush to a river nearby and the Samurai pursue them. Suddenly, Rikichi gives forth a cry and rushes toward the burning hut in front of which stands the woman. When the woman sees Rikichi she runs back inside to her death. It is clear that she is (was) Rikichi's wife. Unable to control himself in battle, he has run to her. Heihachi, seeing this, rushes over to him. Heihachi drags Rikichi back to safety behind some rocks in the river, but a shot rings out and Heihachi falls dead. We do not see the gun, we merely hear the shot; the visual cause-and-effect has been denied us. All that Heihachi, the other Samurai, and we hear, is a loud report and then Heihachi falls. It is ironic that Heihachi should die in this manner, for he who preferred to run from enemies he could not kill dies at the hands of an enemy he could not even see.

Rikichi's rash action is inappropriate for a battle situation. He has given in to his feelings. So too, Heihachi who should have known better. Another level of irony then, for it is Heihachi's very humanity here that causes his death.

Heihachi's death weighs heavy on Kambei and the other Samurai. It brings home their own mortality, a mortality stressed by the grave-side ceremony they hold. Heihachi is buried in a mound placed at the top of a hill, his sword stuck in it as a marker. When some of the farmers are killed, they too will be buried on this hill, although at a lower level. Samurai and farmer who joined together in battle are joined together in death.

The farmers and the Samurai are linked together at the end of section three and the beginning of section four in two other ways. The first is via the banner made by Gorobei. <u>Farmer, Samurai, and Kikuchiyo (who gets his own symbol) are joined on a banner, a pennant which is flown in the midst of battle. This banner joins them together and gives the fighters a flag, an objective symbol of their union</u>. The other union is the relationship between Katsushiro and Shino. Kyuzo, for instance, is humanized for us when he spots the two youngsters in their forest retreat. Later, Katsushiro and Shino will consummate their affair, much to the dismay of Manzo and the amusement of the other Samurai. However, this union does not particularly bring the Samurai and the farmers together; its function is rather to demonstrate, as we will see, the ultimate irreconcilability of the two groups.

In the fourth and final section, Kurosawa drops the alternations between comedy and drama, between stasis and tension, and gives us a compressed, tense, and exciting view of battle. The fascination with process, however, is not abandoned as Kurosawa traces the strategy and its results.

Kambei's idea is to let the brigands enter the fortress-village one at a time so that the farmers can kill them. This works splendidly for the most part. Following a few instances of battle, Kambei is shown marking off the number of brigands killed on a chart he has made. Two problems complicate the plan: the rifles and the increasing ferocity of the brigands' attack. The first part of the problem is alleviated by Kyuzo who goes out into the night and returns with a rifle. That is further aided by Kikuchiyo's similar act. Yet, unfortunately, one more rifle remains in the brigands' hands.

<u>The death of the Samurai is ironic, for the ones who die all die by gunfire.</u> Men who live by the sword and see the sword as their "soul," are killed by guns. Further, those who die are the ones who are flawed. Gorobei dies because his interest in the fight was only to be near Kambei, not to help the farmers. Similarly, Kyuzo was only interested in perfecting his skill with his sword so that his death is doubly ironic, for he dies by another means entirely. And poor Kikuchiyo, who would have hated to die in a "dung heap" like that, has his worst fear come true. His flaw, if one could call it that, was ultimately in trying to be something he could not be. The irony of their deaths adds to the element of "nostalgia" that the film communicates.

The final shots indicate that now the farmers are safe. They no longer need the Samurai. Kambei proclaims that the farmers are the ones who won. The farmers, like the land they work, will go on forever. Kambei, Shichiroji, and Katsushiro leave. The final shot is a pan up to the hillside where the four graves, those of Heihachi, Gorobei, Kyuzo, and Kikuchiyo, with swords in them, become a part of the timeless landscape. This engenders on the formal level, the feeling of *mono no aware* that places *Seven Samurai* within the Nostalgic Samurai sub-genre.

Seven Samurai must also be understood in relation to the nature/culture dichotomy. I have already mentioned that the initial synthesizing between Samurai and farmers occurs through the medium of weaponry, which is to say, culture. The Samurai who represent culture, in some sense "lose"; it is, as Kambei says, the farmers who are the winners and it is the farmers who are linked quite obviously to nature. The brigands are associated with culture, for they have arisen due to cultural forces. The country has been plunged into civil war due to man's greed and ambition. These bandits operate within a cultural context of lawlessness and greed. But the farmers, associated with nature, must bring in other cultural forces to deal with them. Like fighting fire with fire, culture cancels culture, so to speak.

Nature itself becomes a force in the final battle. The rain and the mud aid the farmers, for the brigands are unable to see clearly and their horses are unable to gallop as fast or to secure firm footing. Nature aids the farmer, culture cancels culture, so that the farmers emerge as truly the only winners.

The scene in which the Samurai leave the village also emphasizes the return of the nature/culture dichotomy. The farmers return to their fields, planting a new crop in a ritualistic dance in which the Samurai are neither invited nor welcome to participate. In this scene the youths Katsushiro and Shino exchange glances; the imploring question is silently asked, will Katsushiro stay? In fact, such an option is never presented seriously, for Katsushiro could not possibly stay. He has not simply become a man over the course of the film, by way of his first sexual encounter and his first kill, he has become a Samurai. If Kikuchiyo, one-half of the "youth" image in the film, could not cross class/culture boundaries, neither can Katsushiro. This inability to make the transition due to circumstances is another contributing factor to the feeling of *mono no aware,* for even if Shino and Katsushiro wanted to remain together, their cultural differences prevent it.

It is worth noting here that the very excellent American Western based on Kurosawa's film, *The Magnificent Seven,* combines the youth figures into one person, Chico, the farmer's son who joins the gunfighters' cause. Chico, at the end of the film, does indeed stay in the village. He has not been killed like Kikuchiyo for trying to change his circumstances of birth, nor is he prevented by circumstances of birth from remaining behind. Chico does hang up his guns to become a part of the society he has helped defend. (Never mind the inferior sequel, *The Return of the Seven!*) Katsushiro cannot. Moreover, Katsushiro's place in the future is equally tenuous, for what chance does he have to seek a position? In some sense, Heihachi, Gorobei, and the others are better of, for the future belongs to the farmers.

Ultimately, the farmers synthesize the nature/culture dichotomy for us by keeping firmly in both worlds. The farmers, not the Samurai, are the true recipients of the myth-structure in the film. Let us recall that modern man begins when he changes from a predator to a tiller of the fields. Farming harmonizes nature and culture by bringing culture to nature to increase yield and keep the soil fertile. In *Seven Samurai,* the predators (brigands and Samurai) kill each other, leaving the farmers in peace to pursue their harmonious ends. The farmers sing a song of peace and joy while the Samurai walk down a lonely road to an unknown fate. If we are left feeling nostalgic at this ending as the graves fade from view, we can look forward to a happier film in *The Hidden Fortress.*

The Hidden Fortress

Of all the period films Kurosawa directed, *The Hidden Fortress* is perhaps the most clearly dependent on a number of motifs common to formula films popular in the West. *The Hidden Fortress* is simple, direct, and lighthearted, content, for the most part, to offer up a rousing entertainment. Despite some undertones that distinguish it from the average formula tale, the film emerges as primarily a rousing action-comedy.

The Hidden Fortress is basically structured as an adventure film, for it is mainly concerned with a caper, a quest. Its focus of attention is on a group who tries to get from one place to another, while another group is out to stop them. This simplicity of structure enables Kurosawa to develop characterization via action so that the film falls neatly into the adventure genre as defined by Cawelti. "The true focus of interest in the adventure story is the character of the hero and the nature of the obstacles he has to overcome."[39] In this manner, *The Hidden Fortress* may be considered an adventure film like many a Western, war drama or caper film.

The similarity of structure to Western adventure dramas extends to a similarity of setting. The typical structuring device of a caper film is the crossing of a frontier, a border. If Kurosawa used the idea of a frontier in *Seven Samurai* and created a moral frontier, *The Hidden Fortress* actually uses a physical one. In order to justify such a border, Kurosawa again situates his story in the pre-Tokugawa era of civil wars. However, the moral frontier aspect is deemphasized so that the attention on action is allowed to dominate, creating a dynamic and enjoyable work which can be appreciated solely on this physical level.

However, the deemphasis of the moral frontier does not mean that Kurosawa has abandoned the attempt to transcend mere formularity. *The Hidden Fortress* can also be seen as a big-budget remake of *They Who Tread on the Tiger's Tail*. The earlier film was also a caper film involving a quest to cross a hostile border, yet it introduced an important undercurrent, that of the dialectic between Feudal and Modern. Also, if *Tiger's Tail* was restricted in its use of space due to budgetary constraints, *The Hidden Fortress* positively revels in space with the adoption, for the first time, of the CinemaScope ratio (a ratio Kurosawa will use to superb effect in *Yojimbo, Sanjuro, High and Low,* and *Dersu Uzala*).

The key similarity between *Hidden Fortress* and *Tiger's Tail* lies in the similar origins of the dialectic Feudal/Modern. In the earlier film the dialectic arose by the introduction of the modernist figure, Enoken, into an essentially Feudalist setting. In opposition to Enoken were the warriors who posed as monks. By introducing the two opposed images within the same film, Kurosawa created the "binary bundle"[40] Feudal/Modern. In *Hidden Fortress* there are similarly two opposed figures who correspond to each side of the dialectic. On the one hand there are the two peasants, on the other the general. Initially, the opposition seems to be on the basis of class, just as it seemed in *Seven Samurai*. However, the characteristics of the peasant-heroes define them as modernist, just as Enoken's actions did in *Tiger's Tail*.

The two sets of heroes who come into diametrical opposition in the film also correspond to the two types of heroes present in the adventure formula. There is the "super hero with exceptional ability" or the hero who is "'one of us,' a figure marked, at least at the beginning of the story by flawed abilities."[41] The peasant-heroes are like us; the general is the very model of a super hero. These two heroes, the Modern and the Feudal, are both synthesized and not synthesized by the action of the film. A kind of synthesis is achieved by the film's title in Japanese which is *Kakushi Toride no San-Akunin (Three Bad Men in a Hidden Fortress)*. As Richie notes[42] the three bad men are the peasants and the general, each bad despite their very different attitudes and actions. However, the dynamics of the film mitigate against the synthesis. The presentation of the two types of heroes varies; the peasants are never redeemed in the sense that their motives never change nor do their attitudes. Neither are they unmasked nor exposed. Rather, they get what they ultimately want without a corresponding elevation of status, including moral or ethical status. More to the point, the "badness" of the super hero is never allowed to interfere with our admiration and respect for him. Beyond his inhabitation by the dynamic Toshiro Mifune, the super hero who ignores the feeling of *ninjo* in order to benefit the clan has performed his duty in a manner the Japanese audience in particular wholeheartedly approves of. Kurosawa's own ambivalence toward Feudal ethics, seen in *Seven Samurai,* reappears here.

The narrative strategies employed by *Seven Samurai* reappear here as well. Initially, we are presented with the two peasant-heroes with whom we sympathize, just as we first side with the farmers in *Seven Samurai*. Then, when the super hero is introduced, we shift our allegiance and become ambivalent toward the peasants. The phenomenological link formed between the audience and the oppressed class in *Seven Samurai* reappears here to. In fact, the link is even more strongly forged, for Kurosawa frequently uses point-of-view shots to reveal the super hero. This phenomenology also helps introduce the Feudal/Modern opposition, just as it did, to a lesser extent in *Seven Samurai.* We will notice later on that in *Yojimbo,* when we are not asked to sympathize or relate to the non-Samurai non-heroes, the first person we "meet" in the film is the *yojimbo* himself. Once again, Kurosawa introduces a source of tension as we identify with both types of heroes representing both Feudal and Modern values.

If Kurosawa withholds the formulaic redemption of the ordinary, "one of us," heroes, he never condemns them either. This humanistic slant on the flawed characters distinguishes the film as well. Their cowardice, their greed, their lack of commitment must be seen in the light of the chaos, confusion and moral decay that surrounds them. The entire first section of the film detailing their hardship and oppression wins us over to their side providing a suitable, understandable explanation for their actions. On this level, the "moral frontier" reoccurs, even if it is transcended through action.

The moral confusion, the utter chaos, and the idea of the physical border are all introduced formally in the first shot of the film. This opening shot, a complicated, hand-held tracking shot, is the longest single take in Kurosawa's work until the very different, but much longer, opening shot of *Kagemusha.* The hand-held camera in the 'Scope ratio follows the two peasant-heroes as they discuss their unfortunate situation. Their conversation informs us that they were unwilling foot-soldiers who fought many battles, all on the losing side. They would dearly love to go home but must cross a guarded border to do so. The verbal information combines with the disturbing dynamics of the framing to reinforce each other.

The 'Scope ratio emphasizes offscreen space, a strategy that further reinforces the idea of crossing a border, in this case, the border of the frame. In this opening shot, for instance, from offscreen right comes a running figure followed closely by mounted warriors who surround the man on foot and kill him. Still within the same shot, they ride off screen. In addition to introducing the use of offscreen space, the shot has a thematic value for we understand that we are thrust into a time of surprising violence, when from any side death can strike.

The use of offscreen space introduces another dialectic into the film, that of one between an "open" style and a "closed" as Braudy defines them.[43] Braudy notices this technique; "Kurosawa's camera in the first scenes of *The Hidden Fortress* (1962) [*sic*], for example, stays close to his characters not to confine them but to surprise us (and them) by what else is in the world."[44] However, by working in genre, Kurosawa also adopts, implicitly, the idea of the closed world of the formula film. In this sense, Kurosawa, as I have mentioned earlier, looks forward to (or is contemporary with) the New Wave filmmakers of France and Germany.

Offscreen space will play an important part in the next sequence as well, a sequence which introduces the frontier aspect. The two peasants climb to the top of a ridge only to see, via a point-of-view shot, a well-armed border patrol. Other peasants similarly anxious to cross, inform them that an incoming fog will provide cover for their escape. The fog rolls in, and in a series of long and medium-long shots, the men seem certain to cross the border. When the fog lifts however, the men find themselves in serious danger. The camera reframes, revealing that the men are face to face with the border guards. The fog obscured their vision; off-screen space surprised them.

The two heroes separate; they have had enough of each other and they split up. In two separate vignettes, each man is captured and made a slave, forced to dig for gold to support the army of the clan that has imprisoned them. The lust for gold, introduced in this manner, is to become the defining characteristic of these two seemingly luckless men.

A slave revolt frees them from their bondage, a revolt which begins with the suddenness and the fury of a tropical storm and ends with equal speed as calm returns. Kurosawa films the scene in a manner reminiscent of Eisenstein (as he will do again in a crucial segment of *Kagemusha*). The slaves rush toward their captors on a downward diagonal slope; the camera too, assumes a diagonal view of the action. In a reverse of the Odessa Steps sequence, the slaves rush down toward their oppressors who fire up at them. The cutting alternates between long shots of the entire scene and close-ups of details which are related metonymically to the main action. In the midst of this confusion, the two heroes meet again and huddle in a crawl-space on the stairs. The camera fixes on them as the crowd sweeps past them out of frame. The static camera angle on them again reinforces the offscreen space as peace and tranquility come over the scene.

Though they are still frightened of what might happen next, of what will enter the frame, they decide to remain behind and search for the gold. When they do finally find it, they are revealed as petty and greedy, unwilling to share with each other, and willing to risk their lives to find more. The manner in which they find the gold is rich with mythic overtones. The two men, preparing to cook dinner, start a fire. For some reason, however, the wood will not burn. Upon examining the wood they discover a bar of gold has been hidden in it. Thus, an object of culture, hidden in a part of nature, prevents that part of nature from fulfilling its cultural task, that of transforming the raw into the cooked. Too, gold per se has worth only on the cultural/conventional plane. As a metal it has no useful, logical possibilities, for it cannot be used for cooking, for weaponry, or for building. Its value is totally dependent upon man's agreed assignation. The gold has however, transformed two scared but sensible men into two greedy and foolhardy men.

With the introduction of the gold comes the introduction of the super hero, played by Toshiro Mifune. Through his mere presence, and an abundance of low-angle shots, he intimidates the two men, eventually convincing them out of a combination of their own lust for wealth and his charisma and physicality, to risk a dangerous journey through hostile territory.

The super hero is a famous general, something he tells the two men, but, considering the confusion of the times in which they live, they do not accept. We, however, know this to be true. We also know that the woman who accompanies the men on the dangerous trek is, in fact, a princess, the leader of the clan of which Mifune is the general. The relationship between the general and the princess has a number of similarities to that of Yoshitsune and Benki in *They Who Tread on the Tiger's Tail*. The general is respectful and mindful of his place but is willing to offend her for the greater good of the clan. Just how much he is willing to sacrifice for their cause is made clear in the confrontation between the princess and the general over the execution of the general's sister. His sister had substituted for the princess to fool the rival clan in order to aid their escape. The general seems unconcerned when he learns of her death; the princess is upset at the idea and angry at the general's reaction. Obviously, the general suppresses his sadness while the princess, who is only a teenager, gives in to her feelings.

In order to escape across the border, the three men and the princess pose as wood-gatherers; the princess, who would be unable to disguise her patrician speech, also plays dumb. The two peasants are never entrusted with any of this information. It is not until the journey is over do they learn the whole truth. The general relies on their greed to overcome their cowardice. It never occurs to him to trust them. The two peasants are thus doomed to remain in their station on the ethical, moral, and heroic level in the film.

A variety of dangers confront them along the way, and at each turn the general shows his courage and steadfastness, while the peasants reveal their cowardice. One action sequence in particular must be mentioned, for it contributes to the film's functioning on a number of levels. That is the sequence in which three mounted warriors overtake the party traveling on foot. The general manages to kill two of them, but the third gallops off screen right. The general grabs one of the other horses and takes off in hot pursuit, his sword held ready at his side. He soon overtakes the rider and kills him, but as the camera pans right with him he suddenly finds himself riding right into the armed border-camp. Off-screen space has been his undoing.

This border-camp is under the command of another famous general, one who recognizes Mifune immediately and challenges him to a duel with spears. After an exciting few minutes, Mifune defeats the general and spares his life. This same general later in the film manages their capture. When he confronts his prisoners they notice a long, ugly scar on his face. He has been disgraced by Mifune. The general tells Mifune that he was wrong to spare his life. The princess, however, tells this scarred warrior that his clan leader did him a grave disservice; the disgrace is not his but his lord's. The nobility of Mifune and the princess inspires him to spare their lives and to help get them and their gold across the border. In a rousing action climax the peasants cross first, followed by the horses carrying the gold, followed by a mounted party consisting of the rival general, Mifune, and the princess. Before too long the two peasants get their reward in gold as they learn the truth about their fellow traveling companions.

The peasants remain unchanged; the general and the princess are restored. From the peasants' point of view and our identification with them, *The Hidden Fortress* may be seen as a fairy tale or folktale for "folktales often exemplify... a kind of wish fulfillment fantasy.... The discovery of treasure, or the winning of great rewards for apparently small actions (but often highly moral ones....) are more typical of European peasant tales than those of the myths of aristocratic societies or primitive ones...."[45] It is this fairy-tale aspect, more than the mythic structuring of the Modern/Feudal dialectic, that distinguishes the film and has made it so attractive here in the West (and in Japan where it was awarded the *Kinema Jumpo* #2 for the year).

If the two peasants are never redeemed, never elevated above their base instincts (for they are never really given the chance), then perhaps we should recognize the implicit impossiblity of truly synthesizing the Modern/Feudal dialectic. The Feudal hero in *The Hidden Fortress,* despite his being a "bad man," is bigger, stronger, more brave, more intelligent, more *competent* than we could ever be. He was (literally) born into the role. Modern man does not belong in the Feudal age, just as he did not in *They Who Tread on the Tiger's Tail.* When confronted with Feudal ethics and the sacrifices that must be made to uphold them (whatever their validity), modern man comes up short. Thus one-half of the film mitigates against the escapist element of the adventure formula as it is usually structured here in the West. We do not feel the catharsis of transformation. On the other hand, the Feudal hero certainly does succeed so that Kurosawa has it both ways in the film.

The Hidden Fortress is Kurosawa's second, and final, Nostalgic Samurai Drama. By situating the film in the chaos of pre-Tokugawa Japan he offers us the deeds of heroes at a time when such deeds were still possible, when such actions truly meant something. The nostalgia that one feels, however, is less tinged with *mono no aware* than in *Seven Samurai*. *The Hidden Fortress* does end happily, with an uplifting note of restoration and reward. Despite the odd and disturbing ambivalence introduced into the film, *The Hidden Fortress* can be read as an old-fashioned caper adventure whose intent is to leave us feeling invigorated as the good guys win in the end.

Yojimbo

Yojimbo marks a turning point in Kurosawa's career and in the Japanese Cinema. With *Yojimbo* Kurosawa helps usher in the sixties, becoming an important thematic part of the generation that would erupt in violence later in the decade. His film can be seen as an integral part of Japan's self-examination and self-criticism that is a part of its own "New Wave" that began in the sixties. *Yojimbo* also gives rise to two significant exploitation forms that dominate Japan's output in the sixties and seventies, the Sword Film and the *yakuza* Film. With *Yojimbo*, Kurosawa solidifies his reputation and influence in the West as the sixties saw three of his films transformed into Westerns: *The Magnificent Seven* (from *Seven Samurai*), *The Outrage* (from *Rashomon*), and *A Fistful of Dollars* (from *Yojimbo*).

Yojimbo also marks the full flowering of Kurosawa's genius as it becomes the first of four masterpieces that he produces between 1960 and 1965. Yet, after producing ten films in the 1950s and these four in the first half of the decade, Kurosawa is unable to release a single feature in the second half of the decade.

Yojimbo marks a turning point in Kurosawa's use of the East/West, Feudal-Modern dialectic as he becomes more vicious and satirical in his themes. Because it is so clearly dependent on a number of Western formulas and structures, it has, therefore, been the most misunderstood of his genre films. Even so perceptive a writer as Noel Burch sees *Yojimbo* as "nothing more than a fusion of the latter day *chambara* tradition with the Hollywood Western...."[46] Although it is dependent on Western structures and sword-play dramas, it transcends them. *Yojimbo*, in fact, is closer to the modern Gangster film and the Hard-boiled Detective story than it is to the Western. In many respects, *Yojimbo* is an adaptation of Dashiell Hammett's novel *Red Harvest*, although its origins in pulp fiction are equally as easily transcended, just as they are in *High and Low*.

High and Low transcends its origins in formula fiction through a keen humanism; *Yojimbo* through its use of modernism. *Yojimbo* employs a number of modernist techniques, particularly black comedy and self-reflexivity, as it emerges as a satire on Japan's rush toward Western-style capitalism. Its use of the American Ganster film combines with its modernism to create a work of great subtlety and wit, a work which must be analyzed as both a formula film and a modernist effort.

Yojimbo is brought in line with the Gangster film/Thriller, as Colin McArthur calls the genre,[47] by its structuring of its conflict and the use of a setting closer to the Gangster film than the Western. If *Seven Samurai* utilizes the Western idea of the frontier in the form of a moral frontier and *The Hidden Fortress* in the form of a physical frontier, *Yojimbo* presents us with an economic frontier. *Yojimbo* is situated at a frontier in Japanese history equally as chaotic and volatile as the setting of *Seven Samurai* and *The Hidden Fortress*, namely, the end of the Tokugawa regime. It is a time where East meets West literally, as Admiral Perry's Black Ships demand such a meeting. It is a time of re-evaluation and of destruction. Traditional social classes are being realigned; traditional ties becoming undone. Japan must catch up with the

West, which means that she must move from agriculture to industry; that is, from nature to culture.

The frontier *Yojimbo* utilizes is the frontier of the Gangster film, a frontier of economic striving and of class conflict; of families at war and of a struggle between familial ties and the sense of self. *Yojimbo* introduces this rift in tradition when its hero, known only as *yojimbo* ("bodyguard"; at one point he jokingly calls himself *kuwabatake sanjuro,* "30-year old mulberry field," but nobody else does) comes upon a domestic quarrel. The son of a peasant family who operates an inn wants to leave home. His father and mother try to talk him out of it but he is implacable. He wants to head for "the town" because there are opportunities to make money, to make something of himself. Thus, we have a reversal on both the mythos of the Western film and the tradition of the Japanese family. The pre-modern tradition of Japan was the ancestral business, the inheritance of both title and trade from one's father. The son in *Yojimbo* is ready to break away from this tradition, ready to ignore familial and class ties, in the hopes of economic advancement. Too, this is a reversal of the Western myth where the city is a place of confinement and the frontier, the open spaces, are to be prized. "Go West," is the credo of the Western; "Go East" (to the industrial cities) the credo of the Gangster film.

The city, or the town, in the Gangster film is the place of hope, for it is free of class-based ties, especially if you carry a gun. The great equalizer of the city is ability, which in the Gangster film is the ability to use a gun. Remember too, the corollary of the Gangster film is the Musical where it is not ability with a gun that counts, but ability to sing (dance, write, etc.) that becomes the great equalizer. In *Yojimbo,* this equalizer is the sword. Samurai, *ronin,* peasant, or merchant can make a name for himself if he can wield a sword. Although this is true to a certain extent in the Western film, the lack of class ties, of family ties (there are few real names in Westerns) enables people to join the community; in the Gangster film it enables them to become rich. That difference is the crucial one.

The town itself in *Yojimbo* also represents a break from Japanese tradition and represents an alignment with the Western industrial (capitalistic) city. The city is the archetypical setting for the Gangster film/Thriller. Its importance in *Yojimbo* is not physical (for the little town in which the action occurs is hardly the city of the Gangster film or that of Kurosawa's own Gangster film/Thrillers *Stray Dog* and *High and Low*) but rather, again, economic. The traditional Japanese village is agriculture based. It is barter-centered and provides a central location for meeting, rather than the dominant dwellings. The town in *Yojimbo* is not agriculture-centered. Its chief products are silk and sake, two commodities that are culture-based, not nature-based. Both silk and sake represent the literal transformation of nature into culture, and both commodities take on worth according to convention. The town in *Yojimbo* is, therefore, denatured, a place where culture and convention dominate. Further, the town is caught in the middle of a war, a war for control of the lucrative silk trade; a war, that is, waged for economic profit. This economic-based structure, rather than agriculture-based organization, which is also the foundation of the town in the Western genre, brings *Yojimbo* into the realm of the modern city and hence the territory of the Gangster film.

The warring factions in the town are comparable to economic conglomerates so that *Yojimbo,* like many a Gangster film, can be seen to be symbolic of capitalism. As Cawelti points out, "The drama of the criminal gang has become a kind of allegory of the corporation and the corporate society."[48] However, more significant, more insidious, is that the gangs are not simply conglomerates, not simply a collection of people with similar goals. Rather, the two gangs are family-centered. The traditional idea of "warring clans" (the title of an eccentric Sword film by Kihachi Okamoto) which would otherwise have great validity is undercut here because of the strictly economic basis of the struggle.

The idea of the family-as-gang is a significant part of the American Gangster film as exemplified by the phenomenally successful book and two-part film *The Godfather*. The Don, or godfather, is the symbol of authority by virtue of his place as head of the family, an authority derived from the cultural tradition of Italy and other Mediterranean societies dominated by strong father-figures. The mythos of the family-gang provides a strong dramatic structure in the film, for it brings to bear a pressure on the individual members of the family related to the Japanese idea of *"giri."* In *Yojimbo,* however, it is, perversely, not family ties that bind the two gangs, it is greed. Though they are families, such ties can be ignored when it comes to money. This destruction of the traditional family is apparent in the scene of the hostage exchange (a scene which derives its strength also from the "doubling" aspect of the family, for during the exchange we are confronted with the young mother who is held captive against her will). When the son of one of the factions is reunited with his parents, he is not met with relief. Rather, his mother vilifies him for his cowardice. He has disgraced the family and more importantly, his family-gang has lost its tactical advantage, which means that it suffers economically.

The families that are introduced in *Yojimbo* have all been destroyed by the new form of cutthroat economics. The son leaves his rural home for the town; the town itself is destroyed because of two families at war over profits; a young mother has been torn away from her family as repayment for her husband's gambling debts. The bodyguard himself acts as both destroyer and restorer of the family in the film. The modern families, that is, the two warring gangs, are destroyed; the young mother is reunited, through the *yojimbo's* efforts, with her family; the young boy whom we met at the start is spared from the carnage at the end and told to go home to his parents. This kind of "conservative" element to the film introduces an undercurrent of ambiguity, one that plays against the satire and black comedy.

The bodyguard is similarly shown to fit right into the economic basis of the film. His services are offered to the highest bidder. Unlike the Samurai bodyguards in *Seven Samurai,* he is available for a price, a high price. The moral/ethical positions of the two gangs do not enter into his decision. And they do not, significantly, for neither side is right. Each side wants control of the profitable silk trade strictly for profit. The bodyguard, thus, becomes analogous to the hired gun in the Gangster film and not the Western. *This Gun for Hire* (1942) is the title of a classic Gangster/Thriller. The hero barters his deadly skill, preying on each gang's desires for control.

The basic situation that motivates the plot in *Yojimbo* is adapted from Hammett's *Red Harvest*. Given the economically driven factions in *Yojimbo,* the film is already aligned with the Gangster film. The utilization of *Red Harvest* brings *Yojimbo* into the territory of the Hard-boiled Detective film as well. Of course, there is one difference between *Yojimbo* and the Hard-boiled Detective film, namely, that there is no mystery. Although that might appear to be a crucial difference, it is not. The Hard-boiled Detective story shifts its emphasis from the solving of a crime (the main structural pattern of the Classical Detective Story) to the taking of "a personal, moral stance toward the criminal."[49] The focus of the Hard-boiled Detective story is on character not on process. And although we have seen how Kurosawa can become fascinated by process (and we will see it again in the next chapter), in *Yojimbo* he abandons that interest.

Red Harvest, although it involves a mystery of sorts, concentrates on character and character-interaction. The detective, known only as "the Continental Op," just as the hero in Kurosawa's film is known only as "*yojimbo,*" comes to take on the Hard-boiled Detective's typical role of "judge, jury and executioner" as he "embodies the threat of judgment and execution...."[50] So too, the *yojimbo*. The Continental Op ends up "cleaning up the town," as does the *yojimbo,* and the Continental Op takes a kind of perverse satisfaction out of violence. So too, clearly, does the bodyguard.

The motivation for the detective's involvement in *Red Harvest* is economic—it is his job. The motivation for the bodyguard is similarly economic, at least that is how he presents his motivation to the two gangs, a motivation they can understand. The Op comes into a city not too dissimilar from the one in *Yojimbo*. The city of *Red Harvest* is called "Personville," and given the nickname "Poisonville" out of a combination of dialect and description. The name "Poisonville" for "Personville" is indicative of the fact that the town's troubles are caused by people. The town in *Yojimbo,* similarly is in the grip of man's greed. Personville's man-related problems are given objective correlatives by Hammett through the Op's descriptions of the town. "The city wasn't pretty.... The first policeman I saw needed a shave, the second had a couple of buttons off his shabby uniform.... After that I stopped checking."[51] And there is also this: "Poisonville [was] an ugly city... set in an ugly notch between two ugly mountains that had been all dirtied up by mining. Spread over this was a grimy sky that looked as if it had come out of the smelter's stacks."[52] The city's ugliness is directly attributed to man in the form of industrialization (i.e., culture).

The town in *Yojimbo* similary has none of the picturesque aspects of the typical Japanese rural village. There are no lushly wooded forests surrounding the town. Instead, the town is approached via dusty roads with no planted fields in sight. Instead of the architecturally harmonious Japanese home with its beautiful gardens, the town is constructed of bland wooden shacks and is dominated by a multi-story warehouse that is both ugly and large. And if the bodyguard's first sight is not a policeman with a shabby uniform, it is of a mangy dog carrying an arm in its mouth. And the first person he speaks to in the town, the one who tells him that if he is looking for work as a paid killer he should cut off an arm or two, is in fact, the town magistrate.

The utilization of the Hard-boiled Detective form as adapted from *Red Harvest* enables Kurosawa also to take a satirical/ironic stance. The ending of *Red Harvest*, although it too has an undercurrent of irony, is basically the ending to a job well done. The Op tells us that "Personville, under martial law [develops] into a sweet-smelling thornless bed of roses."[53] The end of *Yojimbo* is, however, the conclusion of a job too well done, for the bodyguard has seen to it that the town is virtually deserted! In breaking the grip of violence formed by monopoly capitalism, the *yojimbo* has destroyed the city. His parting remark that now the town will be peaceful and quiet is wickedly ironic, for there is almost no one left alive. His moral judgment has been swift and complete. This "detective" is so hard-boiled that he can destroy a whole town in his guise of judge, jury, and executioner; he is a logical, if satirical, extension of the pulp hero.

Further, the destruction of the economically driven town is a comment on the city's image in the Gangster film. If the Gangster film essentially utilizes an image of the city as a place of nightmare (the *noir* elements), it never calls for a pastoral solution. That is, the Gangster film does not postulate the mythos of the Western. The "moral" or "reformist" Gangster film calls for law and order, for honest politicians and police, to clean up the city. In *Yojimbo* the solution is to destroy. Again, a kind of conservatism, or reactionary attitude emerges. Yet, this conservative nature must be pitted against the modernist techniques employed.

Yojimbo can be viewed as a comedy, a black comedy about death and destruction.

> Black humor... is a kind of comedy that juxtaposes pain with laughter, fantastic fact with calmly inadequate reaction, a cruelty with tenderness. It requires a certain distance from the very despair it recognizes, and it seems to be able to take surprises, reversals and outrages with a clown's shrug.[54]

It is worth noting that Kurosawa and Kon Ichikawa (in his films *A Crowded Streetcar* and *The Wanderers*) are the only pre-New Wave directors to utilize this modernist comic technique, and of the New Wave directors, only Oshima (in *Death by Hanging* in particular) has similarly utilized the technique.

The first instance of a dark (if not black) humor occurs at the start of the film. The bodyguard, whom we judge to be a *ronin* by virtue of his sword and his shabby dress, seems to be at a total loss about where to go and what to do. From the Japanese viewpoint, this is highly ironic or even absurd in the literal sense of the word, for to be without a goal or aim is to be cut off from your roots and from society. Of course, the *ronin,* or wave man, buffeted about by fate, cut off from his past, is a figure of pathos and tragedy in the Samurai film. But in *Yojimbo* such aimlessness is played for laughs as the *yojimbo* picks up a stick and tosses it in the air. He follows the direction in which it points. His cavalier, unconcerned attitude also distinguishes his odd action.

The tossing of the stick recalls, interestingly, the scene in John Ford's *Young Mr. Lincoln* in which Abe lets the spirit of Ann Rutledge guide his falling stick toward the correct path. However, there is no guiding spirit to aid the bodyguard. His action is perhaps somewhat closer in spirit to the exchange between Alice and the Chesire Cat in *Alice in Wonderland.* Alice, at a loss as to where to go, asks the cat what direction she should take. "Would you tell me please, which way I ought to go from here?" she asks. The cat replies, "That depends on where you want to go." Alice answers that it does not matter much where, to which the cat responds, "Then it doesn't matter which way to go!"[55] In *The Annotated Alice,* Martin Gardner[56] glosses this passage with a comment about a similar exchange in Jack Kerouac's *On the Road* (which he does not much admire) and John Kemeny's essay *A Philosopher Looks at Science.* Gardner, however, seems to have missed the existential, absurdist implications of the passage, something that Kurosawa's scene amply elucidates.

Black comedy, the comedy of death and destruction, reappears permanently when the bodyguard comes to town. The first scene that confronts him is of a dog carrying a human arm in his mouth. The shock effect of this scene is mitigated and turned into comedy in two ways. The first is the jaunty, bouncy, entirely inappropriate music on the sound track. The second is, to anthropomorphize the dog for a moment, the utterly serene and contented look on the dog's face. The hero's own duplicity in the dark tone of the film follows hard upon this scene. Told by the town magistrate that if he wants to make an impression on the gang bosses he should cut off an arm or two, he does exactly that. In a calm, cool and detached manner, he confronts three seemingly tough gang members, killing one, knocking one out, and neatly slicing off the sword hand of the third. The black humor of the situation is compounded by the *yojimbo's* following the advice given to him literally, as if his actions were indeed merely the action of a clown shrugging.

In a sense, the reaction of the mother whose son has been returned to her following the hostage exchange, can also be seen to be an instance of black humor. The expected reaction, that of a tearful reunion, is not delivered. Instead the exact and surprising opposite occurs. We laugh partly out of surprise and partly out of a sense of the outrageousness of the situation.

Irony and black humor also arise when the bodyguard performs one of the few acts of kindness and compassion in the film. He decides to reunite the woman held hostage by one of the gangs (the Ushi-Tora gang) with her husband and child. He tells the gang members that their rivals will no doubt try and recapture her so they better get the woman out of town. He then proceeds to follow them, killing all her captors. The wife and her family are most grateful to him, but in a gruff manner (combining that is, cruelty with tenderness) tells them to be on their way. In wishing to thank him later on for his efforts, they land him in trouble. For his act of kindness, he is mercilessly beaten by the Ushi-Toras. His singular act of goodness puts him in the only real jeopardy he ever faces. In trying to do good in a world gone bad, he suffers.

The apocalypse the hero brings about as first the one clan destroys the other, and then is destroyed by him, is also handled blithely by the bodyguard. His jaunty "goodbye" as he walks away from the town seems highly cavalier considering the town is now all but deserted.

The black comedy of the film is aided by the self-reflexivity, and the link forged between the central character—the *yojimbo*—and the audience. Marsha Kinder has pointed out in *Throne of Blood* "Kurosawa creates a self-reflexive tension between performance and observation—a pattern that he uses again in *Yojimbo*."[57] First we are asked to identify with the bodyguard (a change from the shifting identifications of *Seven Samurai* and *Hidden Fortress*) as our first live-action shot in the film is a close-up (in 'Scope) of him. This identification with him is never abandoned as Kurosawa motivates much of his cuts by using point-of-view shots. For instance, the all-important shot of the dog carrying a hand in his mouth is shown from the bodyguard's point of view. This tension between performance and observation is similarly structured around the *yojimbo's* creation of action and his subsequent observation of it. Perhaps the most spectacular (and amusing) instance of this in operation is the sequence in which the bodyguard has maneuvered both sides into fighting by his promise of siding with them. At the last minute he backs out of the action, preferring to watch it from a vantage point high above the ground. As the two sides prepare to fight, the bodyguard enjoys the spectacle, as do we. First, by means of cross-cutting from his point of view, we see each side trying to egg themselves on. Then Kurosawa cuts to a high angle shot which encompasses an empty screen seen from the bodyguard's vantage point. The sides of the screen, the offscreen space, then become the focal points. We see hesitant swords gingerly enter each side of the frame. Still on a static shot, we see the two gangs slowly and comically enter the frame.

The pattern of initiating action and then watching the results on the part of the bodyguard makes us identify with him as he comes to stand for us. His moral judgments, his ethical stance, must be ours. Although he initiates action and then stands back from it, he also gets involved. He becomes an integral part of the action when he takes matters into his own hands. And if his action is extreme, if he literally cleans up the town in darkly comic excess, he still has been moved toward action. In this manner, Kurosawa's use of black humor mirrors that of the important American novelists of the sixties, such as Ken Kesey, John Barth, Kurt Vonnegut, and Stanley Elkin, who similarly recognized the absurd state of affairs but whose heroes nonetheless act. The difference here, though, is that Kurosawa seems to find specific causes for the feelings of alienation and loss of control. He finds, perhaps, that the economic motivation of Japan has ignored the human angle, that the drive toward "corporate families"[58] has left behind the traditional family, and so he has his hero restore the family in this film. Kurosawa's use of black humor is primarily humanistic and not, as it first seems, nihilistic, for "the black humorist can never deal from a superior position; he is always a part of his own subject matter. He must recognize the insanity that surrounds him, and he must recognize his own contribution to that insanity...."[59] Although *Yojimbo* initiates the nihilistic Sword film, it must still be distinguished from it. Its graphic violence, its shift from societal codes to a distinct lack of codes, its shift from pathos to black comedy, still have a firm basis in the primacy of the worth of the individual. We should always remember that by using the Western formula of the Gangster film/Thriller and the Hard-boiled Detective story, Kurosawa's excesses here must be seen as primarily satirical. He, as any good black humorist might, has extended the conventions to their (il) logical conclusions. Like the bodyguard himself who follows the magistrate's advice literally and cuts off an arm, Kurosawa has taken the underlying mythos of the American formulas literally. But his message is conservative and redemptive; it is, still and all, humanistic.

Sanjuro

Sanjuro is the last true Samurai film that Akira Kurosawa has produced. In some ways the film is a summing up of the various themes he has introduced in his earlier works yet it also contains much that is new and surprising. If *Sanjuro* is perhaps the only period film he has produced which firmly fits into the mainstream of Japanese film genre, it also continues his unique exploration of the East/West dichotomy. And if *Sanjuro* is a more gentle comedy than its predecessors, it also has its moments of raucous satire and darkly comic gloom. Like the best of Kurosawa's films, it is filled with ambivalences, but its formal perfection is unmatched. Perhaps even more so than *Yojimbo*, *Sanjuro* is a comedy of manners and mismatches that is mirrored on the formal and narrative levels.

Sanjuro continues to use the idea of the frontier as its structural base, situating itself (although not explicitly) at the end of the Tokugawa era. But the frontier that Kurosawa uses differs from the earlier ones, for the frontier in *Sanjuro* is an aesthetic frontier. *Sanjuro* is a film about the replacement of one type of aesthetic code with another; about one set of rules coming head-to-head with another. Kurosawa uses the conflict between codes as a source of dramatic tension and a source of humor. The differing codes stand as symbols for the changing nature of society. These changing codes also have implications vis-a-vis the Americanization of Japan, something that will be explored later.

Sanjuro builds upon the code of ethics known as Bushido while it also uses a great deal of the aesthetics of Zen. The two codes are opposed in the film to the private, personal code of the hero, known only as Sanjuro or Tsubaki Sanjuro (and portrayed by Toshiro Mifune). Bushido and Zen Aesthetics are institutionalized in the film, as is another kind of code which might be called "honor among thieves." It is the institutional nature of the codes that interests Kurosawa as he explores the manner in which such codes interfere with the accomplishments of tasks and the attainment of goals. He is concerned with the manner in which codes, inappropriately applied, lead to deemphasis of the human will. Once again, *Sanjuro* operates from a firmly humanistic base.

The characters with whom the hero interacts are, unlike the ones in *Yojimbo,* true Samurai. They have position and status and they are proud of both. They would gladly die for the cause of their clan. Perhaps they would die too willingly, for their very willingness to honor the code of Bushido makes them reckless and thoughtless. Their deaths, in one sense, become their goal, rather than the reinstatement of their clan-leader. It takes an outsider to steer them right.

Because of their subscription to a code, to a set of significations, they mistrust the one man who can help them. The fact that Sanjuro is a *ronin,* an unattached Samurai, disturbs the young Samurai's sense of order. Further, he is dirty, grubby, ill-mannered, and gruff. This, too, goes against their sense of order. They see his clothes and apparent attitude as an objective correlative, which indeed it is, but his actions do not correlate to what they infer. When he asks them for money following his rescue of them from the magistrate's henchman, their mistrust of him is complete. Bushido does not allow for the pursuit of money; a Samurai, even a *ronin,* cannot accept payment for his services. Most of the young Samurai are therefore not able to trust him because he does not appear to subscribe to their codes.

The lack of trust on the part of the young Samurai becomes a constant source of dramatic tension. Their misunderstanding (misreading) of Sanjuro leads to trouble and almost to the defeat of their plans. Their reliance on an objective code prevents them from seeing the true nature of their would-be rescuer. His actions are a mystery to them, for they never trust their instincts; that is, they leave their human connections behind and rely solely on social (civil) codes.

The difference in social codes between Sanjuro and the young Samurai is also exacerbated by a difference in experience. Sanjuro is a battle-scarred fighter, a swordsman of masterful skill who has learned his skill the hard way. The Samurai are well trained, perhaps, but all their experience, so to speak, has been in the classroom. Their abilities have never been tested in nature, in real situations. While they would plunge head-long into a trap, Sanjuro can spot it a mile away. While they trust the magistrate because he is handsome and well-spoken, Sanjuro instinctively mistrusts the man. Sanjuro, like Kambei in *Seven Samurai,* can spot a master swordsman immediately; the young Samurai cannot distinguish a lamb from a wolf. The discrepancy in their abilities is the discrepancy between theory and practice, between socialized codes of behavior and naturalized codes of action. *Sanjuro* is an explication of the dangers and problems that arise when theory and practice do not coincide.

Juxtaposed against the relationship between Sanjuro and the Samurai is the relationship that develops between Sanjuro and the magistrate's chief henchman (Tatsuya Nakadai). The henchman subscribes to a code of "honor among thieves," or, more significantly, a code of mercenary values. The henchman thinks Sanjuro is a kindred spirit because he is a *ronin* and because he possesses an anarchic nature. Too, Sanjuro, like himself, is an expert swordsman, which implies that everyone else is fair game. The very things that the young Samurai mistrust about Sanjuro endear him to the henchman. Just as the Samurai misjudge Sanjuro because of their institutionalized codes, the henchman thinks he has Sanjuro figured out via his own (different) set of codes. Bad attracts bad, he thinks, and it is this belief that proves ultimately to be his undoing. The henchman is equally guilty of misjudging Sanjuro's behavior. If the young Samurai believe Sanjuro to be lying when he is telling the truth, the henchman believes Sanjuro to be telling the truth when he is lying. His set of beliefs does not permit the possibility of a set of actions *meaning* something else, just as the Samurai are unable to think differently.

Theory and practice constantly collide, an idea also seen clearly in the exchanges between Sanjuro and the chamberlain's wife. With Sanjuro's help the young Samurai rescue the wife and daughter of the chamberlain who had been prisoners of the magistrate. Sanjuro has had to kill two of their guards while the Samurai make a prisoner of the third. The old woman is quite distressed at the deaths, and she speaks her mind strongly on the subject. Sanjuro is a little nonplussed but accepts her criticism mutely. In order to escape from the compound, they must climb a stone wall. The two women are unable to jump high enough to reach the top so Sanjuro offers himself as a footstool. The older woman refuses, claiming it would be "impolite." Indeed it would be impolite, but the need for hurry, one should think, far outweighs the

Toshiro Mifune (left) stars as *Sanjuro* with co-star Yuzo Kayama.

need for politeness. Yet the woman's aesthetic code interferes with the more logical or natural code that should enter in here. Sanjuro is able to convince her to accept his inconvenience by reminding her that if they do not hurry he may be forced to kill again. This prospect inspires her to place one aesthetic value before another, and up over the wall she goes, apologizing all the while for her rudeness.

On the other hand, the old lady's sense of values, of aesthetics, is not without a certain legitimacy. We see this in the sequence of the young Samurai's celebration when they discover the chamberlain's hidden whereabouts. In the midst of their celebrating, they notice their prisoner is leaping for joy along with them. He has left his place of imprisonment (a closet) and instead of escaping has literally joined their cause. When asked why he did not run away, he says it is because it never occurred to the old lady that he would. They also notice that he is wearing the best kimono of their leader (Yuzo Kayama) as he tells them the old lady lent it to him because his was dirty. His sense of propriety and aesthetics have been influenced by her as he found validity in her actions, and by extension, feels the young Samurai's cause to be the right one.

The chamberlain's wife also introduces the Zen Aesthetic of the paradox of the "undrawn sword." She tells Sanjuro that the very best swords remain in their scabbards. She compares him to a drawn sword and would prefer that he were not that way. In the light of the narrative action, Sanjuro's keeping his sword sheathed would have meant defeat for their cause, again indicating that an aesthetic idea cannot always work in practice. *Sanjuro,* in this fashion, is the paradox of the whole Zen Swordsman sub-genre of the Samurai film, for there too, the heroes never manage to keep their swords sheathed—which is exactly the way the audience wants it.

Sanjuro's judgments and actions all prove correct and cogent. His instinctual mistrust of the magistrate and his siding with the chamberlain are rewarded. His acting like a "drawn sword" literally saves the day time after time, although at the end of the film when challenged by the henchman he prefers to keep his sword sheathed. Unfortunately, the henchman's anger at having been fooled is too great and he challenges Sanjuro to a fight. He loses, in one of the most shocking (and thrilling) climaxes in Kurosawa's canon. Although Sanjuro's feat impresses the Samurai, Sanjuro cannot be persuaded by them to remain. There is no place for him in the new (or restored) society he has helped bring about. Sanjuro is not a man at peace with the cultural codes that will be in force, nor is he, according to Zen, at peace with himself. He has his own codes, his own rules of behavior, and he cannot conform to the new ones the chamberlain and his society will create. On the aesthetic frontier of the film, Sanjuro is an outsider and seems doomed to remain that way.

Kurosawa has stated[60] that he made *Sanjuro* as a sequel to *Yojimbo* and had not even intended to direct it but did so at the studio's insistence. He feels, he says further,[61] that while *Yojimbo* is a film for kids, *Sanjuro* is a film for adults. One knows what he means, for *Yojimbo* is filled with a raucous, anarchic sense of humor and has an undisciplined, carefree look to it, one which is in keeping with the theme. *Sanjuro*, with its gentle humor that arises due to the aesthetic juxtapositions, is a film of seemingly greater subtlety. Its control over its formal elements is both complete and obvious. The world in which Sanjuro moves is the refined world of *tatami* mats and tea ceremonies and camellias, hardly the hard-boiled look of *Yojimbo*. Yet, *Sanjuro* can also be seen as the children's film while *Yojimbo* with its black humor and self-reflexivity, can be seen as the more adult effort.

If we understand *Shane*, for all its formal brilliance, to have an essentially child-like appeal, so too, we should see that same appeal in *Sanjuro*. Through a profound similarity of structure, both films utilize the child's point of view in their narrative so that their subjects take on something of the nature of folktales. *Sanjuro* and *Shane* use children (or youths) as structuring principles to create mythic images that reflect a specific ideology. Both films use a similar tone and a similar ending to comment upon the importance of myth-images and heroes in today's world.

Shane, in the film of the same name, is first seen by little Joey Starrett as he stands gazing off into the horizon. He spies Shane, framed between the antlers of a deer, seemingly to have come out of nowhere. Shane's entrance from out of nowhere, and his link with nature, imbue his image with strong and archetypical mythic overtones. Shane rides toward the camera continually seen from Joey's point of view. When he nears Joey, he is seen from a low-angle shot which further mythicizes/heroizes him in both Joey's and the audience's eyes.

Similarly, the hero in *Sanjuro* is introduced via the point of view and the mediation of youngsters. The Samurai are sitting in the room of a temple as their leader brings them up to date on the situation. Suddenly, a voice calls out to them, a voice that springs from out of nowhere and seems to be everywhere at once. A sliding screen is opened and in walks Sanjuro himself, seen as in *Shane,* from a low-angle shot that duplicates the youths' point of view.

Both Shane and Sanjuro take on the role of mentor/teacher for the respective youngsters in the films. This teacher/disciple aspect is a common structuring device of the Western as it appears in many of the classic films. (e.g., *Red River:* Tom Dunson and Matthew Garth; *The Searchers:* Ethan Edwards and Martin Pawley; *Ride the High Country:* Gil Westrum plus Steve Judd and Heck). Shane shows little Joey how to wear a gun and how to shoot; Sanjuro teaches the Samurai that you cannot judge a man by his looks. Too, the respective heroes take on an added stature through the eyes of the youth-figures so that they become our mentors, our teachers, as well.

Both Shane and Sanjuro become juxtaposed against other father-figures in the two films. Shane is constantly compared to Joe Starrett by little Joey. He asks Shane if Shane can beat up Joe Starrett and finds the well-dressed gunfighter a more appealing romantic figure. Similarly, the young Samurai, although they are ambivalent toward Sanjuro throughout much of the film, are finally won over by him and at the end are ready to forsake the chamberlain to follow him. Of equal importance, the two heroes have a healthy and genuine admiration for the father-figures against whom they are juxtaposed. Shane agrees to work for Joe Starrett out of respect for what Joe is trying to accomplish. Together, the two men are able to uproot a tree trunk that has been plaguing the Starretts. Shane further insists on fighting Wilson, the gunman, even though Joe insists that he should be the one to face him. Shane even resorts to "cheating" in their fight when he hits Joe with the butt of his gun. Sanjuro instinctively admires the chamberlain and says so to the young Samurai. Further, both Shane and Sanjuro recognize their own alienation from the events they help bring about and both leave, out of respect for their peers. Shane knows he has no place anymore at Starrett's side, while Sanjuro respects the chamberlain too much to remain in his domain.

Both films also introduce an antagonist who is related thematically and structurally to the hero. In *Shane* that is Wilson, in *Sanjuro,* the henchman. The heroes take on stature and ability in direct proportion to their antagonists. This is further impacted by the youths' own reactions to the antagonists' abilities. Little Joey is almost as fascinated by Wilson as he is with Shane; the young Samurai fear the henchman almost as much as they do their own ally Sanjuro. Eventually, both Shane and Sanjuro will meet face to face with their respective antagonists and their contests will be witnessed, in each case, by their young protegees.

The relationship that Stevens and Kurosawa develop can be schematized as follows:

Shane : Joe Starrett as Sanjuro : Chamberlain
Shane : Wilson as Sanjuro : Henchman

It is also worth noting that the relationship between Sanjuro and the henchman has something in common with the typical hero/villain relationship in the films of Anthony Mann. Toshiro Mifune and Tatsuya Nakadai in both *Yojimbo* and *Sanjuro* can be seen to be related to the relationship between Jimmy Stewart and Arthur Kennedy in *The Man From Laramie* and *Bend of the River*. Both linked pairs share similar backgrounds and abilities and both are attractive and intelligent. The one goes bad not because he is evil but because he misplaces his sense of humanism. The hero kills his antagonist somewhat reluctantly or only when he is convinced of the villain's unredeemable nature.

Shane and *Sanjuro* end in the exact same manner. Shane, having killed Wilson before Joey's admiring gaze, rides off into the sunset; Sanjuro, having killed the henchman before the young Samurais' admiring gaze, walks off down the road into the sunset. Both Shane and Sanjuro insist that the youngsters return to their homes; both head off for a lonely horizon, knowing there is no place for them in the societies they have helped forge.

The similar endings, combined with the mediation of the heroes through the eyes of youth, give *Shane* and *Sanjuro* a similar elegiac tone. On this level, *Sanjuro* has much in common with the Nostalgic Samurai genre and with many another Western besides *Shane*. The clear and concise narrative pattern of each film has presented clear and precise visions of heroes operating in a clearly-defined moral universe. The tragedy and/or pathos of *Sanjuro* is an aesthetic issue. Right and wrong not only exist clearly in the mind of Sanjuro himself, but, for the first time in Kurosawa's Samurai films, in the narrative as well. Both *Sanjuro* and *Shane* can be reduced to a remarkably similar plot synopsis as well. A hero comes from seemingly out of nowhere and from unknown origins. He barely has a proper name, while each film takes its name eponymously. The hero becomes involved in a conflict in which he has no personal stake but which has clearly demarcated lines of right and wrong (more clearly, surprisingly, in *Sanjuro*). He risks his own life for the cause of others when he faces down a deadly and skilled antagonist. He defeats his opponent and rides (or walks) off into the sunset. In the meantime, he has affected and influenced the life (lives) of members of a younger generation. The elegant simplicity of both plots and the clear demarcation between right and wrong, good and bad, call forth a simpler, more understandable time.

Both *Shane* and *Sanjuro* are structured in important ways around the Nature/Culture dialectic. Shane, the natural man/outsider, comes riding in from the wilderness in his buckskin suit. This natural man aids the transition from nature to culture when he aids the farmer Joe Starrett who is engaged in the process of fencing off his land. Starrett's wife Marion is also a contributor to this process as she plants her flower garden (nature/culture = desert/garden). Shane, who also combines aspects of nature and culture (he is an excellent dancer, for instance), realizes that the cultural side of the dialectic is the inevitable victor in the battle. And although he combines both traits within himself, he is still linked more closely with nature. The same is true of the hero in *Sanjuro*. His dirty clothes and ill-manners link him with nature, although his deadly skill with a sword gives him a link with culture. In *Sanjuro*, the hero's task is to *restore* culture to the town. Nature, in the form of greed, has been let loose. It takes an outsider, a man with a natural code of ethics and aesthetics, to restore culture to its place of prominence. Sanjuro also recognizes his implicit links with nature, and so he too leaves the newly acculturated state he has helped form.

The use of the nature/culture dialectic in *Sanjuro* can be seen to be Kurosawa's repositioning of the East/West dichotomy. Japan represents nature, the West culture, so that the eponymous hero of this film marks the first instance of a Kurosawa hero in a period film helping bring about a synthesis of the two forces. Culture should be brought about, or restored, however, not on economic lines (the lines of the magistrate and his henchman) but along the lines of more reasonable codes. Even if the traditional Japanese hero, the hero armed with sword, has no place in the new society, a new kind of hero, one with a sheathed sword might be able to fit in. Like the Western, then, it takes men with weapons and with violence to tame the frontier even though there is no place for them in it.

Yet, the question remains, for all the remarkable similarities between *Sanjuro* and *Shane,* is Kurosawa's film a Western? If the two films were oral tales, then my structural analysis has been unable to distinguish them. The two films seem mere variations. Yet *Sanjuro* is clearly not a Western for one simple reason: it does not look like one. "The element that most clearly defines the Western is the symbolic landscape in which it takes place and the influence this landscape has on the characters and actions of the hero."[62] The Western film is defined as much by John Ford's fabulous vistas of Monument Valley, Anthony Mann's majestic mountains, and Budd Boetticher's barren, harsh landscapes as the narrative patterns or their character relationships. *Shane,* for instance, lovingly reveals the mountains, forests and lakes that surround the Starrett homestead. *Sanjuro,* curiously perhaps, is, in fact, the most restricted of Kurosawa's period films. Much of the film takes place indoors; those scenes which are not confined to traditional Japanese *tatami* rooms (an index of the "aesthetic frontier") take place in spaces defined by buildings: gardens, alleys, streets. And if *Sanjuro* is marked by its use of the CinemaScope aspect ratio, this ratio does not reveal space. It helps constrict it. The landscape of *Sanjuro* is the aesthetic hand of man, not the wild but soon-to-be tamed wilderness of the American West.

There is another important difference between *Shane* and *Sanjuro,* one that points up to an extraordinary, perhaps even fundamental difference between the Samurai film and the Western in general. And that is the place of romance.

I pointed out in my discussion of *Seven Samurai* the essentially non-romantic relationship between the young Samurai Katsushiro and the young farming girl Shino. Unlike the American remake of the film, the two youngsters do not remain together. The role of the women in *Shane* compared to *Sanjuro* is similarly significant. In both *Shane* and *Sanjuro,* the father-figures are married; i.e., there are mother-figures in the film. But in *Shane,* Starrett's wife Marion is also a potential source of sexual tension. Much is made, subtly it is true, of the attraction between Shane and Marion. At the end of the film Marion tells Shane not to fight Wilson if he is doing it for her. Similarly, Joe Starrett says that if he goes against Wilson and loses, he knows Shane will take care of Marion and little Joey. But in *Sanjuro* there is no such tension between the hero and the wife of the man he respects. "*Sanjuro* introduces a woman who is . . . a match for the *ronin* hero. . . . But she is merely a peripheral character, and Kurosawa gives her no name. She is also a woman of late middle age, having long passed the time when she could use her sexuality against men."[63] Although I disagree with Mellen's characterization of the woman as "peripheral," Mellen is quite right about her lack of sexuality. The younger woman, the chamberlain's daughter, is a sexual being (a highly sexual being, in fact). There is a lovely little scene when the girl tells her mother that she and her fiance, Yuzo Kayama, have come to the barn very often. After making love, it is implied, she falls asleep on her lover's arm. The old woman's only reaction to that is that it is rude to use his arm for a pillow! This younger woman, however, betrays not the slightest interest in her rescuer on the romantic level.

Noticing the total lack of romance in Kurosawa's Samurai films, one becomes hard pressed to find many examples of romantic love in all of the Samurai form. There is passion to be sure; even eroticism, but rarely true love as it is expressed in the Western.

The myth of romantic love is one of the important characteristics of the Western because it also comes into conflict with the genre's adolescent appeal. The myth of romantic love, we should note, is a strictly Euro-American idea, one that begins not coincidentally, with the rise of the bourgeois class in the eighteenth and nineteenth centuries. "The belief in love between man and woman as the supreme happiness is neither a classical concept nor a Christian one."[64] The myth initially arises with the tradition of Courtly Love in the eleventh century, a myth, however, in which physical consummation with the love object was *not* desired. Its true solidification occurs with the rise of the middle class as it becomes structured into the bourgeois form par excellence: the novel. The connection between the novel and the cinema (for which a case can be said as the new bourgeois convention) finds support in a parenthetical remark by Fiedler: "We still live in the Age of the Novel (and the cinema which is its child)."[65] If D.W. Griffith is the acknowledged father of the narrative cinema, we should recall once again that he works firmly within the bounds of the nineteenth-century melodrama and the novels of Charles Dickens.

The Western genre has roots firmly within the novels of James Fenimore Cooper and comes to fruition with the "dime novels" and pulp fiction of the late nineteenth and early twentieth centuries.[66] As a popular formula it is characterized by the tension between the Sentimental Love Religion and the Adolescent Retreat from Woman. The Sentimental Love Religion is the new American Secular Religion, a new Christianity "where tears are considered a truer service to God than prayers, the Pure Young Girl replaces Christ as the Savior [and] marriage becomes the equivalent of bliss eternal."[67] Many a Western hero hangs up his guns upon finding the love of a good woman (not until, however, he has used those guns).

On the other hand, the Western formula is also a ritual reenactment of the archetype of Huck Finn, wherein the hero "lights out for the territories" and thereby escapes the control and domination by women. The Western form manifests a great deal of ambivalence toward women. Woman is divided into two images, the archetypes of the Virgin and the Whore. On the one hand there is the virginal girl from the East, typically a school marm as established in one of the founding works of the Western form, Owen Wister's *The Virginian*. On the other hand there is the saloon girl, a fallen woman who might be either good or bad, but who rarely gets the man. We can note this classic dichotomy in John Ford's *My Darling Clementine* in the conflict between the blonde/virginal Clementine, newly arrived from the East and the dark/whorish Chihuahua, associated (via Mexico) with the Wild West. The typical Western hero either avoids true involvement with women or is "trapped," "hooked," by one and forced to hang up his guns.

The Western hero is usually more at home among Indians than he is with women. That is, he is more at ease with nature than he is with culture. The archetypical figure of Cooper's Natty Bumpo and his Indian friend Chingachgook characterize many a Westerner's preferences for life in the Wild West. Similarly, Huck Finn and Nigger Jim escape from the control of women by heading for the territories together.

Japan's middle ages had its own tradition of Courtly Poetry but it was not dedicated to hopeless cases of romantic infatuation. The low status of women in Europe which translated to a high status in the literature found its opposite in Japan. Though women rarely held political office, she was an acknowledged force behind the scenes. Too, the European tradition of Courtly Love was also a disguise for homosexual passion, a passion which had to be repressed. In Japan, no such repression was needed (although in contemporary films it has gone unacknowledged). Even so sketchy a book as James Clavell's *Shogun* points out the similarities between the Samurai and the Spartan warrior of Ancient Greece. On the whole, the lack of sexual repression in Japan, whether heterosexual or homosexual, found poetry and proto-novels such as *The Tale of Genji* and *The Pillow Book of Sei Shonagon* prizing aesthetics as an end in itself. While Europe's rising bourgeoisie created the novel for its own amusement, the Japanese merchant middle class created the Kabuki and Puppet theatre where romantic love was expressed as tragic passion, when it arose. This same sense of doomed love dominates the Samurai film on the rare occasions it even appears. Although one can argue that today's Japanese have similarly adopted the Sentimental Love Religion (to a certain extent) it has not found its way into the Samurai film.

Ultimately then, though *Sanjuro* adopts a Western formula as directly as any Kurosawa film, including *Yojimbo* and *High and Low,* it remains an essentially Japanese work structured around the individual whose personal codes can find no institutionalized equivalent. Despite its comic style, its willingness to undercut its own seriousness, as witness Sanjuro saying "Don't follow me, I'm in a bad mood," after slicing open the henchman, it seems a film of ambivalence. If he has helped bring about the Westernization of Japan, there is no place for him. If he has much to teach the youth of Japan, how are they to learn when there are no more pure chances for heroism? The new society is completely cultured, dominated by aesthetic codes learned in classrooms. There is no real place for a gruffy, grubby, anarchic spirit like Sanjuro. If the bodyguard in *Yojimbo* is very likely to come across another Western-style gangland town, is Sanjuro going to meet up the likes of the chamberlain and his wife again? Even more than Shane, this Sanjuro, this thirty-year-old who is closer to forty, is a man without a country.

Kagemusha

Marsha Kinder in her review of *Kagemusha*[68] rightly understands the film as being about the act of signification. If on the surface *Kagemusha* seems to depart from Kurosawa's humanistic tragi-comedies, a closer reading reveals that he has simply changed the mode of its presentation. Here signification replaces emotion, not on the level of plot necessarily, but phenomenologically. *Kagemusha* is clearly as stylized and formalized a film as Kurosawa has ever produced (excepting *Throne of Blood* perhaps), yet, as in *Dodeskaden,* there is still a strong undercurrent of concern for the human condition.

I call *Kagemusha* a tragedy of signification, for Kurosawa has detailed the manner in which signs come together to shape events. As in *Sanjuro,* Kurosawa foregrounds the film in a typically Japanese context. A society which places such great emphasis on signification has now been given a film which demands an acknowledgment of this fact. The tragedy in *Kagemusha* arises within the nexus of an individual confronting a series of signs, of signifying practices, and then losing sight of their (and his) nature. In *Kagemusha* the bonds between signified and signifier are broken apart and reformed (re-signified) *as signs* but the central character, caught up in this process as a sign himself, becomes unable to distinguish between them.

There are two planes in which the process of signification is examined in *Kagemusha:* the manner in which signs influence others and the manner in which signs influence the conception of the self. A single figure, that of the *kagemusha,* the shadow warrior, becomes intimately connected with both processes as he becomes a sign used to affect the actions and perceptions of others and as he himself, in the process of becoming such a sign, is reinterpreted.

The opening, pre-credit sequence introduces the idea of explicating the signification process and the idea of signs. In the single longest take in all of Kurosawa's work, we are introduced to Shingen Takeda (Tatsuya Nakadai) and what we should call the "sign" of Shingen Takeda. Three apparently identical men sit facing the camera. They are framed asymmetrically with two of "him" in the background slightly off-center to the left, and one similarly dressed but behaviorally different Shingen in the foreground screen right.

Kurosawa's camera distance does not immediately reveal that the "Shingen Takeda" sitting screen left is not an identical twin, but rather a similarly dressed and reasonably representative image. However, this Shingen is, in fact, portrayed by another actor (Tsutomo Yamazaki). Thus we are introduced already to two important motifs of iconicity—dress and behavior. The Shingen sitting far left dresses and acts like Shingen, despite the fact that a closer examination shows the two men to be different; the Shingen sitting screen right dresses the same and looks the same, but acts differently, even though he is in fact the same as Shingen by virtue of being portrayed by the same actor.

Through conversation we learn that the non-identical Shingen Takeda is Shingen's brother Nobukado who is a *kagemusha*, a shadow warrior, for Shingen himself. The figure sitting in the foreground is a thief who bears a strong (identical, of course) resemblance to Shingen and who will be recruited as another *kagemusha*, another shadow warrior. This thief will be saved from crucifixion in exchange for assuming the role of *kagemusha*.

We should note here that the idea of an exact double, a shadow warrior, if you will, is a common motif in Western stories. This idea forms the drama of the swashbuckling classics *The Prisoner of Zenda* and *The Man in the Iron Mask*, as well as informing a lesser work like *Royal Flash*. Woody Allen puts the idea of *kagemusha* to excellent comic use in *Love and Death* as his hapless protagonist unknowingly attempts to assassinate a phony Napoleon. The difference between the use of the double in Kurosawa and in the West, lies, as one might expect, in the significance of the loss of the self. If the thief in *Kagemusha* will come to accept his role, eventually, as a complex signifier of the original, his Western counterpart can never do so. Even the temporary loss of one's actual identity as defined by others is a major trauma to the Western hero. The quest to end the charade and reestablish his true self becomes equally as important as the need for the role-switch. The thief in Kurosawa's Japanese film becomes admirable precisely for this ability to deny his true self and redefine it. The fact that his true self gets lost when the signified to which he is linked is himself de-signified (by his death and its acknowledgment) makes the shadow warrior a pathetic figure but still a heroic one. In the West he might be looked upon as absurd.

The camera position of this extraordinary opening shot remains static throughout its entire duration. This static camera, combined with the long-take employed, bring this shot in line with the so-called "realist" mode of the cinema,[69] so that Kurosawa informs us that, via this technique, what we are seeing is "real." Though we know that the appearance of two Tatsuya Nakadais in the frame is an optical illusion, the style asks us to reject that fact. By extending the scene for this length of time Kurosawa generates a dynamic tension by confronting us with the literally impossible within a literal (realist) frame. Although Kinder finds this single-actor-dual-role within this shot to be of primary significance as it relates to the filmmaker's ability to play with

Photo from *Kagemusha*.

signification, I think this technique is the literalization of the idea of doubling within a semiotic context. The real and the impossible coexist, yet both are merely signs to be interpreted.

It is important that this sequence take place before the opening credits of the film. The idea of signification per se has been presented before the context in which it will appear. We are thus given privileged information about not simply the roles and identities of the two shadow warriors, but about the way signification will structure the film as a whole. Throughout the film we will continue to receive information regarding the "truth" behind the signs that confront us; we will always be one step ahead of the protagonists who will struggle to come to terms with the signifying practices at work.

Kagemusha is structured by a series of situations in which the operation and importance of signs is both implicitly and explicitly acknowledged. The influence of signs upon action is, for instance, one of the key reasons that Shingen Takeda justifies the need for a shadow warrior. Shingen, we realize, is a master warlord not simply for his tactical knowledge of the battlefield, but for his tactical control of signs. His armies, for instance, go to battle under a series of flags, or banners, which have symbolic importance. Shingen's presence on the battlefield is also important (and hence the need for the shadow warrior). It is crucial that Shingen appear to be solidly behind his men when they do battle. To this end, he has a special chair upon which he sits to oversee his men.

Shingen understands the importance of signs in the film's first key plot point: the siege of the castle. Each night, Shingen learns, the sound of a melodious bamboo flute can be heard emanating from within the castle walls. One particular night Shingen determines that if the flute is heard, his siege of the castle will be ineffective; if he does not, then the castle will fall. He has his attendants set up his sedan chair (his "sign" while leading his troops in battle) and he will listen for the flute. The flute begins to play signaling that the castle will stand; a shot rings out and someone is apparently hit.

This sequence is one of the most densely impacted in the film for its multi-varied presentation of significance. First, the flute-as-index is introduced. The playing of music while under siege implies (signifies) the ability of the men playing and listening to such music to withstand the assault. Shingen's personal appearance on the scene implies (signifies) his own understanding of the flute's significance. The bringing of his sedan chair to the castle implies to Shingen's men that their leader, "the mountain," is with them. The sound (with no image) on the sound track signifies a gunshot; the resultant activity outside the castle walls implies (signifies) that someone of importance has been hit. Two sounds are used, then, as signifiers; two sounds become indices of a host of signifieds, not the least of which is the possibility that Shingen himself has been shot. The truth behind the signifier of the shot occupies a central place within the plot, for Shingen's enemies Nobunaga and Tokugawa are possessed by the need for certainty. As long as they see the "sign" of Shingen, that is Shingen or his *kagemusha*, they are paralyzed with uncertainty. Shingen knew that such would be the case and planned for that contingency by developing the thief as his identical double insofar as possible. Shingen then is a master strategist precisely because he acknowledges the importance of signs and is able to manipulate their significance.

The influence of signs upon the actions of others is balanced in the film with the influence of signs upon the self. This, in turn, is then turned outward again to the influence of the self-as-sign upon others. There are four areas of signs and sign-production which are introduced to demonstrate the process of re-signification: (1) Physical resemblance, which includes dress; (2) physical action which includes behavioral indexes; (3) verbal and aural signs; and (4) indexical and "supra-iconic" (a term introduced to imply instinct, a key element to the tragedy of signification in *Kagemusha*).

The transformation from thief to warlord for the most part takes place offscreen, a curious omission, considering the primary importance such a transformation occupies in the plot and in the film's schema. I tend to think that perhaps some of the missing twenty minutes from the original version to the American-release version (the latter is the version under analysis here) contained some of this process. Nevertheless, we are introduced to the reconstituted sign of Shingen Takeda on all four planes of sign production.

Dress and costume have enormous significance. As I have shown earlier in chapter 2, the signs of the Samurai possess a life of their own. Family crests, banners and heirlooms, all icons of societal structures, literally (metonymically) become the things themselves. On this level, the implication becomes "one who dresses like a warlord must therefore be a warlord." Given the thief's physical resemblance to Shingen Takeda, a resemblance in costume would transform him into an exact double. The introduction of the *kagemusha* by Nobukado is done in just this manner.

Although we have seen the thief dressed as Shingen in the opening section, Shingen's generals have not seen him. Nobukado introduces him in a highly dramatic manner. On a windy night as the generals argue back and forth a figure dressed in Shingen's fierce battle garb and mask appears. He sits on Shingen's stool and pauses. The generals are puzzled for they are sure they know (as do we) that Shingen is dead. The figure then removes the mask and the generals are astounded as Shingen seems reincarnated before their eyes. Significantly, the American sub-titled version of the film flashes a title beneath this seated figure informing us that this is "the thief." Although the old cliche that all Japanese look alike is literally true with regards Shingen and the thief, we have seen Shingen's corpse (contrary to Marsha Kinder's contention in her article[70] that we have not). The fear on the part of the American distributors that we would confuse who was who extends even further, as they choose to identify characters who do not even remotely resemble Shingen nor are intended to! These titles are noteworthy insofar as they point up to the fears and narrative naïveté of commercial distributors. The privileged information Kurosawa gives his audience is enough to unravel the puzzles of *Kagemusha;* these titles cannot be truly included in an analysis of Kurosawa's film, but are important to note in comparing Western and Japanese differences.

This basic iconic level which includes physical resemblance and dress, can succeed only at a distance. That is, the *kagemusha* can fool some of the people some of the time, but he cannot fool all of the people all of the time. Not unless he can act like Shingen Takeda, that is. Kurosawa has introduced certain physical habits, or "signs," of Shingen, primarily in the opening scene and in the scene between Shingen and his top general. As Kinder points out, one of his most distinguishing traits is the twirling of his mustache.[71] There is also a certain posture and facial attitude (which both imply, that is, are indices of, a certain mental attitude). The transformation from thief to Shingen occurs on this level in the sequence in which Nobukado introduces the *kagemusha* to Shingen's retainers. They are employed and enjoined to teach the thief how to *act* like the warlord. The thief is initially playful, bold, and somewhat conceited in their presence. The pages and bodyguards frown and show their displeasure by their formal posture. The thief, clearly somewhat abashed, assumes a more relaxed and modest position, pulling Shingen's little table over to him to lean on just as we saw Shingen do earlier. His physical resemblance combines with this attitudinal, indexical resemblance, to elicit surprised shock from the retainers.

Dress and behavior are still not enough to transform the thief into the very image of the warlord. He must also master verbal signs. Perhaps on this level it is fortunate that the Japanese are not a people who normally prize facile conversation and rhetoric. But it does play some importance as we saw in *The Hidden Fortress* where the princess, who would be unable to disguise her patrician speech, was forced to play dumb. The *kagemusha* can get by, it seems with a mere phrase or two as long as they derive from what might be called another indexical sign. The thief is told to keep in mind the fact that Shingen Takeda is called the mountain, a metaphor which the thief must use in all his actions.

Before turning to the fourth level of sign, we must again return to speculation about the excised twenty minutes for the American-release print. The transformation from thief to warlord, the movement that is, from low to high, takes place at the level of sign. A similar transformation from commoner to royalty at this level, occupies a central place, for instance, in Mark Twain's *The Prince and the Pauper*. Behavioral differences distinguish the otherwise identical twins, the prince and the poor slum child. What makes a prince, or a gentleman, is the acting like one, the adoption of the signs of the class. In Japan, with its cultural codes of speech and its tradition of class, such a transformation would be infinitely more complex and so its lack of examination is surprising. Further, on the comic level (a level so important previously to Kurosawa) this transformational process would have provided numerous and natural opportunities for gags. Speculation has it that when Kurosawa replaced the original star of the film, Shintaro Katsu, with Tatsuya Nakadai, some of the comedy was dropped.[72] While this seems not unlikely, one should also recognize Nakadai's substantial abilities as a comic actor (as seen, for instance, in Okamoto's eccentric Sword Film *Kill!*). Whatever the case, the absence of this process and the absence of humor do substantiate the claim that Kurosawa is exploring signification as such and not how signifying practices arise.

The first three levels of sign may be understood to be "presentational" modes. The thief is presenting himself as Shingen; he is acting like Shingen by duplicating Shingen's modes of behavior. What happens however, is that the thief comes to identify with Shingen, internalizing Shingen's values, as for example, coming to love Shingen's grandson. The transformation of the thief occurs from the outside in, much like the acting style of the classic British theatre (as distinguished from "the method.") An actor like Sir Laurence Olivier, for instance, will begin to build a character from the outside, finding a walk, a facial type, and a mode of speech. Most of these traits can be found through references in the text, of course. In this manner, the thief is building his version of Shingen in the same way, with the original, real Shingen as "the text." The method, as proposed first by Constantin Stanislavsky and popularized by Lee Strasberg, asks that the actor create his character from the inside, finding emotional equivalents to the experiences of the character. However, a similar phenomenon arises in the British and the American methods. Both actors will find themselves having "internalized" their characters despite the differences in character-origination. So too, has the thief in *Kagemusha*. Looking, dressing, acting and speaking like Shingen, he becomes Shingen. He does not lose himself in the sense of becoming an amnesiac, nor, on the other hand, is there an internal conflict along the lines of *Seconds*, a brilliant, under-appreciated look at a different kind of "shadow warrior." The thief simply comes to internalize Shingen to a greater degree than he has internalized the identity-sign of the thief. We should realize that the thief is never identified by anything but this kind of generic title. He is given no name, which is to say that he is identified by what he does. When he steals, he is a thief; when he plays the warlord, he is a warlord. This is quite a radical conception of the sense of self, one very different from what we find in the West, but not so far removed, in signification at least, from the Western genre.

The thief has been used by Shingen's generals as a potent sign to influence the actions of others, but in the process has himself been transformed. The tragedy of *Kagemusha* ensues when the thief is designified as a meaningful sign to others, but fails to designify his sense of a new self. Throughout the film there is a tension between the thief as signifier and Shingen as signified. Those who know the truth behind the thief are constantly concerned about their secret;

that is, they worry about maintaining the signifier-signified relationship. Those who do not know the truth, which is whether the real Shingen is dead or alive, wish to discover the truth and also emphasize the signifier-signified relationship, but they seek to know the true status of the signified. Essentially, they are unconcerned about the signifier insofar as it is divorced from a signified. This points to an important conception of the way human knowledge is understood epistemologically. Kurosawa uses a number of examples to demonstrate this.

Shingen's bitter enemies, the warlords Nobunaga and Tokugawa (figures every Japanese audience member knows as well as Americans know Washington and Lincoln, for instance) are passionately, even obsessively, concerned about whether the Shingen they see after the shooting at the castle is the real Shingen or not. Despite the fact that it is clear that Shingen is not the warlord he once was (inexplicably lifting the siege of the castle, staying only in his own fief), they are still unable to act definitively until they are sure of his status. Shingen's (or what *may* be Shingen's) actions are not sufficient for their certainty. What influences them is the conception they hold of the "sign" of Shingen. Even when that sign seems to differ from their previously understood concept, they are paralyzed, unable to act, based upon this idea. The only way they can free themselves from their conception is to break the signifier-signified relationship *at the level of the signified*. However, most human action and knowledge is generated *at the level of the signifier*. In this case, the cinema offers us a privileged text to explore this paradox. Perhaps only in art can there exist a certainty with regards the signified.

Another example of the idea of Shingen-as-signified is seen in the relationship between the thief (in his role as Shingen) and Shingen's embittered son. The thief has embarrassed the son at the first clan meeting; the thief enrages Shingen's son when he appears on the battlefield, dressed of course, as Shingen. The son, through sound martial strategy, is able to lay siege and conquer a castle that eluded his father. But the credit for the victory is laid at the feet of the thief-Shingen. By his mere appearance he receives the credit. The gap between Shingen's real ability and the thief's tactical ability is enormous, yet it is overcome merely by the thief's presence in full battle regalia. The thief, accompanied by Shingen's retainers flying Shingen's banners, resembles Shingen in every way; therefore, Shingen must be present. Therefore, the battle is won by Shingen. The son's reaction to the thief duplicates his reactions to his father; in a strange way, he hates the thief as he hates his father. Even certainty regarding his father's death does not change his feelings. The signified "Shingen" still *means* the same to him.

The thief is unmasked (designified) at the fourth level of sign production and consumption—the indexical and "supra-iconic" by which I mean non-objective signs, signifiers which can be explained but not necessarily perceived by all. Although the thief has mastered a number of indexical signs, such as

Tatsuya Nakadai, in his guise as the shadow warrior, comes to love Shingen's grandson in *Kagemusha*.

behavior and speech, a physical index has been overlooked. In the sequence in which the thief is introduced to Shingen's mistresses, we are introduced to one type of "supra-iconic" sign or indexical sign—sex. Nobukado forbids the thief to sleep with either of Shingen's mistresses on the assumption that during the process of love-making they would recognize that something was amiss. This implies that there is a certain way about Shingen during the act of sex that the thief would be unable to duplicate. Even if he could master Shingen's technique (indexes), assuming it could be isolated and defined, the assumption is that the women would "know" that the thief is an imposter. At this level, we should recall Shingen's grandson's reaction to the thief at first meeting in which the little child called out "That's not my grandfather!" The little boy has his immediate (and true) perception redefined, a redefinition which takes place not at the level of icon or symbol, but at the indexical and supra-iconic level. He comes to love the thief in his guise as Shingen, therefore he wants to believe that the thief is truly his grandfather.

A horse, however, unmasks the thief. The thief, apparently having internalized his role as the warlord too deeply, tries to ride the horse that only Shingen could master. The horse throws him. This would be, perhaps, damaging enough, but when the thief's shoulder is exposed, one and all notice the lack of a battle scar.

There are two types of sign at work here—the supra-iconic or instinctual and the indexical. The horse senses or feels that the rider on his back is not his master. The thief, in this manner, has not been able to internalize Shingen's own internal structures. The thief duplicated the exteriors, the signs, but could not reach the depths, "the truth," behind the "real" Shingen. On the indexical plane, Shingen's mistresses and retainers not privy to the charade discover that the thief is missing Shingen's battle scar. The generals, so concerned with the exteriors, the easily perceived signs, have neglected the level of signs just below the exteriors. This same idea appears in *Royal Flash* in which Captain Harry Flashman is kidnapped and forced to impersonate a duke. The duke, however, has a nasty fencing scar on his cheek. Flashman's kidnappers remedy this lack with one flick of a saber. The generals in *Kagemusha,* however, simply forgot Shingen's shoulder wound.

The battle-scar on Shingen's shoulder can also be understood metaphorically as well as indexically. As an index it stands for the fact that Shingen is a warrior, much the way callouses on one's hands might imply one is a laborer. Yet, metaphorically, the scar indicates that Shingen has been touched, or marked, by battle, that a warrior has seen more (and differently) than someone else. If the carrying of a sword does not necessarily make one a fighter, the "carrying" of a scar perhaps does; and this scar indicates that a potentially radically different world-view is held by the person so marked.

Once the shadow warrior is designified, a funeral is held for Shingen. This funeral finally satisfies Nobunaga and Tokugawa that Shingen is dead.

Although they themselves never see Shingen's body, his funeral, the public declaration that he is dead, finally enables them to designify Shingen Takeda. Nobunaga, learning of the truth does not perform, as Kinder says, "a strange ritualistic dance,"[73] but rather chants a "death poem" very much within the mainstream of Buddhist thought. At this point, I must digress for a moment, and point out the typically Japanese attitudes conveyed by Nobunaga. Nobunaga is shown to be sympathetic to Christianity, even going so far as to have his final battle with Shingen's troops blessed by a Portuguese Priest (doubtless a Jesuit). He carries a number of Portuguese and Christian signs with him into battle; he is also a devotee of Portuguese wine as seen in an amusing bit between himself and Tokugawa. Yet, upon learning of Shingen's death, he does not offer up a prayer to the Christian God, but rather immediately reverts to the Buddhistic tradition of Japan. This mirrors the traditional Japanese ability to combine Shinto, Buddhism, and even Christianity (Catholicism) into worship. The chanting of a poem on this occasion also recalls the tradition of courtly poetry extremely common among the aristocracy of the Heian period. The dance and chant that Nobunaga performs might also be understood to be a ritualistic cleansing of Shingen's signified from his mind.

Once Shingen's shadow warrior is dismissed, the film heads inexorably (and quickly) into the final, climactic scene, a scene once again devoted not to action and/or humanism, but to signification. The son, disobeying his father's prime order, takes his troops out of his fief to meet Nobunaga's men in battle. As they travel out of their territory, they are met by the sight of a huge rainbow. This rainbow is a complex "sign" here because it *may* mean something or it may not. Two interpretations are offered by characters within the film. The son sees the rainbow as a portent of victory; the generals see it as Shingen's way of saying "go no further." Yet the rainbow may also mean nothing; after all, it is a *natural* occurrence, signifying, perhaps only that it has rained earlier, hardly a "sign" in the semiotic sense. The variety of interpretations, including the negative, non-signifying one, reminds us of the arbitrary nature of the sign. Signs are culturally determined, particularly indexical and symbolic signs (the latter strictly cultural in origin). Yet, when confronted with a natural phenomenon, the characters in this film try to make it "mean" culturally.

From the Japanese viewpoint, the taking of natural signs for cultural significance is highly important. In *Kagemusha,* for instance, we have been exposed to the banners of the Takeda clan and their symbolic importance. Mountain, wind, fire, and forest are all natural "signs" which have been transposed to culture-specific meanings. In Japan this is quite frequent in general, especially as seen in family crests. Therefore, in one sense, it is "natural" that Shingen's men would seek significance from a natural occurrence. Yet the potential exists that the rainbow, in fact, means nothing at all.

The final battle, the final scene in fact, is the last, and as Kinder says, the most "bold"[74] usage of signs. The entire scene is filmed as if Kurosawa were forced to use "creative geography" due to budget. That is, he shows men shooting and men reacting to the shooting, *but he never shows a single man fall in battle*. There are three planes of action to this battle—Nobunaga's troops dug in behind a fence; Shingen's charging cavalry and infantry; Shingen's generals watching from a hill-top. Kurosawa, however, only shows two planes, namely the men firing and the generals reacting. This is a very oblique way to show the scene, a way that contradicts virtually every epic film ever made, except one—*October*. Eisenstein's experimental film was similarly concerned with signs, so that his editing patterns duplicate the idea of battle without showing direct cause-and-effect. In fact, the editing employed by Kurosawa in this scene is certainly "Eisensteinian" in tone and spirit. All we see are montages of rifles being fired (photographed to emphasize the diagonal form) and horrified looks on the generals' faces.

This pattern is reversed when the thief rushes on to the battlefield. Now we see the fallen men as the thief runs about; now we *hear* the sound of rifle-shots and we see the thief fall, but we do not, this time, see the riflemen. The thief, mortally wounded, rushes to the river (and so ties together Shingen's associations with water as seen in the lacquer jar in which Shingen is buried in the lake, and the expressionistic dream sequence) and retrieves Shingen's banner. Holding onto the banner he dies, a meaningless death, except now this signifier is symbolically reunited with his signified.

In the above sequence, it would have been entirely possible to film the battle scene with no charging soldiers, just men shooting and men reacting, and no doubt the scene was filmed in such a manner. Creative geography, however, puts the two ideas together, that of the charging cavalry we have earlier seen rushing screen left and the soldiers firing offscreen right. Just as the characters in *Kagemusha* react to certain signs in a culturally determined way, so too, do we. Given the signs of men shooting at something we cannot see, and men reacting to something we still cannot see, we draw certain conclusions which are culturally based in the sense that we have a "filmic competence" that allows us to read these signs in the correct manner. Kurosawa is not denying us the direct cause-and-effect of men shooting and men dying in the spectacular tradition of epic and action because of budget (the film was already the most expensive ever made in Japan), but because he is once again, and finally, demonstrating the all-important function of signification. We believe according to convention and learning; one who can manipulate our conventions is thus a very powerful and significant person. In the case of the plot of *Kagemusha* such a person was Shingen Takeda; in the case of the film, such a person was Akira Kurosawa.

Kagemusha has one more crucial significance to make. And that is that Kurosawa has made a Samurai film in which *no one dies by the sword*.

Kagemusha thus denies the myth of the Samurai film in one bitter stroke. Situated in the era just before the Tokugawa, *Kagemusha* already points up to the obsolescence of the true Samurai. That is, although the mythos of the Samurai film relies heavily on the obsolete warrior in time of peace, Kurosawa is pointing out that the warrior who carries a sword in time of *war* is also obsolete (a theme alluded to in *Seven Samurai,* of course). Perhaps the most telling indication of this is the sequence in which the peasant-soldier demonstrates how he shot Shingen. The elaborate reconstruction of the process is in keeping with Kurosawa's typical fascination with process for its own sake, "as if in a courtroom" as Kinder says.[75] But the scene is also used to demonstrate that there is no "Bushido" at work any more, no elaborate ritualistic fights between two deadly swordsmen. Now it is a matter of technology and ingenuity (one is tempted to say "Yankee ingenuity," and perhaps Kurosawa would not mind). To Kurosawa, the Samurai film, perhaps even his own, is a mere sham, a disturbing message perhaps, but one that Kurosawa is clearly (and none too obliquely) delivering in *Kagemusha.* The man who has done so much to bring the Samurai film into serious study now repudiates it and it is perhaps this, more than anything else, that disturbs one about *Kagemusha.* It is a masterpiece, a consummate work of film art, and a modernistically important work. But it is also a sad work, for in showing so clearly that film, history, and myth may be reduced to mere signification, Kurosawa is denying us a sense that these are also more than signification. In this fashion, *Kagemusha* clearly recalls another late work by an old master, John Ford's *The Man Who Shot Liberty Valance.* These two respected artists of the cinema, near the end of illustrious careers, reflect on the genre they have forged, on the myths they themselves have promulgated, and reveal a profound sadness bordering on despair. Ford tells us that "when the legend becomes fact, print the legend," and then proceeds to reveal the *fact.* Ford practically deconstructs the modern Western, formally by refusing to shoot in exteriors and repudiating color, and thematically by foregrounding the desert/garden antinomy (which is perhaps the central mythos of the Western) in the symbol of the cactus-rose. In revealing the superficiality and essential hollowness of Western legend as well as Ransom Stoddard's (Jimmy Stewart) and Tom Doniphon's (John Wayne) complicity in forging that legend, Ford seems to be decrying his own complicity in mythicizing the West. *Liberty Valance* emerges as a meta-Western, a bitter critique; so too *Kagemusha* destroys the myth of the Samurai film by making it obvious, by focusing on the mythicization process and the filmmaker's complicty in it. *Kagemusha,* like *Liberty Valance,* is a brilliant film, but it is clearly a film whose maker has lost some of his joy.

Conclusion

What can we conclude from these analyses of Kurosawa's period films? Perhaps the main idea to be gleaned is that there is perhaps a more suitable narrative structure for genre films than for other works. If we recognize that *Seven Samurai, Yojimbo,* and *Sanjuro* are—as I have tried to show—the richest, most elaborately structured, and successfully realized of Kurosawa's period films, we should also realize that they have the same basic narrative pattern. All three films use the formula of the stranger coming into a situation, solving it and moving on. This pattern informs many of the great Westerns and is certainly one of the most significant of Kurosawa's borrowings. The idea of the stranger who is juxtaposed against two opposing forces allows Kurosawa to embody the idea of a dialectic while also allowing for the idea of synthesis. Kurosawa builds an identification between audience and protagonist who is caught (usually by choice) in the middle. In *Seven Samurai* we identify with men who find themselves in the middle of a battle between farmers and brigands; *Yojimbo* finds a hero playing two opposed economic forces against each other; *Sanjuro* has a hero stepping into a struggle within a clan.

When the object of our identification chooses to side with one force over another, or chooses *not* to side at all as in *Yojimbo,* we are given a view of some sort of synthesis.

The use of a stranger as such, is a significant choice, and another important link with the Western. In Japanese society it is almost impossible to be a stranger. In feudal times one was born into a fairly rigid social class; in modern times one is always confronted by the need to identify oneself with a group.[76] Yet in the Western genre, almost everyone is a stranger. Kurosawa thus gives a Western audience a figure most familiar to them while delivering a "Western" figure to the Westernized Japanese.

The idea of the stranger should also be recognized for its existential implications. Everyone is a stranger; all situations present one with moral/ethical choices. By typically denying his characters a past (as well as a viable present and future), Kurosawa literalizes this existential situation. The forces that the stranger confronts, which are in dialectical opposition, are thus presented without societally imposed values but are rather, as we have seen, situationally oriented.

Aside from the importance of the stranger, this man-in-the-middle structure recalls other classic Westerns which use that pattern. Once again the man-in-the-middle allows filmmakers the perfect opportunity to explore "dialectics." Virtually every great Western (with some exceptions) uses this structure. For instance, *Red River* pits Matthew Garth against Tom Dunson but also finds him juxtaposed against Dunson's men. *The Searchers* finds Ethan Edwards in the middle between the Indians on the one hand, and the settlers on the other. (Synthesis, so to speak, in *The Searchers,* is in the figure of Martwin Pawley, who is part Indian.) *The Man Who Shot Liberty Valance* uses the figure of Ransom Stoddard as the medium between Tom Doniphon and Liberty Valance. *Shane,* of course, uses both the stranger and the idea of the man-in-the-middle.

There is yet a third significance to Kurosawa's borrowing of this Western pattern and it lies in the idea of "professionalism." To a certain extent, this idea of professionalism is countermanded by Kurosawa's films, for although his heroes are motivated by payment of a sort, whether it be three meals a day as in *Seven Samurai* or the few coins Sanjuro takes in that film, they transcend it. Many Western films do not so much transcend the idea of professionalism as revel in it. Although *Shane* certainly transcends it, think of Hawks's classic *Rio Bravo.* These men do not back down because they are emotionally involved. They do not back down because it is their job not to. The highest compliment one can pay to another is the saying, "He's all right!" which simply means he is good at what he does. Kurosawa's men operate in this kind of universe, even if their ultimate reasons for staying, for dealing with the situation, transcend professionalism. There is the same kind of respect for ability found in Kurosawa as in Hawks; there is a similar kind of relationship between hero and villain as found in Mann and Boetticher, a relationship which begins at the level of *competence.*

We can perhaps say that this kind of structure is most suitable for this kind of genre film. The same structure works well in the Hard-boiled and Classical Detective stories, but not as well in the Gangster film, for instance. The use of this structure fosters a dialectic of its own which further enriches the films. By utilizing the stranger, or the wanderer, motif there is an implicit dialectic between the nomad/settler forces. This dialectic is enhanced in the Western by the frontier setting; in the Samurai film it is enhanced by the setting in the Tokugawa era, but we should recognize that the nomad motif tends to be "grafted" on by Kurosawa and others more deliberately than in the Western film. This choice of narrative pattern and its effectiveness enables *Seven Samurai, Yojimbo,* and *Sanjuro* to succeed as formula works first. Kurosawa transcends formula then by introducing new elements within the dialectics presented and by seeking non-formulaic solutions. But we should never overlook the firm grounding in genre.

Photo from *High and Low*.

4
Implications for Further Study

There are a number of areas of concern that arise from the implications of this study. An examination should now be made, in the light of the methodologies and the findings expounded upon earlier, of Kurosawa's formula films which fall within the broad expanse of the *gendai-mono,* or modern story. The non-formulaic works of Kurosawa should also be examined from the point of view of how American motifs and popular structures have been utilized. It also seems that the converse of this study might also be undertaken, i.e., the influence of Akira Kurosawa on American popular formulas.

Perhaps the most immediate concern that my study points towards is the examination of Kurosawa's modern stories that, a priori, seem derived quite clearly from American formula tales: *Drunken Angel, Stray Dog, The Bad Sleep Well,* and *High and Low.* Initially, as we did with the Samurai film it might behoove us to question the existence of a Japanese gangster or thriller form within this (these) genre.[1] Within this comparative context one could then determine the manner in which Kurosawa utilizes American forms and Japanese forms, and the manner in which he diverges.

What seems quite clear is that there really is no "native" Japanese Gangster genre. As a formula in popular literature and film it seems absent from pre-war texts. This is to say that it appears that the Gangster film and its subsidiary forms like the Crime Thriller and Caper film are post-war phenomena. In some sense, the Gangster film as it is currently (vaguely) defined is, like the Western, a specifically American formula, one that intends to act as a "paradigm of the American dream.... Our involvement with the gangster rests on our identification with him as the archetypal American dreamer whose actions and behavior involve a living out of the dream common to most everyone who exists in the particular configurations and contradictions of American society...."[2] Although certainly the French and the Italians are also adept producers and consumers of Gangster films, I think it is clear that they are derivative of American formulas. This too, might make a valuable study.

If it is true that the Japanese have no native Gangster or Thriller formula, they do have a native cultural product which has given rise, in the post-war era, to a distinctly Japanese formula related to the Gangster film, but far different:

the *yakuza* tale. *Yakuza*, or gamblers, as a sub-culture existed in Japan long before the post-war era but it is not until the early sixties that the *yakuza* film, as such, begins. Although Kurosawa's gangsters and gamblers, his criminals and cops, do not by any means fall within the bounds of the *yakuza* genre (although his *Yojimbo* serves as a structural archetype and model), it would be most helpful, in the light of this new study to be undertaken, to explore the genre of the *yakuza*. I will, therefore, briefly outline some of the major issues of concern in defining the form.

"In the early sixties... samurai films were declining in popularity and the studios sought ways to update them for new audiences.... Toei studios took the lead. The transformation *jidai-geki* to *yakuza-eiga* can first be seen in the '*Jirocho*' series produced by Toei from 1962 to 1963."[3] Schrader thus supports my contention that the *yakuza* film is an extension of the Samurai film and gives logical plausibility, at least, to *Yojimbo* (1960) leading to *Yakuza* (1962). While Schrader is correct that Samurai films were declining in popularity, as Silver's Samurai film listing of the years 1959 compared to 1963-64 will attest,[4] it is also true that contemporaneous to the *yakuza-eiga* is the Sword film. It is also worth noting that Hideo Gosha directed his first feature, *Three Outlaw Samurai,* in 1964, so that if the sixties saw a decline in the number of Samurai films, they also saw some of the best and most interesting of them as well. What is undeniable is that the *yakuza* film came to popularity, and, at least for the moment, seems definitely to have overtaken its period-based cousin in popularity.

Schrader sees the *yakuza* film as introducing a new structuration of the *giri/ninjo* conflict. "The *yakuza-eiga* has two primary themes: duty *(giri)* and humanity *(ninjo)*.... The Samurai film, of course [sic] had only one theme, *giri-ninjo;* the Siamese twin themes of duty and humanity were so interlocked as to be indistinguishable."[5] It seems that Schrader here thinks of the Samurai film as a uniform whole apparently without permutations and that the separation of *giri* from *ninjo* in the *yakuza* film is an important distinguishing trait. Yet if my contention about the Sword film is correct, and remember the two forms arise simultaneously, the *giri/ninjo* dichotomy cannot be so easily understood.

If the Sword film was shown to have a basic morphology, perhaps the same can be said of the *yakuza* film. Burch points out in his discussion of *Throne of Blood* that every *yakuza* film ends with a ritualized climax where the hero and/or his gang march to the final conflict.[6] This alone, however, cannot be used to distinguish the form, for not only do *yakuza* films tend to end in this manner, but so does every Sword film as well as every other sub-genre in the Samurai film (not to mention Westerns, as well!). The "shoot-out" has become so much of a cliche in every one of these forms that it took the *outre* style of Sergio Leone to inject some new life into it, especially the three-way gunfight in

The Good, the Bad and the Ugly and the protracted face-to-face confrontation at the climax of *Once Upon a Time in the West*. Kurosawa, too, recognized the cliche status of the climactic face-off, hence the incredible duel at the end of *Sanjuro*.

We are led closer to morphology of the form with Schrader. He claims that there are "twenty or so basic *Yakuza* set pieces ... every *Yakuza* film will have six to ten of them."[7] I think, in fact, that there is even a more specific morphology to the form and a further study will demonstrate that.

There is a very important similarity between the *yakuza* film and the Sword film, that of the relationship between hero and henchman. Typically, the two are "brothers" in the sense of belonging to the same *yakuza* group, a group to whom one owes complete and total loyalty. Usually, the hero will attempt to break away from the group while his *yakuza*-brother remains. A bloody battle involving the two is inevitable.

The most essential difference between the Sword film and the *yakuza* film is the organizational setting. The hero in the Sword film is, or shortly becomes an outsider which *begins* the dramatic action. The *yakuza* hero begins as a member of a group; becoming an outsider causes the climactic *end* of the drama. The strict adherence to group loyalties and the code of the *yakuza* demanding absolute obedience of the *kobun* to his *oyabun* (boss) have been perceived as a contemporary return to feudalistic ideals. This has worried some social critics of the Japanese cinema. "Tado Sato's lengthy essay, 'Reflex of Loyalty,' sees the *yakuza-eiga* as having created a new situational morality where duty can be 'more important' than humanity—thus opening many new doors to old forms of fascism."[8] This idea of feudalism remaining an essential feature of Japanese society is supported by Richard Tucker, speaking in another context entirely.

> The characters in Kurosawa's films interact with their environment; they are realistic in that they condition and are conditioned by the social context in which they live. Now while Richie has made this point, he has chosen to ignore the nature of that social structure. For this society is seen by a Japanese and since it derives from Japanese culture it is not suprising to find that the structure is feudal.[9]

Unfortunately, Tucker's implicit definition of feudal is not only suspect, it seems rather entirely off the mark.

> A close regard for the central characters within Kurosawa's world will show that in every case there is a relationship which is in essence feudal. The master-pupil situation, one in which values of humanist tendencies are slowly absorbed by the pupil through observation of the master, is central to each of the films....[10]

While Tucker's observation regarding Kurosawa's film is an acute and important one, is a master-pupil relationship in essence feudal? The same kind of master-pupil structure is most important in Westerns as well, yet no one would call the Western genre a "feudalist" one.

Yet despite Tucker's strange definition of feudalism, it is true that much of the feudal ethos remains in contemporary Japan. But the question now is, is Sato correct that the essential "message" of the *yakuza-eiga* is one of fascistic feudalism?

I think the answer is no, that the *yakuza* film, like the Gangster film and other formula films, is an attempt to relieve societal tensions. The central fantasy of the *yakuza* film is the rebellion from a confining, self-defining group. The most common motif of the *yakuza* film is the realization on the part of the central protagonist that his life has been wrong. His gang, his boss, have been wrong. The hero's subscription to a code which places group loyalty before humanity has turned him into something less than human. For instance, we see this clearly in Hideo Gosha's masterful *yakuza* film *The Wolves* (1966). (A similar index runs throughout Gosha's Samurai films as well, especially *Sword of the Beast,* and *Three Outlaw Samurai* whose Japanese title *"Sambiki no Samurai"* indicates their dehumanization in the choice of *"sambiki"* instead of *"sannin"* which would be correct in referring to people.) The group, the organization, then, has been wrong in making such demands upon its members.

Of course, the *yakuza-eiga,* like the Sword film, can be perceived as bleak and nihilistic. Both forms are given to graphic displays of violence and both revel in virtual bloodbaths. But while the Sword film usually allows its outcast hero to survive, the *yakuza* film is not so generous. The realization on the hero's part that he has subscribed to a hollow, dehumanizing code almost always ends in his death. Schrader implicitly recognizes the importance of this fact when he says that *"Socho Tobaku (Presidential Gambler)* is the richest and most complex *yakuza-eiga* made to date, yet it is also the darkest and most pessimistic. Both duty and humanity end in death; no middle road is offered."[11] I submit here that it is precisely *because* it is the "darkest and most pessimistic" that *Presidential Gambler* is one of the most significant films in the genre. It is worth noting that in Schrader's own *yakuza* film, *The Yakuza* (1975), written with his brother Leonard, his American and Japanese gangsters both survive (minus the pinkies of their left hands, the *yakuza*'s sign of repentence). If the Japanese seem to expect or demand the death of the *yakuza* hero, Americans, typically, prefer a live one.

If Schrader is correct that "*Yakuza-eiga* is probably the most restricted genre yet devised,"[12] we also are faced with another possible clue to the form's functioning. If the typical Japanese who finds *yakuza* films ritualistically satisfying also feels his life is restricted, it would be likely that he would achieve catharsis from a genre similarly closed in. It is also of prime importance to note that *yakuza* films, like the classic Gangster films, are situated in cities. The postwar emergence of the city-based *yakuza* film also corresponds to the urbanization of Japan. "From 1950 to 1960 population steadily gravitated toward large cities. . . . if a city with a population of 100,000 or more is taken to be an urban center, then urban center populations in 1960 amounted to 41% of the total population in 1960 and then reached 52% in 1970."[13] Fukutake then goes on to note that if cities of 50,000 or more are added to this number, the urban population reaches 80% by 1970.[14] Although traditionally Edo (Tokyo), Kyoto, and Osaka have been among the largest cities in the world, at the time of the Meiji Restoration, using the same standards of urban populations, less than 10% of Japanese lived in cities.[15] Industrialization followed by the post-war economic depression turned Japan, like America, into a nation of cities.

Another factor that might help understand the popularity of the *yakuza* film is the essentially feudalistic nature of Japanese corporations, which might be what Tucker had in mind. Monopoly capitalism, the growth of giant corporations and the Japanese tendency toward lifetime employment with the same company[16] might also help understand the dynamics of the genre.

With these suggestions in mind a detailed analysis of the Japanese *yakuza* film could shed some light on Kurosawa's forays into crime thrillers.

It is quite obvious from Kurosawa's own remarks that Western formula writings have influenced the construction of his crime films. Concerning *Stray Dog* he has said, "I am very fond of Georges Simenon and I wanted to do something in his manner."[17] As Richie further elaborates on Kurosawa's attraction to the story structure of *Stray Dog* he also brings Kurosawa in line with John Ford. "One of the reasons, perhaps, that Kurosawa has been so fond of the films of John Ford is that they, like his, are about moral battles and often incorporate all the elements of the great quest. When he heard the anecdote (*Stray Dog* is based on a true story) Kurosawa first thought of Simenon for all detective stories are variations of the quest."[18] Certainly, however, the clearest example of a direct influence and an explicit use of formula lies with *High and Low*.

Kurosawa took the bones of Ed McBain's 87th Precinct novel *King's Ransom* (1959) and fleshed-out McBain's basic structure. As in *Rashomon*, the additions to the original source are perhaps more significant than the similarities. Kurosawa keeps the basic plot line from *King's Ransom* intact. A shoe manufacturing magnate on the verge of a business coup thinks that his son has been kidnapped and is being held for ransom. It develops that the kidnapper (who is not related in any way to the forthcoming business transaction) has snatched the wrong child and is holding his chauffeur's son. However, the kidnapper nevertheless demands that the industrialist pay the ransom or the child will be killed. If he pays the ransom he loses his only chance to own the factory outright, which is his lifetime dream; if he does not pay, the boy will die.

This ethical dilemma obviously held much fascination for Kurosawa. Many of his earlier films are built around strictly ethical premises, especially

Ikiru (1952) and *The Bad Sleep Well* (1958). There is also the implicit structuration of materialism versus humanism, certainly an important motif in his own films.

There are three planes of action in *King's Ransom:* the businessman's household, which includes his treacherous assistant who sells him out; the police and their procedures; the kidnappers, here two men and a woman. This third plane of action includes the detailing of the relationship between the kidnappers and their hostage and the dynamics of the kidnappers' own interactions. The three spheres are presented in a kind of "parallel editing," of a "meanwhile back at the ranch" structure. The plot turns on the defection of the female kidnapper who then convinces her boy friend to inform the police of their whereabouts. Although it is not especially important in terms of the plot, we should note that the businessman's name is King so that the title is a pun.

Kurosawa's *High and Low* also has three planes of action. Here, however, they are distinct, following chronologically and progressively from high to low. The Japanese title of the film, *Tengoku to Jigoku,* which, as Richie points out, is better translated as "Heaven and Hell," "suggests an extreme opposite that merely "High and Low" does not."[19]

The first section of Kurosawa's film takes place in the home of Gondo (the "King" of the novel). This section, which is filmed entirely indoors, and for the most part in one room, uses the CinemaScope frame to great advantage in suggesting both openness and enclosure at the same time. Gondo's home is situated, as is King's, on top of a hill overlooking the crowded city below. As in the novel, we are first introduced to Gondo and his business associates. Soon the film takes a surprising turn when the kidnapping is announced. This first section comes to an end when Gondo, finally, decides to pay the ransom.

Section two of *High and Low* might be called "middle," and is essentially structured as a "police procedure" thriller. This lovingly detailed sequence, like the previous revelations of the way the ransom money is delivered to the kidnappers, once again reveals Kurosawa's fascination with process. We have still not seen the kidnappers.

Section three is the "low" and concerns the examination of the kidnapper and his milieu. The view shifts away, temporarily, from Gondo and the police. This section and the entire climax involving the capture of the criminal diverge totally from McBain. We are confronted with the kidnapper's situation as we see the slum he lives in, how the heat oppresses him as he stares out of the window looking up at Gondo's obviously air-conditioned home. Although the shooting style of sections one and two are quite different, we are still not prepared for the incredible, highly expressionistic *"Walpurgis nacht"* sequence at the climax of the film. *High and Low* is quite dispassionate in its shooting style, as for instance, when examining Gondo's ethical dilemma there are no camera or editing clues to sway our sympathy. Yet in this sequence the inner-city night life seems to be seen from the point of view of the disturbed kidnapper even though there are no "point of view" shots as such.

This sketchy examination of *High and Low* suggest some of the main areas of exploration. A detailed examination of the differences between *High and Low* and *King's Ransom* would prove as illuminating, I think, as the comparison between *Sanjuro* and *Shane* attempted earlier. As in the earlier comparison, the use of sexual tension in the two works is at variance. King's assistant in *King's Ransom* is a charismatic, ambitious businessman. McBain details a relationship between this assistant and the wife of King's neighbor. The equation of sex and power, the idea as well, of "illicit sex," is very much a part of the pulp tradition in which McBain is working. Sex, in this fashion, is equated with power, decadence, greed, and lust. In *High and Low* there is no corresponding sexual encounter, and the assistant is rather more colorless and forgettable.

The lack of sexual tension among the major characters here, as well as in *Sanjuro* compared to *Shane,* may have implications for the metaphorical function of sex in the Japanese cinema. One might wish to examine, for instance, the ways in which sex is used in the political films of Nagisa Oshima, especially *Diary of a Shinjuku Thief* (1969), *The Man Who Left His Will on Film* (1970), and *In the Realm of the Senses* (1976). We might also look toward the role of sex in *Yakuza* films or the way sex is thought of in the *"pinku"* films.

I have suggested as well, that the influence of American popular formulas or structures on Kurosawa's non-formulaic works might also prove enlightening. Two films of prime importance here would be *Ikiru* and *Red Beard* (1965), both of which were extremely popular in Japan as they received the *Kinema Jumpo* #1 Award, and both were, and remain, popular in America. These films might first be related to their Japanese antecedents, perhaps in the *shomin-geki* formula, and then might be compared to the melodrama. The potential use of Western popular formulas in such successful, essentially non-formulaic work, has implications for narrative theory. Just as we saw that an appropriate model for constructing a successful Samurai film lay in using the motif of the stranger, so we might see that the structure of the melodrama is appropriate for detailing the struggle of an individual who is put through a series of experiences which reshape his attitudes.

We must explore whether or not Kurosawa's non-generic films are essentially "dialectic" in nature. Certainly, their different structural patterns do not oppose two forces mediated by a third, outside, force. In this fashion, binary oppositions which exist are structured into the texts in a different manner from the Samurai films. In fact, in *Ikiru* and *Red Beard* (as well as *I Live in Fear* and *The Bad Sleep Well*) the hero forms one side of an antinomy which is itself built around action/non-action, involvement/non-involvement, honesty/corruption (and more). Already we can see that the mediation so crucial to a strategy of distanciation and ambiguity in the Samurai films is lacking in the (supposedly) non-formulaic work. And we also want to ask, to inquire into, the appearance (or not) of the fundamental East/West tension so important to the Samurai films. In other words, how does structure and the notion of dialectic lead to a definition of genre?

Another implication of this study—another area for future exploration—is obvious and has always been obvious, throughout this work: the influence of Kurosawa on the West and on, in particular, the Western film. (We might note, simply in passing and to proclaim yet one more area of study, how much of *Hidden Fortress* forms the basis of *Star Wars,* and how *Seven Samurai* was also the basis for *Battle Beyond the Stars*—the Samurai film as science fiction!)

For the moment I would like to deal briefly with two films which owe a debt to Kurosawa and *Seven Samurai: The Magnificent Seven* and Sam Peckinpah's *The Wild Bunch.* Using methodologies outlined in the previous chapters, we can see the clear and coherent ways that technical and thematic strategies developed by Kurosawa were easily and astutely transformed by his Hollywood counterparts. Such methodologies also help us account for the artistic superiority of *Seven Samurai* over *The Magnificent Seven* and help us to understand why *The Wild Bunch* is so successful and meaningful a transformation of Kurosawa's epic original.

We have seen above how the Samurai film, like the Western, situates itself at a frontier. In the Western this site of action is usually a literal frontier, a genuine outpost at the farthest reaches of civilization, while the Samurai film tends to use a metaphorical frontier—moral or ethical realms. The discussion of *Seven Samurai* noted that Kurosawa's film was situated in the chaotic pre-Tokugawa era of civil war and banditry. Kurosawa subtly pointed out a disturbing paradox: in a time of universal warfare, unemployed Samurai *(ronin)* roam the land. These *ronin,* dreaming of bright futures as clan retainers, are faced with ethical choices; in the breakdown of traditional authority such choices are interiorized. This interiorization, this "existentialism," already imparts Kurosawa's heroes a commonality with the Westerner.

Related to the interiorized moral systems of a chaotic period is the idea of crossing class boundaries. Distinctions between Samurai and peasant, held up as fairly absolute in theory, become, in practice, no longer so clear. As we have seen, the character Kikuchiyo is able to cross such a boundary, although at a severe price.

John Sturges' *The Magnificent Seven* is already situated at a frontier (it is a Western). As such, its characters too are confronted with moral choices in a land where law has yet to be established. More significantly, the film adopts the notion of crossing class boundaries when the film's characters cross a literal boundary: the Mexican-American border. There is no class hierarchy in the Western, of course, but there is a cultural—specifically, a *technological*—

boundary involved. The American gunmen, with their superior technology help the Mexicans. The haves help the have-nots.

As we saw in *Seven Samurai,* this same sort of technological boundary operated. In both films, access to technology and the knowledge of how to use it rests only in the hands of one class or group. The individual films detail the ethical choices the members of the group must make.

There is something else operating here, however, something which at times threatens to overwhelm the "moral narrative" and replace it with another story. This new story is the tale of men in groups, men undertaking a suicidal mission "for the hell of it." I alluded to the concept of "professionalism" at the end of the last chapter, but it returns in a more fundamental way when examining what is borrowed from Kurosawa by Sturges and Peckinpah.

In Will Wright's challenging study of the Western, *Sixguns and Society,* he isolates four variations of the Western formula: the classical, vengeance, transition, and professional variation.[20] Although Wright's selection of Westerns is open to question (comparative performance at the box office), there is much merit in his study. Of particular importance here is the professional variation.

In tracing the changing mythos of the Western, Wright isolates the professional variation as probably appearing with *Gunfight at the OK Corral* (1957) (a John Sturges film). Wright admits earlier traces may be found in John Ford's cavalry trilogy (1948-50), but asserts that the true beginning of the variation is Howard Hawks' *Rio Bravo* (1959). However, using Wright's own list of "functions" (a variation, so to speak, on Propp's *Morphology of the Folk-Tale*), it is clear that Kurosawa's *Seven Samurai* can be considered a professional Western. (Admittedly, it does have something in common with the classical Western, but so, too, does the professional plot. These lists of functions also enable *Sanjuro* to be seen, like *Shane,* as a classical Western.) The requisite functions for the professional Western involve the formation of a group of trained fighters who share respect and loyalty for each other, who exist independently of society and who stay (or die) together at the end. Much of the narrative focus of these films is on how the fight itself is fought—the planning of the campaign, the staging of the battle, and the spectacle of the final confrontation. This focus demonstrates both the professionalism of the men and pushes other issues (like morality) into the background. Although Wright does not discuss *The Magnificent Seven* (it did not gross enough money, one assumes, in its year of release), it is obviously a professional Western.

Sturges' film, like Kurosawa's strives to be "more" than merely a Western, for it tries to deliver two "messages"—one narrative, the realm of morality, and one spectacle, the realm of genre. The superiority of Kurosawa's film is not a function of its being the original (for there is nothing *necessarily* better in being an original, it just seems to work out that way) nor of any notion that Sturges' film "borrows" without sufficient mythical grounding in American culture (the way we might say that Martin Ritt's *The Outrage* borrows all the wrong things from *Rashomon*). This is only to say that at some level we can separate the meaning of a work from its artistic or rhetorical plane, although ultimately we must allow style and technique to reenter the picture.

But is this entirely true? Is *Seven Samurai* a better (more powerful, richer, more engaging) film than *The Magnificent Seven* because Kurosawa is a better (more competent, innovative, daring) filmmaker than Sturges? Not entirely, for there is another element which *Seven Samurai* explores that *The Magnificent Seven* ignores. It is precisely this "missing" element which Peckinpah fills in in *The Wild Bunch*.

What Kurosawa recognizes, that Sturges does not, is that the utilization of superior technology brings with it a quality of alienation. As Kambei notes at the conclusion of *Seven Samurai,* "We've lost again ... the farmers are the winners." The farmers' victory stems from the fact that they plant roots into the land, roots which anchor them physically and metaphysically. The existential way of life of the Samurai precludes them, *by definition,* from planting roots. To live existentially is to be alienated. And it is precisely the use of (advanced) technology which is responsible for their alienation. Advanced technology leads to the formation of new forms of social groups. The farmers, born and nourished by the land, maintain a traditional, communal society. But the Samurai must forge (like a smithee of the soul) ever new and changing social models.

Peckinpah is keenly aware of this alienating factor, perhaps even more so than Kurosawa. Technological modes occupy an important part of the subtext of *The Wild Bunch*. This subtext, which is intimately bound up with the much discussed "demythological" workings of the film, is unaccounted for (and unaccountable by) Wright's narrative morphology. He sees *The Wild Bunch* as a professional Western, but seems not to recognize the manner in which it differs from the earlier variations.

The concept of class boundaries, transformed into borders in *The Magnificent Seven,* also appears in *The Wild Bunch,* which takes place along the Mexican-American border and also involves technologically superior gunmen aiding a Mexican group. However, *The Wild Bunch* also adds another kind of border or boundary: a temporal one. The members of the wild bunch, aging gunfighters all (except, significantly, the Mexican member), see their day passing. The film is set in 1912, a time when the frontier was tamed and the day of the gunman was fast drawing to a close. What Peckinpah is concerned with is how such men cope with changing times. And what he clearly shows us is how the changing times are a function of changing technology. Automobiles and machine guns are the most blatant symbols of advanced technology in the Western; they make the classic Western horse and sixgun obsolete. Indeed, when Pike Bishop (William Holden) is found dead following a massive shoot-out and slaughter-fest, his sixgun still remains in its holster, undrawn. The change in transportation and weaponry has brought about a change in group relationships. From the Western "gang" dependent upon charismatic leadership and "the code of the West," Peckinpah shows the evolution toward the modern military/industrial complex. "The army" is now the dominant mode of organization and even if the wild "bunch" are shown to be superior (more professional) to the army, we also know that their kind of group dynamics are doomed. (They do all die at the end.) Not only are they doomed; they were always doomed. They were doomed the minute they opted for an existential life and the sacrifice of traditional communal values for technological ones. (One shudders to apply this precise notion to one's own life and society.)

Of course, *Seven Samurai* has many such ironies of its own. If Pike Bishop's sixgun never left his holster, then we will recall how each of the Samurai killed die by gunshots. The sword gives way to the gun, the Samurai to the foot-soldier; the sixgun gives way to the machine gun, the bunch to the army. Technological modes change and so (or hence) do group dynamics. To live a technological life is to accept alienation as a condition of existence.

The ordinary professional Western disguises this alienated condition by appealing to the spectacle of the film and by stressing the professionalism of the heroes as a transcendent value. It is Kurosawa's genius to be able to romanticize the inner strength of character of his heroes while at the same time recognizing their ironic components. It is this ability to mythicize and demythicize in the same film, at the same time, that accounts for the richness of Kurosawa's film and, indeed, for Peckinpah's.

Obviously much yet remains to be said about the specific influence of Kurosawa's Samurai film upon Peckinpah's Western, and much about Kurosawa's cinema upon Peckinpah's. In particular, a study dealing with cinematic creators should pay attention to primarily cinematic devices. That such a need exists may be shown by pointing out the somewhat shocking weakness of some prior thinking on the subject.

Paul Seydor, who has written the most detailed and intelligent full-length study of Peckinpah's films, recognizes implicit similarities between *Seven Samurai* and *The Wild Bunch*. Seydor asserts that "*The Wild Bunch* [is] the best film since *The Seven Samurai* about men whose lives and work involve violence and killing."[21] Seydor also notes that Peckinpah has expressed admiration for Kurosawa's work going so far as to say that *Rashomon* is one of his favorite films.[22] However, in tracing Peckinpah's indebtedness to Kurosawa, Seydor woefully misrepresents one of Kurosawa's formal devices: "Kurosawa has photographed violence in slow motion, but that is a superficial link at best to Peckinpah, who...inflects the device with a degree of psychological subtlety and nuance, and with a range of expressiveness that is simply absent from Kurosawa, for whom slow motion serves a largely pictorial function."[23] While Peckinpah's use of slow motion is complex (it owes much to Eisenstein), Seydor is quite wrong about Kurosawa.

My discussion of *Seven Samurai* elucidated the two most spectacular uses of slow motion in the film: Kambei's killing of the thief and Kyuzo's duel. Although both utilize slow motion, their effects, as I noted differ. The pictorial beauty Seydor speaks of does appear in the scene of Kyuzo's duel, but its pictorialism is not done for its own sake. It is better to say that the scene transfers the death from the human plane to the aesthetic one, exactly in keeping with Kyuzo's character. In the former usage, slow motion permits our emotional entry; in the latter it forbids it. This is a far cry from mere pictorialism. If Peckinpah's use of slow motion differs from Kurosawa's, such a difference need not be evaluative.

What I would like to suggest, in concluding, is what I hope was apparent all along, and what I hope is even more apparent now: namely, that Kurosawa's films are worth studying, that this study has been worth undertaking, and that such studies (and more) that I have called for are similarly perceived to be of value. Since the middle 1970s Kurosawa's cinema has been devalued in the sparse critical literature produced on the Japanese cinema. Kurosawa has been displaced, to all intents and purposes, by the so-called "modernists" of the Japanese cinema, Ozu, Mizoguchi, and Oshima.[24] While I entirely support the projects undertaken by writers such as David Bordwell, Kristin Thompson, Stephen Heath, and Edward Branigan, under the impetus of Noel Burch's *Theory of Film Practice,* I decry the absence of Kurosawa. And this is not to call for the case of Kurosawa's modernism, which is what Burch does in *To the Distant Observer.* Instead, it is a call to appreciate Kurosawa precisely for his classicism and precisely for his manifestation of what used to be called (before it became "bourgeois") "humanism."

While I would agree that humanism, as such, is not a standard of directorial value (is Renoir a better director than Hitchcock because he is a humanist and Hitchcock is not?), it can be a standard of a work's worth, its importance for detailing what used to called "the human condition." I found flaws in *Rashomon, Throne of Blood* and, to a lesser extent, *Kagemusha* on the basis that to a large extent the films concentrated on formal aspects at the expense of human concerns. The over-attachment to form seems an implicit denial of the value of human action. I would like to equate a "formalist" style with Leo Braudy's notion of "closed" style (without denying the "openness" of the films of Ozu or Oshima, an openness which is a function of *narrative* denial and the refusal of "the principle of the inclusion of the viewer in the diegesis"[25]). Braudy declares that the open style in filmmaking is implicitly more humanistic than the closed.

The so-called "humanistic" impression given by Renoir's films derives from the open and contingent relation between people, places and things within his narratives; the frequently attacked "inhuman" quality of Lang's films derives from his insistence on a total visual schema of every person, place or thing in his films.[26]

Braudy maintains that Kurosawa subscribes to the open style.

> Renoir, Rossellini, Visconti, De Sica, Antonioni, Fellini, Satyajit Ray, and Akira Kurosawa elaborate the possibilities of the open film.[27]

This is true, as we have seen with respect to *The Hidden Fortress* and *Yojimbo*, where the CinemaScope ratio is used to emphasize the presence of offscreen space, a characteristic of the open film. However, it is also true that the use of genre is characteristic of the closed style of filmmaking. It is likely that Kurosawa elaborates the possibility of Braudy's conception of the "open world and [the] enclosed story."[28] Yet I would like to submit that if genre films are, as Braudy says, "closed by convention,"[29] this mitigates against a true humanism arising.

If the world of genre is a world of preconceived narrative patterns, characters and motifs, there seems little chance for unique individual action. The individual character in a formulaic work is bound by the content-determined structure of the film to fit into symbolic or archetypical categories. Human action is thus fore-doomed, as it must subscribe to generic conventions. Kurosawa may be said to create a dialectic between the open and the closed styles, yet to the extent that he stays within formula bounds it may be true that he is not a humanist.

Yet if Kurosawa *is* a humanist, it may be important to explore in greater degree the relationship between humanism and genre. It might be fruitful, for instance, to examine the idea of "tragedy" as a genre. Tragedy, in the classical sense, is certainly a formulaic structure wherein a hero struggles mightily to achieve a degree of self-determination yet who is ultimately bound to fail. However, it seems certain that many tragedians are great humanists. We would have to expand our conception of humanism or of genre in order to see the conjunction of the two.

I have pointed out some of the existential implications of Kurosawa's work, especially in *Yojimbo*. It might be useful in the context of exploring the question of humanism arising in genre to address this issue in more detail. In a sense, according to the existentialists, all life is formulaic, leading to an inevitable end, which may or may not be particularly heroic. If existentialism is brought to bear on the issue of genre and humanism, it is entirely possible that notions of genre and humanism will have to be expanded. It is possible that there might ultimately be no such thing as a non-formulaic work; alternately, humanism may be said to arise precisely to the extent that the narrative structures of films are formulaic. Kurosawa's works address these issues quite clearly and are worth exploring in further detail.

Kurosawa's cinema, in the light of these implications, takes on ever more complexity and richness. Kurosawa is a filmmaker worth exploring in detail not because he utilizes an open or a closed style, but because he sets the two forms in opposition. He is an important director because he deliberately uses American and Japanese formulas and transcends them. Kurosawa's films are valuable for the stories they tell, the characters they reveal, and the manner in which they are delivered. In-depth studies of his *oeuvre* must reveal the significance of his patterns, not just their appearance. By his bold experiments in films like *Rashomon, Seven Samurai, Throne of Blood, Yojimbo, Sanjuro,* and *Kagemusha,* Kurosawa has shown both the strengths and weaknesses of formulaic structures, formalist experimentation and humanistic conceptions of character. Further studies must show how certain narrative patterns, character traits and formal means can be used most appropriately in certain kinds of films. Through the study of Kurosawa's films we can learn not only about one of the world's leading directors but about the nature and power of the cinema.

Notes

Chapter 1

1. Audie Bock, *Japanese Film Directors* (New York: Kodansha International Ltd., 1978), p. 163.
2. Arthur Knight, *The Liveliest Art: A Panoramic History of the Movies,* Rev. ed. (New York: Macmillan Publishing Co., 1978); Jack C. Ellis, *A History of Film* (Englewood Cliffs, New Jersey: Prentice-Hall, 1979).
3. Knight, p. 212; Richard N. Tucker, *Japan: Film Image* (London: Studio Vista, 1973), p. 116.
4. Bock, p. 163.
5. Related in J.L. Anderson and Donald Richie, *The Japanese Film: Art and Industry* (Rutland, Vermont: Charles E. Tuttle, 1959), p. 24.
6. Ibid., p. 28.
7. David Bordwell, "American Influences on Pre-War Japanese Cinema," Panel: Japanese Cinema, Ohio University Film Conference, 25 April 1981.
8. Anderson and Richie, p. 429, chart I.
9. Donald Richie, *Japanese Cinema: Film Style and National Character* (New York: Doubleday Anchor Books, 1971), p. 221.
10. Anderson and Richie, p. 162.
11. Richie, p. 200.
12. Hideo Gosha receives some interesting in-depth discussion in Alain Silver, *The Samurai Film* (New York: A.S. Barnes, 1977), pp. 108-63.
13. E.g., Jack Shadoian, *Dreams and Dead Ends: The American Gangster/Crime Film* (Cambridge, Massachusetts: The MIT Press, 1977); Will Wright, *Sixguns and Society: A Structural Study of the Western* (Berkeley: Unviersity of California Press, 1975).
14. Noel Burch, *To the Distant Observer: Form and Meaning in the Japanese Cinema* (Los Angeles: University of California Press, 1979), p. 291.
15. Richie, p. 198.
16. Ibid., p. 200.
17. Ibid., pp. 172-73.

18. Andrew Sarris, "Towards a Theory of Film History," in *Movies and Methods: An Anthology,* ed. Bill Nichols (Berkeley: University of California Press, 1976), p. 246.
19. Anderson and Richie, p. 315.

Chapter 2

1. John G. Cawelti, *Adventure, Mystery, and Romance* (Chicago: University of Chicago Press, 1976), p. 35.
2. Ibid., pp. 34-36.
3. Edmund Leach, *Claude Levi-Strauss* (Middlesex, England: Penguin Books, 1970), pp. 58-59.
4. Claude Levi-Strauss, *Structural Anthropology,* vol. 1, trans. Claire Jacobson and Brooke Grundfest Schoepf (New York: Basic Books, 1963), p. 216.
5. Ibid., p. 229.
6. Leach, pp. 63-64.
7. Roland Barthes, *Mythologies,* trans. Annette Lavers (New York: Hill and Wang, 1972), p. 109.
8. Ibid., p. 114.
9. Ibid., p. 128.
10. J.L. Anderson and Donald Richie, *The Japanese Film: Art and Industry* (Rutland, Vermont: Charles E. Tuttle Co., 1959), p. 60.
11. Ibid., pp. 74-75.
12. W.G. Beasley, *The Modern History of Japan,* 2d ed. (New York: Praeger Publishers, 1973), p. 321.
13. Anderson and Richie, p. 64.
14. W.G. Beasley, "The Samurai Tradition," in *The Japan Reader I: Imperial Japan,* ed. Jon Livingston, Joe Moore, Felicia Oldfeather (New York: Pantheon Books, 1973), p. 16.
15. Ibid., p. 17.
16. Ibid., p. 18.
17. Ann Douglas, *The Feminization of American Culture* (New York: Knopf, 1977).
18. Robert Warshow, "Movie Chronicle: The Westerner," in *Focus on the Western,* ed. Jack Nachbar (Englewood Cliffs, New Jersey: Prentice-Hall, 1974).
19. H. Paul Varley, *Japanese Culture: A Short History,* Expanded ed. (New York: Praeger Publishers, 1977), p. 23.
20. George Sansom, *A History of Japan to 1334* (Stanford: Stanford University Press, 1959), p. 124.
21. Noel Burch, *To the Distant Observer* (Los Angeles: University of California Press, 1979), p. 47.
22. Ibid., p. 69.
23. Roland Barthes, *Image, Music, Text,* trans. Stephen Heath (New York: Hill and Wang, 1977), p. 175.

24. Anderson and Richie, pp. 58-60.
25. Ibid., p. 160.
26. *"Mono no aware,"* like many Japanese aesthetic terms is difficult to translate. For further discussion see Varley, p. 48; and *Sources of Japanese Tradition,* vol. 1, Ryusaku Tsunoda, Wm. Theodore de Barry, Donald Keene (New York: Columbia University Press, 1958), pp. 172-74.
27. Ivan Morris, *The Nobility of Failure: Tragic Heroes in the History of Japan* (New York: New American Library, 1975).
28. Beasley, *The Modern History of Japan,* pp. 299-300.
29. Ibid., p. 300.
30. Varley, p. 196.
31. D.T. Suzuki, *Zen and Japanese Culture* (Princeton: Princeton University Press, 1959), p. 63.
32. This account of Musashi's life is drawn primarily from Alain Silver, *The Samurai Film* (New York: A.S. Barnes, 1977), p. 94.
33. Cf. *The Portable Jung,* ed. Joseph Campbell (New York: The Viking Press, 1971).
34. Silver, pp. 183-85; Joan Mellen, *The Waves at Genji's Door* (New York: Pantheon Books, 1976), pp. 118-20.
35. Vladimir Propp, *Morphology of the Folk-Tale,* ed. Louis A. Wagner, trans. Laurence Scott (Austin: University of Texas Press, 1968).
36. Cf. Levi-Strauss, "The Structural Study of Myth," in *Structural Anthropology,* vol. 2; and Joseph Campbell, *The Hero with a Thousand Faces* (Princeton: Princeton University Press, 1949).
37. Claude Levi-Strauss, "How Myths Die," in *Structural Anthropology,* vol. 2 (New York: Basic Books, 1976), p. 398.
38. E.g., Will Wright, *Sixguns and Society* (Berkeley: University of California Press, 1975).
39. Barthes, *Mythologies,* p. 141.
40. Ibid., p. 142.
41. Ibid.
42. Ibid., p. 147.
43. Ibid., p. 148.
44. Ibid., p. 151.

Chapter 3

1. Peter Wollen, *Signs and Meaning in the Cinema* (Bloomington: Indiana University Press, 1972), p. 168.
2. Donald Richie, *The Films of Akira Kurosawa* (Los Angeles: University of California Press, 1965), p. 10.
3. Bradley Smith, *Japan: A History of Art* (New York: Doubleday and Company, 1964), p. 251.
4. Richie, p. 11.

5. Ibid.
6. Ibid., p. 196.
7. Smith, p. 259.
8. Andrew Sarris, "Notes on the Auteur Theory in 1962" in *Film Theory and Criticism*, ed. Gerald Mast and Marshall Cohen, 2d ed. (New York: Oxford University Press, 1979), p. 663.
9. Donald Richie, *Japanese Cinema* (New York: Anchor Books, 1971), p. 198.
10. Patricia Erens, *Akira Kurosawa: A Guide to References and Resources* (Boston: G.K. Hall, 1979), p. 28.
11. Richie, *Films of Akira Kurosawa*, p. 196.
12. H. Paul Varley, *Japanese Culture: A Short History* (New York: Praeger Publishers, 1977), p. 204.
13. Audie Bock, *Japanese Film Directors* (New York: Kodansha International, 1978), p. 172.
14. Ibid., p. 171.
15. Ibid., p. 172.
16. Noel Burch, *To the Distant Observer* (Los Angeles: University of California Press, 1979), p. 299.
17. Wollen, p. 168.
18. Richie, *Films of Akira Kurosawa*, p. 14.
19. Bock, p. 165.
20. Ivan Morris, *The Nobility of Failure* (New York: New American Library, 1975), pp. 67-105.
21. Richie, *Films of Akira Kurosawa*, p. 31.
22. Ibid.
23. Bock, p. 167.
24. Richie, *Films of Akira Kurosawa*, p. 34.
25. Burch, p. 296.
26. Bruce Kawin, *Mindscreen: Point of View in the Cinema* (Princeton: Princeton University Press, 1978).
27. Makoto Ueda, *Modern Japanese Writers and the Nature of Literature* (Stanford: Stanford University Press, 1976), pp. 111-14.
28. John G. Cawelti, *Adventure, Mystery and Romance* (Chicago: University of Chicago Press, 1976), p. 80.
29. Ibid.
30. Ibid., p. 84.
31. Ibid.
32. Burch, p. 298.
33. Ibid., p. 310.
34. Richie, *Films of Akira Kurosawa*, p. 115.

35. Burch, p. 310.
36. Charles Barr, "CinemaScope: Before and After," in Mast and Cohen, p. 156.
37. Richie, *Films of Akira Kurosawa*, p. 117.
38. D.T. Suzuki, *Zen and Japanese Culture* (Princeton: Princeton University Press, 1959), p. 128.
39. Cawelti, p. 40.
40. The term is adapted from Claude Levi-Strauss, *Structural Anthropology*, vol. 1, trans. Claire Jacobson and Brooke Grundfest Schoepf (New York: Basic Books, 1963), p. 211.
41. Cawelti, p. 40.
42. Richie, *Films of Akira Kurosawa*, p. 119.
43. Leo Braudy, *The World in a Frame* (Garden City, New York: Anchor Press, 1977), pp. 44-51.
44. Ibid., p. 49.
45. G.S. Kirk, *Myth: Its Meaning and Function in Ancient and Other Cultures* (Berkeley: University of California Press, 1970), pp. 38-39.
46. Burch, p. 318.
47. Colin McArthur, *Underworld USA* (New York: The Viking Press, 1972).
48. Cawelti, p. 77.
49. Ibid., p. 143.
50. Ibid.
51. Dashiell Hammett, *Red Harvest* (New York: Vintage Books, 1956), pp. 3-4.
52. Ibid.
53. Ibid., p. 199.
54. Raymond M. Olderman, *Beyond the Waste Land: A Study of the American Novel in the Nineteen-Sixties* (New Haven: Yale University Press, 1972), p. 26.
55. Martin Gardner, *The Annotated Alice* (New York: Bramhall House, 1960), p. 88.
56. Ibid., p. 89.
57. Marsha Kinder, "Throne of Blood: A Morality Dance" in *Literature/Film Quarterly* 5, no. 4 (1977), p. 340.
58. Chie Nakane, *Japanese Society* (Berkeley: University of California Press, 1979), p. 96.
59. Olderman, p. 28.
60. Andrew Sarris, ed. *Interviews with Film Directors* (New York: Avon Books, 1967), p. 307.
61. Ibid.
62. Cawelti, p. 193.
63. Joan Mellen, *The Waves at Genji's Door* (New York: Pantheon Books, 1976), p. 53.
64. Leslie A. Fiedler, *Love and Death in the American Novel* (New York: Stein and Day, 1966), p. 46.
65. Ibid.

Notes for Chapter 4

66. Cawelti, pp. 194-215.
67. Fiedler, p. 45.
68. Marsha Kinder, *"Kagemusha"* in *Film Quarterly* 34, No. 2 (1980-81), pp. 44-48.
69. Cf. Andre Bazin, "The Evolution of the Language of Cinema" in *What is Cinema?* vol. I, ed. and trans. Hugh Gray (Berkeley: University California Press, 1967), pp. 23-40.
70. Kinder, *"Kagemusha,"* p. 46.
71. Ibid.
72. Personal discussion with Prof. Keiko McDonald, 27 December 1980.
73. Kinder, *"Kagemusha,"* p. 48.
74. Ibid., p. 46.
75. Ibid., p. 45.
76. Nakane, Chapter Four.

Chapter 4

1. The Gangster Film is hardly well defined. As witness I point toward two books, both influential, which use different titles for the form: Jack Shadoian, *Dreams and Dead Ends: The American Gangster/Crime Film* (Cambridge, Massachusetts: The MIT Press, 1977); Colin McArthur, *Underworld U.S.A.: The Gangster Film/Thriller* (New York: The Viking Press, 1972).
2. Shadoian, p. 2.
3. Paul Schrader, *"Yakuza-eiga:* A Primer," *Film Comment* 10 (Jan.-Feb. 1974), p. 10.
4. Alain Silver, *The Samurai Film* (New York: A.S. Barnes, 1977), pp. 220-28.
5. Schrader, p. 11.
6. Noel Burch, *To the Distant Observer: Form and Meaning in the Japanese Cinema* (Los Angeles: University of California Press, 1979), p. 317.
7. Schrader, p. 14.
8. Ibid., p. 11.
9. Richard N. Tucker, *Japan: Film Image* (London: Studio Vista, 1973), p. 82.
10. Tucker, p. 83.
11. Schrader, p. 13.
12. Ibid.
13. Tadashi Fukutake, *Japanese Society Today* (Tokyo: University of Tokyo Press, 1974), p. 63.
14. Ibid.
15. Ibid.
16. Chie Nakane, *Japanese Society* (Berkeley: University of California Press, 1979), p. 96.
17. Donald Richie, *The Films of Akira Kurosawa* (Los Angeles: University of California Press, 1965), p. 58.

18. Ibid.
19. Ibid., p. 160.
20. Will Wright, *Sixguns and Society: A Structural Study of the Western* (Berkeley: University of California Press, 1975).
21. Paul Seydor, *Peckinpah: The Western Films* (Urbana: University of Illinois Press, 1980), p. 94.
22. Ibid., p. 135.
23. Ibid., p. 263.
24. Modernist criticism includes such articles as Kristin Thompson and David Bordwell, "Space and Narrative in the Films of Ozu" *Screen* 17, No. 2 (Summer 1976): 41-73; Edward Branigan, "The Space of *Equinox Flower,*" Ibid.: 74-105; Stephen Heath, "Anato Mo," *Screen* 17, No. 4 (Winter 1976-77): 49-66.
25. Burch, p. 159.
26. Leo Braudy, *The World in a Frame* (New York: Anchor Books, 1977), p. 55.
27. Ibid., p. 98.
28. Ibid., p. 94.
29. Ibid., p. 112.

Bibliography

Books

Anderson, Joseph, and Donald Richie. *Japanese Film: Art and Industry.* Rutland, Vermont: Charles E. Tuttle, 1959. Reprinted, Princeton: Princeton University Press, 1982.
Barthes, Roland. *Image, Music, Text.* Translated by Stephen Heath. New York: Hill and Wang, 1977.
──────. *Mythologies.* Translated by Annette Lavers. New York: Hill and Wang, 1972.
Bazin, Andre. "The Evolution of the Language of the Cinema." In *What is Cinema?* by Andre Bazin, Vol. I, translated and edited by Hugh Gray, pp. 23-40. Berkeley: University of California Press, 1967.
Beasley, W.G. *The Modern History of Japan.* 2d ed. New York: Praeger, 1963, 1973.
──────. "The Samurai Tradition." In *The Japan Reader I: Imperial Japan 1800-1945,* edited by Jon Livingston, Joe Moore, Felicia Oldfeather, pp. 15-18. New York: Pantheon Books, 1973.
Bock, Audie. *Japanese Film Directors.* New York: Kodansha International, 1978.
Braudy, Leo. *The World in a Frame: What We See in Films.* New York: Anchor Books, 1977.
Burch, Noel. *Theory of Film Practice.* Translated by Helen R. Lane. New York: Praeger, 1973. Reprinted, Princeton: Princeton University Press, 1981.
──────. *To the Distant Observer: Form and Meaning in the Japanese Cinema.* Los Angeles: University of California Press, 1979.
Buscombe, Edward. "The Idea of Genre in the American Cinema." In *Film Genre: Theory and Criticism,* edited by Barry Grant, pp. 24-28. Metuchen, New Jersey: The Scarecrow Press, 1977.
Campbell, Joseph. *The Hero with a Thousand Faces.* Princeton: Princeton University Press, 1949.
──────, ed. *The Portable Jung.* New York: The Viking Press, 1971.
Cawelti, John G. *Adventure, Mystery, and Romance: Formula Stories as Art and Popular Culture.* Chicago: University of Chicago Press, 1976.
Douglas, Ann. *The Feminization of American Culture.* New York: Knopf, 1977.
Ellis, Jack D. *A History of Film.* Englewood Cliffs, New Jersey: Prentice-Hall, 1979.
Erens, Patricia. *Akira Kurosawa: A Guide to References and Resources.* Boston: G.K. Hall, 1979.
Fiedler, Leslie A. *Love and Death in the American Novel.* New York: Stein and Day, 1966.
Frayling, Christopher. *Spaghetti Westerns: Cowboys and Europeans from Karl May to Sergio Leone.* London: Routledge & Kegan Paul, 1981.
Frye, Northrop. *Anatomy of Criticism: Four Essays.* Princeton: Princeton University Press, 1967.
Fukutake, Tadashi. *Japanese Society Today.* Tokyo: University of Tokyo Press, 1974.
Gardner, Martin. *The Annotated Alice.* New York: Bramhall House, 1960.
Hammett, Dashiell. *Red Harvest.* New York: Vintage Books, 1956.
Kaminsky, Stuart M. *American Film Genres: Approaches to a Critical Theory of Popular Film.* New York: Dell, 1974.
Kawin, Bruce. *Mindscreen: Point of View in the Cinema.* Princeton: Princeton University Press, 1978.

Kirk, G.S. *Myth: Its Meaning and Functions in Ancient and Other Cultures.* Los Angeles: University of California Press, 1970.
Knight, Arthur. *The Liveliest Art: A Panoramic History of the Movies.* Rev. ed. New York: Macmillan, 1978.
Kracauer, Siegfried. *Theory of Film: Redemption of Physical Reality.* New York: Oxford University Press, 1960.
Kurosawa, Akira. *Something Like an Autobiography.* Translated by Audie Bock. New York: Alfred A. Knopf, 1982.
Leach, Edmund. *Claude Levi-Strauss.* Rev. ed. Middlesex, England: Penguin Books, 1970.
Levi-Strauss, Claude. *Structural Anthropology.* Vol. I. Translated by Claire Jacobson and Brooke Grundfest Schoepf. New York: Basic Books, 1963.
_____. *Structural Anthropology.* Vol. 2. Translated by Claire Jacobson and Brooke Grundfest Schoepf. New York: Basic Books, 1976.
Mast, Gerald, and Marshall Cohen, eds. *Film Theory and Criticism: Introductory Readings.* 2d ed. New York: Oxford University Press, 1979.
McArthur, Colin. *Underworld U.S.A.: The Gangster Film/Thriller.* New York: The Viking Press, 1972.
McBain, Ed. *King's Ransom.* New York: New American Library, 1959.
McConnell, Frank D. "Leopards and History: The Problem of Film Genre." In *Film Genre: Theory and Criticism,* edited by Barry Grant, pp. 7-15. Metuchen, New Jersey: The Scarecrow Press, 1977.
Mellen, Joan. *The Waves at Genji's Door: Japan Through its Cinema.* New York: Pantheon Books, 1976.
Morris, Ivan. *The Nobility of Failure: Tragic Heroes in the History of Japan.* New York: New American Library, 1975.
Nakane, Chie. *Japanese Society.* Berkeley: University of California Press, 1970.
Olderman, Raymond M. *Beyond the Waste Land: A Study of the American Novel in the Nineteen-Sixties.* New Haven: Yale University Press, 1972.
Propp, Vladimir. *Morphology of the Folk-Tale.* Translated by Laurence Scott. Edited by Louis A. Wagner. Austin: University of Texas Press, 1968.
Richie, Donald. *The Films of Akira Kurosawa.* Los Angeles: University of California Press, 1965.
_____. *Japanese Cinema: Film Style and National Character.* New York: Doubleday Anchor Books, 1971.
Sansom, George. *A History of Japan to 1334.* Stanford: Stanford University Press, 1958.
Sarris, Andrew, ed. *Interviews with Film Directors.* New York: Avon, 1967.
_____. "Towards a Theory of Film History." In *Movies and Methods,* edited by Bill Nichols, pp. 238-51. Berkeley: University of California Press, 1976.
Sato, Tadao. *Currents in Japanese Cinema.* Translated by Gregory Barrett. Tokyo: Kodansha, 1982.
Seydor, Paul. *Peckinpah: The Western Films.* Urbana: Unviersity of Illinois Press, 1980.
Shadoian, Jack. *Dreams and Dead Ends: The American Gangster/Crime Film.* Cambridge, Massachusetts: MIT Press, 1977.
Silver, Alain. *The Samurai Film.* New York: A.S. Barnes, 1977.
Smith, Bradley. *Japan: A History in Art.* New York: Doubleday, 1964.
Sources of Japanese Tradition. Vol. I. Compiled by Ryusaku Tsunoda, Wm. Theodore de Bary, Donald Keene. New York: Columbia University Press, 1958.
Suzuki, D.T. *Zen and Japanese Culture.* Princeton: Princeton University Press, 1959.
Tucker, Richard N. *Japan: Film Image.* London: Studio Vista, 1973.
Ueda, Makoto. *Literary and Art Theories in Japan.* Cleveland: The Press of Western Reserve University, 1967.
_____. *Modern Japanese Writers and the Nature of Literature.* Stanford: Stanford University Press, 1976.

Varley, H. Paul. *Japanese Culture: A Short History.* New York: Praeger, 1977.
Warshow, Robert. "Movie Chronicle: The Westerner." In *Focus on the Western,* edited by Jack Nachbar, pp. 45-56. Englewood Cliffs, New Jersey: Prentice-Hall, 1974.
Wollen, Peter. *Signs and Meaning in the Cinema.* Rev. ed. Bloomington: Indiana University Press, 1972.
Wright, Will. *Sixguns and Society: A Structural Study of the Western.* Berkeley: University of California Press, 1975.

Articles

Anderson, Joseph L. "Japanese Swordfighters and American Gunfighters." *Cinema Journal* 12, No. 2 (Spring 1973): 1-21.
Branigan, Edward. "The Space of *Equinox Flower.*" *Screen* 17, No. 2 (Summer 1976): 74-105.
Heath, Stephen. "Anato Mo." *Screen* 17, No. 4 (Winter 1976-77): 49-66.
Kinder, Marsha. *"Kagemusha."* Review. *Film Quarterly* 34, No. 2 (Winter 1980-81): 44-48.
_____. *"Throne of Blood:* A Morality Dance." *Literature/Film Quarterly* 5, No. 4 (Fall 1977): 339-45.
Schrader, Paul. "*Yakuza-eiga:* A Primer." *Film Comment* 10 (Jan.-Feb. 1974): 10-17.
Thompson, Kristin, and David Bordwell. "Space and Narrative in the Films of Ozu." *Screen* 17, No. 2 (Summer 1976): 41-73.

Other Sources

Bordwell, David. "American Influences on Pre-War Japanese Cinema." Phio University Film Conference 25, April 1981.
McDonald, Keiko. Personal Discussion, 27 December 1980, Modern Language Association Conference.

Index

Akutagawa, Ryunosuke, 66
Alice in Wonderland, 103
Allen, Woody, 117
Animal Farm, 73
Anderson, Joseph L., 21, 31
Antonioni, Michelangelo, 145
Ataka, 64

Barth, John, 105
Barthes, Roland, 16, 17, 45, 52, 53
Bazin, André, 72
Boetticher, Budd, 42, 45, 53, 113, 130
Bordwell, David, 144
Braudy, Leo, 94, 144, 145
Branigan, Edward, 144
Bunraku, 28
Burch, Noel, 7, 10, 61, 65, 70, 71, 72, 98, 134
Bushido, 22, 30, 36, 106

Cawelti, John G., 14, 92, 100
Chinese cinema, 13; Kung Fu films, 18
Christie, Agatha, 68
Cimino, Michael, 37
Clavell, James, 115
Cooper, James Fennimore, 114, 115

De Palma, Brian, 68
De Sica, Vittorio, 145
Dickens, Charles, 114
Dostoevsky, Fyodor, 5, 7, 60
Dragoti, Stan, 37

Eisenstein, Sergei, 4, 95, 127, 144
Elkin, Stanley, 105
Enoken (Enomoto, Kenichi), 64-65, 93

Fairbanks, Douglas, 47
Fellini, Federico, 145

Fiedler, Leslie, 114
Ford, John, 7, 8, 51, 53, 58, 59, 76, 79, 103, 113, 115, 128, 137, 141
Fuller, Samuel, 76

Gance, Abel, 58
Gangster films, 7, 16, 42, 43, 44, 98, 99, 100, 101, 102, 105, 130, 133, 136
Gardner, Martin, 103
Gendai-mono, 20, 21, 133
German cinema, 13, 18; Nazi films, 19
Gosha, Hideo, 6, 8, 35, 36, 37, 51, 134, 136
Griffith, D.W., 4, 59, 81, 114

Hammett, Dashiell, 98; *see also Red Harvest*
Hawks, Howard, 7, 8, 51, 53, 57, 58, 59, 61, 76, 130, 141
Heath, Stephen, 144
Hill, Walter, 2
Hitchcock, Alfred, 59, 144

Ichikawa, Kon, 5, 37, 76, 103
Ikehiro, Kazuo, 52
Inagaki, Hiroshi, 2, 31, 32, 33, 35, 40
Indian cinema, 13, 18

Jakobson, Roman, 15
James, Henry, 60
Japan: American occupation of (SCAP), 4, 5, 20, 31; cultural overview, 2-3, 19-20; film industry, 3-4, 8-9, 13, 19; language, 25-27; Meiji Restoration, 3, 20, 22, 58, 63, 137; Tokugawa era, 3, 22-23, 45, 77, 106, 130
Japan-U.S. Mutual Security Pact, 36
Jidai-geki, 20, 76
Joyce, James, 60

Kabuki, 28, 29, 115; *oyama,* 29
Kanjincho, 64

Index

Katsu, Shintaro, 122
Kawin, Bruce, 65
Kayama, Yuzo, 63, 109
Kemeny, John, 103
Kennedy, Arthur, 111
Kesey, Ken, 105
Kerouac, Jack, 103
Kinder, Marsha, 104, 116, 117, 120, 121, 126, 127
King's Ransom, 61, 137-39
Kinoshita, Keisuke, 5
Kobayashi, Masaki, 6, 8, 25, 36, 51, 71, 75
Kurosawa, Heigo, 58

Ladd, Alan, 30
Levi-Strauss, Claude, 14, 15, 16, 51, 52
Leone, Sergio, 134
Lewis, Jerry, 64

Macbeth, 72, 73, 76
Mann, Anthony, 42, 45, 53, 111, 113, 130
McArthur, Colin, 98
McBain, Ed, 61, 137, 139; see also *King's Ransom*
Meiji-mono, 20
Meiji Restoration *see* Japan
Mellen, Joan, 38, 114
Melodrama, 16
Mifune, Toshiro, 63, 70, 83, 87, 93, 95, 96, 97, 106, 111
Misumi, Kenji, 52
Miyamoto, Musashi, 32, 40-41, 42
Mizoguchi, Kenji, 1, 2, 4, 5, 32, 60, 82, 144
Moby Dick, 79
Morphology of the Folk-Tale, 48, 141
Morris, Ivan, 64
Murnau, F.W., 4
Musical films, 16, 99

Nakadai, Tatsuya, 107, 111, 116, 117, 122
Naruse, Mikio, 1
Nelson, Ralph, 37
No theatre, 28, 72
Nobility of Failure, The, 33, 37, 64

Okamoto, Kihachi, 7, 100, 122
Olivier, Laurence, 122
On the Road, 103
Oshima, Nagisa, 25, 60, 103, 139, 144
Ozu, Yasujiro, 1, 2, 4, 5, 16, 25, 29, 33, 34, 144

Palance, Jack, 30
Peckinpah, Sam, 2, 10, 76, 140, 141, 142, 143, 144
Peirce, Charles Sanders, 17
Philosopher Looks at Science, A, 103

Pillow Book of Sei Shonagon, The, 115
Prince and the Pauper, The, 121
Propp, Vladimir, 48, 141

Ray, Satyajit, 145
Red Harvest, 98, 101-2
Renoir, Jean, 144, 145
Richie, Donald, 7, 10, 21, 31, 38, 64, 93, 137, 138
Ritt, Martin, 142
Rossellini, Roberto, 145
Russia: cinema, 13, 18; literature, 61
Russo-Japanese War, 3

Sarris, Andrew, 8
Sato, Tadao, 135, 136
Saussure, Ferdinand de, 17
Schrader, Leonard, 136
Schrader, Paul, 134, 135, 136
Seydor, Paul, 143
Shakespeare, William, 61
Shimura, Takashi, 87
Shinoda, Masahiro, 76
Shogun, 115
Siegel, Don, 63
Signs and Meaning in the Cinema, 57
Silver, Alain, 134
Simenon, Georges, 137
Sixguns and Society, 141
Stanislavsky, Constantin, 122
Sternberg, Josef von, 59
Stevens, George, 58, 79
Stewart, James, 111, 128
Strasberg, Lee, 122
Sturges, John, 10, 140, 141
Suzuki, Daisetz T., 83

Tale of Genji, The, 34, 115
Theory of Film Practice, 144
Thompson, Kristin, 144
To the Distant Observer, 10, 144
Tokugawa era *see* Japan
Truffaut, Francois, 10
Tucker, Richard, 135, 136, 137
Twain, Mark, 121

Uegusa, Keinosuke, 57

Varley, H. Paul, 26
Virginian, The, 115
Visconti, Luchino, 145
Vonnegut, Kurt, 105

Warshow, Robert, 24
Wayne, John, 42, 128
Welles, Orson, 66

Western films, 7, 9, 10, 13, 16, 21, 23, 24, 25, 29, 30, 32, 37, 42, 43, 44, 45, 81, 84, 98, 99, 100, 101, 102, 110, 112, 113, 114, 115, 128, 129, 130, 134, 136, 140, 141, 142; Italian, 16, 21, 52
Wister, Owen, 115
Wollen, Peter, 57, 61
Woolf, Virginia, 60

Wright, Will, 141
Wyler, William, 79

Yakuza films, 6, 7, 8, 10, 51, 98, 134-37, 139
Yamamoto, Kajiro, 62
Yamazaki, Tsutomo, 117

Zen, 39-40, 41-42, 44, 62, 83, 106, 109

Film Title Index

Age of Assassins, 7
Ai no Koriida *see* In the Realm of the Senses
Akahige *see* Red Beard
Akibiyori *see* Late Autumn
All the President's Men, 31

Bad Sleep Well, The, 62, 79, 133, 138, 139
Bandits on the Wind, 33, 35
Battle Beyond the Stars, 140
Bend of the River, 111
Birth of A Nation, The, 81

Chushingura (The Loyal 47 Ronin), 30, 33
Citizen Kane, 62, 65, 66
Cobweb Castle *see* Throne of Blood
Crimson Bat, The, 45
Crowded Streetcar, A, 103

Death by Hanging, 103
Dersu Uzala, 2, 93
Diary of a Shinjuku Thief, 139
Dirty Little Billy, 37
Dodeskaden, 2, 62, 66, 79, 116
Donzoko *see* The Lower Depths
Double Suicide, 28
Drunken Angel, 5, 133

Fistful of Dollars, A, 2, 98
Floating Clouds, 1

Gate of Hell, 1, 32
Godfather, The, 100
Good, The Bad, and The Ugly, The, 21, 135
Gone With the Wind, 21
Great Santini, The, 31
Gunfight at the OK Corral, 141

Hakuchi *see* The Idiot
Hang 'em High, 52
Hara-Kiri, 36, 37, 38, 75
Heaven's Gate, 37

Hidden Fortress, The, 9, 60, 62, 65, 77, 92-97, 98, 104, 121, 140, 145
High and Low, 5, 6, 10, 61, 66, 79, 93, 98, 99, 115, 133, 137-39
High Noon, 38, 81
High Plains Drifter, 52
Horse, 62
Human Bullet, The, 7
Human Condition, The, 51

I Live in Fear, 139
Ichiban Utsukushiku *see* The Most Beautiful
Idiot, The, 5, 60, 61, 66
Ikimono no Kiroku *see* I Live in Fear
Ikiru, 66, 79, 138, 139
In the Realm of the Senses, 139

Jigokumon *see* Gate of Hell
Jeremiah Johnson, 25
Jirocho series, 134
Joiuchi *see* Rebellion

Kagemusha, 2, 3, 9, 30, 66, 75, 79, 83, 94, 95, 116-30, 144, 146
Kakushi Toride no San Akunin *see* The Hidden Fortress
Kedamono no Ken *see* Sword of the Beast
Kill!, 7, 122
Kiru *see* Kill!
Koshikei *see* Death by Hanging
Kozure Ookami *see* Sword of Vengeance series
Kumonosujo *see* Throne of Blood

Late Autumn, 1
Life of Oharu, The, 1
Loyal 47 Ronin, The, *see* Chushingura
Lou Grant, 31
Love and Death, 117
Lower Depths, The, 5, 61

Magnificent Seven, The, 2, 91, 98, 140, 141, 142

Man From Laramie, The, 111
Man in the Iron Mask, The, 117
Man Who Left His Will on Film, The, 139
Man Who Shot Liberty Valance, The, 128, 130
Manin Densha see A Crowded Streetcar
Matatabi see The Wanderers
Miyamoto Musashi see Zen and Sword
Most Beautiful, The, 5
Muho Matsu no Issho see Rickshaw Man
My Darling Clementine, 115

New Tale of the Taira Clan, 32
Ningen no Joken see The Human Condition
No Regrets for Our Youth, 5
Nora Inu see Stray Dog

October, 127
Once Upon a Time in the West, 135
One Wonderful Sunday, 5
Outrage, The, 98, 142

Phantom of the Paradise, 68
Presidential Gambler, 136
Prisoner of Zenda, The, 117

Rashomon, 1, 5, 6, 9, 32, 60, 61, 62, 65-71, 76, 77, 78, 79, 98, 142, 143, 144, 146
Rebellion, 36, 38
Record of a Living Being see I Live in Fear
Red Beard, 62, 63, 66, 79, 139
Red River, 110, 129
Return of the Seven, The, 91
Rickshaw Man, 1, 35
Ride the High Country, 110
Rio Bravo, 42, 130, 141
Roue, La, 58
Royal Flash, 117, 125

Saikaku Ichidai Onna see The Life of Oharu
Sambiki no Samurai see Three Outlaw Samurai
Samurai Rebellion see Rebellion
Samurai Trilogy, 32, 35, 40, 41
Sanjuro, 2, 6, 9, 41, 60, 61, 63, 65, 73, 77, 84, 93, 105-16, 129, 130, 135, 139, 141, 146
Sanshiro Sugata, 5, 9, 32, 62-64, 65
Sanshiro Sugata Part II, 5
Sansho the Bailiff, 21
Scandal, 62, 79
Searchers, The, 110, 129
Seconds, 122
Seppuku see Hara-Kiri
Seven Samurai, 2, 6, 8, 9, 10, 32, 34, 60, 66, 77-91, 92, 93, 97, 98, 101, 104, 107, 129, 130, 140, 141-44, 146
Shane, 24, 30, 61, 110-13, 130, 139, 141
Shichinin no Samurai see Seven Samurai

Shin Heike Monogatari see New Tales of the Taira Clan
Shinju Ten no Amijima see Double Suicide
Shinjuku Dorobo Nikki see Diary of a Shinjuku Thief
Skyandaru see Scandal
Socho Tobaku see Presidential Gambler
Soldier Blue, 37
Star Wars, 140
Stray Dog, 5, 63, 79, 99, 133, 137
Subarashiki Nichiyobi see One Wonderful Sunday
Sugata Sanshiro see Sanshiro Sugata
Suna no Onna see Woman in the Dunes
Sword of the Beast, 136
Sword of Vengeance series, 30, 31, 43, 47

Tenchu, 37
Tengoku to Jigoku see High and Low
They Who Tread on the Tiger's Tail, 5, 9, 64-65, 68, 77, 92, 93, 96, 97
This Gun For Hire, 101
Three Outlaw Samurai, 35, 134, 136
Throne of Blood, 5, 6, 9, 60, 61, 66, 71-76, 78, 79, 104, 116, 134, 144, 146
Tokyo Senso Sengo Hiwa see The Man Who Left His Will on Film
Tora no O o Fumu Otokotachi see They Who Tread on the Tiger's Tail
Tsubaki Sanjuro see Sanjuro

Ugetsu, 35, 82
Ukigumo see Floating Clouds
Uma see Horse
Utamaro and His Five Women, 32

Waga Seishun ni Kui Nashi see No Regrets for Our Youth
Wanderers, The, 37, 77, 103
Warui Yatsu Hodo Yoku Nemuru see The Bad Sleep Well
Wild Bunch, The, 24, 140, 142-43
Wolves, The, 52, 136
Woman in the Dunes, 71

Yakuza, The, 136
Yato Kaze no Naka o Hashiru see Bandits on the Wind
Yoidore Tenshi see Drunken Angel
Yojimbo, 2, 5, 8, 9, 21, 31, 43, 60, 77, 89, 93, 94, 97-105, 106, 109, 115, 116, 129, 130, 134, 145, 146
Young Mr. Lincoln, 103

Zato Ichi series, 6, 43, 44, 45
Zen and Sword, 41
Zoku Sugata Sanshiro see Sanshiro Sugata Part II